Advanced Information and Knowledge Processing

Also in this series

Gregoris Mentzas, Dimitris Apostolou, Andreas Abecker and Ron Young
Knowledge Asset Management
1-85233-583-1

Michalis Vazirgiannis, Maria Halkidi and Dimitrios Gunopulos
Uncertainty Handling and Quality Assessment in Data Mining
1-85233-655-2

Asunción Gómez-Pérez, Mariano Fernández-López, Oscar Corcho
Ontological Engineering
1-85233-551-3

Arno Scharl (Ed.)
Environmental Online Communication
1-85233-783-4

Jason T.L. Wang, Mohammed J. Zaki, Hannu T.T. Toivonen
and Dennis Shasha (Eds)
Data Mining in Bioinformatics
1-85233-671-4

Shichao Zhang, Chengqi Zhang and Xindong Wu
Knowledge Discovery in Multiple Databases
1-85233-703-6

C.C. Ko, Ben M. Chen and Jianping Chen

Creating Web-based Laboratories

With 173 Figures

 Springer

C.C. Ko, PhD
Ben M. Chen, PhD
Department of Electrical & Computer Engineering,
National University of Singapore, Singapore 117576

Jianping Chen, PhD
School of Electrical & Electronic Engineering,
Nanyang Technological University, Singapore 639798

Series Editors
Xindong Wu
Lakhmi Jain

British Library Cataloguing in Publication Data
Ko, C. C.
   Creating web-based laboratories. – (Advanced information and knowledge processing)
   1. Intelligent tutoring systems   2. Computer-assisted instruction – Computer programs
   3. Web-based instruction
   I. Title   II. Chen, Ben M.   III. Chen, Jianping
   371.3′34

   ISBN 1852338377

Ko, Chi C. (Chi Chung)
   Creating web-based laboratories/Chi C. Ko, Ben M. Chen, Jianping Chen.
      p. cm.
   Includes bibliographical references and index.
   ISBN 1-85233-837-7 (alk. paper)
   1. Computer networks–Remote access. 2. Internetworking (Telecommunication)
   3. Internet in education. 4. World Wide Web. I. Chen, Ben M., 1963– II. Chen, Jianping.
   III. Title.

   TK5105.597.K623 2004
   004.6–dc22   2004046865

AI&KP ISSN 1610-3947

ISBN 1-4471-5672-2 Springer-Verlag London Berlin Heidelberg
Springer Science+Business Media
springeronline.com
© 2005 Springer-verlag London Limited 2004
Softcover re-print of the Hardcover 1st edition 2005

Typesetting: Electronic text files prepared by authors

34/3830-543210 Printed on acid-free paper SPIN 10971468

To Our Families

Preface

The Internet extends the power of the personal computer (PC) from being a personal machine to one that is connected to the world. Instead of being able to carry out just some simple gaming, data, and word-processing tasks, a PC using the Internet has access to an increasingly large variety of applications offered by numerous Web sites and application providers. Applications such as purchasing, banking, library access, entertainment download, and tax returns can now be routinely carried out by a low-cost PC with an Internet connection at any time from practically anywhere.

Most of the current applications however are software-oriented in nature and do not involve access to physical hardware or equipment on the server side or remote site. In terms of evolution, this is perhaps not unexpected as it is always easier for programs (software), which are more flexible, to evolve first. From this angle, future development of the Internet may include many more applications where hardware can be controlled or different pieces of hardware can communicate with each other to enable us to have a better working and living environment.

This book is on an application in this direction and involves the creation of Internet remote experimentation for the purpose of education. The design and setup of an Internet system that can control and monitor physical equipment and activities at a remote site is a task that is inherently more difficult than setting up a software-based Web site. Specifically, not only does the Web browser on the user side have to talk to the server on the remote site, but the remote site must also communicate with a variety of instruments under its control and audio/video feedback must be streamed back to the user.

The topics covered in this book are based on the research and development work that we have carried out in designing and implementing a number of Web-based experiments to enhance the learning experience of our students in the Department of Electrical and Computer Engineering at the National University of Singapore. While the book gives examples on Web-based experimentation, it will also suit those who would like to create Internet systems that interact with hardware equipment for purposes such as security, research collaboration, home and office automation, robotics, and so on. The overall design and some of the source code included may be modified or reused to save development time. Furthermore, it can serve as a useful reference for Web site designers, programmers, and administrators.

The book consists basically of two sections. The first section, involving most of the chapters, presents the design and main hardware and software components of the system in a generic manner. The second section, including the last chapter and the appendices, gives a complete implementation example. By illustrating how the various components are integrated together to form a working system, this section may be most useful to programmers, engineers, and researchers.

We are particularly thankful to our research fellow, Dr. Changdong Cheng, and our former graduate students, Feng Gu, Shihong Chen, Yuan Zhuang, Shaoyan Hu, and Vikram Ramakrishnan, for their help and contribution to the launch of the various Internet remote laboratories. We would also like to thank the series editor, Professor Lakhmi C. Jain of the University of South Australia, for his kindly encouragement during the course of preparing this monograph. Last, but certainly not the least, we would like to acknowledge the National University of Singapore and the Singapore Advanced Research and Education Network for providing us with research funds for this project.

Singapore   Chi Chung Ko
April 2004   Ben M. Chen
                                                 Jianping Chen

Contents

1 Introduction

1.1 A Brief Description of the Internet

The Internet is the largest computer network in the world. Technically speaking, it is a network that connects numerous smaller networks and computers worldwide. The Internet had its origin in 1969 under a contract by the Advanced Research Projects Agency (ARPA) and involved the networking of four computers at the University of California at Los Angeles, Stanford Research Institute, University of California at Santa Barbara, and University of Utah.

By 1970, computers from the Massachusetts Institute of Technology (MIT), Harvard, BBN, and Systems Development Corporation in Santa Monica, California, were added to the network. In 1971, Stanford University, MIT's Lincoln Laboratory, Carnegie Mellon University, and Case Western Reserve University became new members. In the months and years to come, many more organizations and universities plugged into the Internet, snowballing its growth to become a global network with millions of computers in practically all corners of the world.

The Internet was designed to provide a network that would continue to work even if some of the sites were destroyed by a major catastrophe such as a nuclear attack. If the most direct route became unavailable, routers would direct traffic around the network via alternate routes. The early Internet was used primarily by computer experts, engineers, and scientists. There were no home or office personal computers, and the system was simply too complicated for ordinary users. The Internet matured in the 1970s as a result of the TCP/IP architecture first proposed by Bob Kahn at BBN and further developed by Kahn and Vint Cerf at Stanford as well as many others throughout the 1970s. It was adopted by the U.S. Defense Department in 1980 and had been universally adopted by 1983.

As the commands for e-mail, FTP, and Telnet were standardized, it became much easier for nontechnical computer users to access and use the Internet in an increasing variety of applications such as communicating with friends and colleagues around the world and sharing files and resources. Libraries, which had been automating their catalogs, took the next logical step and made their automated catalogs available to the world.

While the number of sites on the Internet was small, it was fairly easy to keep track of the resources of interest that were available. But as more and more universities and organizations got connected, this tracking problem became increasingly difficult to carry out. The need therefore arose for tools that could index the resources that were available. The first such effort was undertaken in 1989, as Peter Deutsch and his co-workers at McGill University in Montreal created Archie, an archiver for FTP (file transfer protocol) sites. Basically, the software would periodically reach out to all known openly available FTP sites, list their files, and build a searchable index.

1.2 World Wide Web

In 1989, another significant event took place that made the Internet easier to use. Tim Berners-Lee and others at the European Laboratory for Particle Physics, more popularly known as CERN, proposed a new protocol for information distribution. This protocol, which became the World Wide Web (also known as the Web, WWW, or 3W) in 1991, was based on hypertext. This is a system for embedding links in text for the purpose of linking to other related text. It opens up the possibility of reading and referencing information contained elsewhere. Although initiated before Gopher, the development of the idea was rather slow. The development in 1993 of the graphical browser Mosaic by Marc Andreessen and his team at the National Center for Supercomputing Applications (NCSA), however, gave the protocol a big boost.

Today, the World Wide Web is the most commonly used Internet application. With the power of Web hyperlinks, navigation to other documents in the same directory, on the same Web server, or elsewhere in Web servers located anywhere in the world became a simple, enjoyable, and often productive task.

Web servers and Web browsers now support all major computer architectures and operating systems. The Web allows highlighted words and pictures in a document to link or point to media such as documents, phrases, movie clips, or sound files. The Web can link from any point in a document or image to any point in another document. With a browser that has a graphical user interface (GUI), the links can be activated by simply using the mouse to point and click.

1.2.1 HyperText Markup Language

All World Wide Web pages are written in HyperText Markup Language (HTML). While some files may have different file extensions (such as .cfm or .asp), they are all based on HTML.

HTML is not a real programming language, such as C++ or Pascal, but is a system for describing documents for a Web browser to interpret and display. HTML is a special version of SGML (Standard Generalized Markup Language, used by large organizations for exchanging data) with a focus on hypertext. HTML code is written in ASCII format. This is an important advantage because ASCII can be read under all the common platforms (such as IBM, Macintosh, and UNIX). The current standard defined by the W3 Consortium is HTML 4.0.

Although not an official standard, the earliest version of HTML (1.0) has functionality corresponding to Mosaic, the first popular browser. The first official version of HTML is 2.0, the most basic standard for creating Web pages that can be read by any browser. A more useful and newer standard is HTML 3.2, which was refined from HTML 3.0 because the latter was not widely accepted. With the advent of cascading stylesheets and HTML 4.0, HTML returned (as intended by the W3 Consortium, or W3C) to its real foundations. By its very nature, HTML is a structural but not formatting language. There are tags, such as `<font>` or `<b>`, for formatting text, but these elements were declared "deprecated" by the W3C. Elements not included in the official standard are called "obsolete" elements.

1.2.2 Universal Resource Locator

Each hyperlink in an HTML document is made up of two components – the anchor text or, as it is sometimes called, graphic text, that, when clicked, triggers the hyperlink; and the Universal Resource Locator (URL) that describes the action to be carried out when the hyperlink is activated. From the perspective of the user, this corresponds to "When this link is activated, jump to that resource for more information." The URL describes the protocol used to reach the target server, the host system (or server name) on which the document resides, the directory path to the document, and the document filename.

An example of a URL to a remote resource is given below. The URL points to the home page for the Web-based laboratory in the Department of Electrical and Computer Engineering at the National University of Singapore:

```
http://vlab.ee.nus.edu.sg/vlab/index.html
```

The URL above signifies the use of the HyperText Transfer Protocol (HTTP) to reach a server called `vlab.ee.nus.edu.sg` (with the default port 80) to look for a directory `/vlab/` that contains a hypertext document named `index.html`.

Every file on the Internet is uniquely addressable by its URL. Besides the HTTP access method, the URL may also be used to specify other important Internet protocols such as Gopher, FTP, and Telnet. In addition, gateways or enhanced clients can allow the Web to access other types of servers such as Finger and WAIS.

The URL above is called an absolute URL since it specifies how a file can be found directly. A simplified form of URL, called relative URL, allows one to use a shorter form for referencing other documents on the same server relative to the current document. Relative URLs also allow a Web browser to get direct access to the files on the system that it is running on without using any server name. This uniform naming scheme for resources is what makes the World Wide Web such a rich information environment and explains why so many people consider World Wide Web browsers the universal Internet access tool.

1.2.3 Web Browsers and Web Servers

Like numerous other network applications, the World Wide Web conforms to the client/server model. In the client/server environment of the Web, control lies with the Web browser. The job of the Web browser is to use the initial URL to retrieve a Web document from a Web server, interpret the HTML, and present the document to the user with as much embellishment as the user environment provides.

When the user selects a hypertext link, the process starts all over again – the Web browser uses the URL associated with the hypertext link to request the associated document, waits for the document to arrive, and then processes and displays the new document.

Many Web browsers also allow the user to carry out a variety of tasks with the current document, including printing, saving to disk, sending e-mail messages, searching for text strings, or even examining the HTML code of the source. The server software used with the World Wide Web is referred to as a Web server. Generally, it listens to port 80 by default. When a client requests a specific page, the server retrieves the page and sends it to the client. Web browsers and Web servers communicate by using the HTTP, a lightweight protocol that is conceptually similar to the Gopher protocol. Each request for a document from a Web browser to a Web server is a new connection. When a Web browser requests an HTML document from a Web server, the connection is opened, the document is transferred, and then the connection is closed.

Presently, the most common browsers in the market are Microsoft Internet Explorer and Netscape Navigator. Two first-generation browsers, Viola and Midas, were released in January 1993 for X-Windows. At about the same time, an alpha-version Macintosh browser was released. WWW, a line mode browser, was made available for the public in January 1992 via Telnet. The first popular browser was NCSA Mosaic and supported only HTML 1.0.

When Marc Andreessen, the mastermind of Mosaic, founded Mosaic Communications Corporation (now called Netscape and part of American Online), the well-known Netscape Navigator 1.0 was born and soon controlled 70% of the browser market. Seeing this huge success and potential, Microsoft soon released its own browser, MS Internet Explorer, for free. Subsequent refinements saw these browsers develop into the two most popular browsers currently being used.

Naturally, both Microsoft and Netscape try their best to attract as many users to use their browsers as possible. For Microsoft, Internet Explorer is combined with the Microsoft Windows operating system and is released free of any licensing fees. For Netscape, the source code of Navigator is open and freely available to any user. It is possible to download the source code and make modifications for certain specific purposes.

However, even though both browsers support HTML 4.0 or lower, they do have a lot of significant differences, which sometimes create inconvenience and complications in application development. In particular, for the creation of Web-based laboratories, it is often necessary to choose one of these as the target browsing platform. The development of codes that will work for both browsers may not be advisable from a resource point of view. As an example, out of the Web-based laboratories that have been developed at National University of Singapore, the experiment for the oscilloscope can only support Netscape, while the other experiments support only Microsoft Internet Explorer.

1.3 Overview of Web-Based Laboratories

1.3.1 The Internet for Education

Developed within the midst of universities and government agencies, the Internet has been used for a variety of purposes in education. The Internet provides a convenient multimedia communication channel between teachers and students and between scholars and research centers, in addition to being woven into everyday life and seeing extensive use as a connectivity and reference tool for numerous commercial business and personal applications.

With the Internet, many new, immersing, and innovative ways to enhance learning and expand educational opportunities may become realizable. Distance education and nontraditional classrooms can reach more students with specialized instruction and self-paced learning. Student projects, virtual field trips, and online journals may complement available local resources. Career planning and academic advising increase the versatility of students and make them more aware of available options. Couple these applications with the increase in computer ownership among students, and the Internet is rapidly realizing its potential of becoming a powerful educational tool at the college level.

The integration of the Internet into education is most commonly achieved through the following methodologies:

- Developing a course Web site to centrally house various online functions and facilitate course management.

- Creating a remote laboratory where multimedia animation or simulation is provided to replace physical experiments.

- Developing a Web-based laboratory that enables students to set up parameters and undertake experiments from a remote location.

Course Web Site

This is the most common way to utilize the Internet for education. Successful examples can be found from a lot of sites [1–6].

Simione and Tuttle [1] presented a user-centered Web page construction and maintenance model to develop Web-based course materials at the University of Minnesota College of Education and Human Development (CEHD).

Pascoe [2] not only made use of the Web for distributing course materials but also developed several methods to enable students to interact with the course site to enhance their learning. The methods include interactive exercises, facilities for students to annotate course notes, improved graphics, and automatic feedback tailored to specific student needs.

Rosenblum and Healy [3] developed some Web-based communication tools through a common gateway interface (CGI) program that provides instructors with private course discussion areas. With an intuitive chat interface, these areas allow instructors to give students a platform-independent ability to communicate in as many groups as is needed by the class. These tools open the door to instructors who would like to have a flexible online collaborative learning environment.

Numerous similar Web sites can be found both from the Internet and articles in the literature (see, for example, [4–6]) that exploit this type of teaching or learning methodology. In fact, nowadays, most universities in the world have systems that utilize the Internet as a general communication tool and aid for material download and general learning.

Remote Simulation Laboratory

This is the second most common way to utilize the Internet for education. It is well-known that software demonstrations of abstract concepts can be very beneficial in helping students to obtain a deeper understanding of hard-to-grasp topics. As an example, the concept of frequency content in a time-domain signal can be effectively illustrated by using an interactive multimedia approach where students can change the amplitudes of the various spectral components and view the waveform of the resulting audio signal while listening to it at the same time. This type of illustration can be carried out in class by the instructor or, better still, undertaken by the students individually in the context of playing or experimenting.

Before the advent of the Web, such demonstrations were typically developed in isolation at scattered institutions using locally available software packages. With the Internet, the demonstration programs can be launched and made available to the entire world, allowing more students to have access without the need to waste time developing the software.

Software-based demonstrations can be passive or interactive. The former is simpler in structure but only allows a student to play back prerecorded audio or video. The latter is more interesting from a learning point of view but is also more complicated to develop. Software demonstration can in general be categorized into those that need to be downloaded for execution on a local machine running software such as MATLAB or those that run directly on the Web using Java applets.

Numerous demonstration-based laboratories teaching a variety of topics can be found on the Web from developers all over the world [7, 8]. The simulation laboratory developed at Carnegie Mellon University is a good example. The system has been designed to provide an effective paradigm to use the Web as an education aid for tutoring students on the use of MATLAB and SIMULINK. Students are expected to run MATLAB or SIMULINK in one window of their own computers and a Web browser in another. While surfing the tutorial, the student can download examples from the Web page and run them locally. The tutorials on the Web are designed to help students learn how MATLAB can be used for the analysis and design of automatic control systems. They cover some MATLAB basics and common classical (PID, root locus, and frequency response), modern (state-space), and digital control techniques.

Remote Web-Based Laboratory

The systems above provide students with only theoretical and simulation materials. However, especially in science and engineering, it is more or less universally recognized that effective and efficient learning requires a mixture of both theoretical knowledge and practical exercises. For the purpose of seeing or appreciating how theory can be applied to solving real-world problems, practical exercises or experimentations are essential.

Nevertheless, there are a number of resource issues that need to be tackled in setting up and running laboratory-based experimentation sessions. Firstly, physical space must be available for developing the experimental setups and for students to carry out the experiments in a conductive environment. Secondly, technical manpower has to be deployed to ensure safety and the proper handling of equipment. Thirdly, proper time scheduling has to be in place to ensure maximum usage of the laboratory.

In the context of education, where the teaching of various topics usually follows a certain sequence, it is often desirable and sometimes necessary for certain experiments to be carried out by the entire class within a short span of time, say, a few weeks. This places a lot of constraints on resources, which will inevitably be used poorly or not at all when the experimentation session is over. Also, students taking courses part-time or in the evening or through distance learning may not have the chance to carry out an experiment due to the unavailability of technical personnel and the closure of laboratories.

The idea of having a remote Web-based laboratory corresponds to an attempt to overcome these constraints [9–13] and may well be the next important step in remote distance learning. Such a system will enable students to have access to laboratory experimentation anytime and anywhere via the Internet. Specifically, a properly designed laboratory will allow students to conduct the experiments in as realistic a manner as possible, as if they were working in the actual laboratories. A more advanced system may even have software that monitors logging on and how the instruments are used, enabling the experiment to be graded in a semiautomatic fashion.

In addition to education, a remote Web-based laboratory may also allow researchers in different locations to carry out research and design work co-operatively and remotely at the same time. This can even include the remote monitoring or observation of vital changes at various stages of the experiment over a long period of time. A more extended discussion of a remote Web-based laboratory will be provided in the next section.

1.3.2 Web-Based Laboratories

Performing experiments from a remote location is an extension of remote access that allows interaction with the physical world. This can be achieved by using appropriate electronic control and monitoring systems external to, but controlled by, computers. The combination of these systems and the provision of Internet communications allows a remote user to control and monitor devices and apparatus in the physical laboratory as if they were placed in front of the remote user. This is the concept of Web-based laboratories and the issue to be addressed throughout this monograph.

Typically, after logging on through the Internet, a user will be able to control both the computer and the various equipment in the remote laboratory through an appropriately designed graphical user interface running on the client computer. The interface may include videos or images captured in real time in the laboratory resulting from, say, adjustments made to some apparatus or changes in the dynamics of what is being investigated. A microphone may also be placed at interesting locations to pick up acoustic signals or vibrations in the experiment setup, and data may be captured by some instruments or sensors to be sent back or displayed or downloaded for further analysis by the user on the client computer.

A number of well-established universities, such as Oxford University and Carnegie Mellon University, have been developing and experimenting with the concept of Web-based laboratories. Some of these prototype systems are also open without any restrictions to interested users via the Internet.

The laboratory being developed at Oxford's new Chemistry IT Center allows students to carry out interactive chemistry experiments over the Internet, while at Carnegie Mellon University, two electrical engineering experiments on circuit characterization and motor control are available [14].

At Purdue University, a virtual laboratory called SoftLab has been set up to provide an environment for both physical experiments and numerical simulation [15]. Students are able to remotely control some real instruments after installing SoftMedia, an exclusive software for accessing the service in the laboratory.

Aktan et al. [16] describe a virtual laboratory that enables users to control a three-degree-of-freedom robot arm remotely. A client/server structure is used, but a software X-terminal has to be properly set up. Werges and Naylor [17] describe a virtual laboratory called the Networked Instructional Instrumentation Facility, which is a prototype Web system allowing multiuser access for carrying out measurements within a library of test equipment and devices. Again, the user must install some software built with Java using Microsoft J++ on the client side. Other similar systems can be found in [12, 18, 19].

It is envisaged that remote control and reconfiguration of instrumentation will soon become an increasingly common event for education and in the workplace. The growth of this paradigm is expected to parallel the increasing use of telecomputing and teleconferencing systems.

1.4 Target of the Book

In this book, we aim to explore the philosophy of designing efficient, secure, and convenient Web-based laboratories. Also, while the examples drawn come primarily from an educational and research point of view, the philosophy of creating Web-based laboratories can be readily extended to other fields such as Web-based monitoring systems for homes and the handling of dangerous substances or systems.

To achieve these objectives, we will give a systematic presentation on the principle, structure, and technologies of a Web-based laboratory and its component systems. We will discuss the integration of the important hardware and software systems, the design and development of some interfaces and components for use in typical Web-based laboratories, and some advanced topics such as multicast and impact on education.

In particular, we will cover the following fundamental topics that are needed for the creation of Web-based laboratories:

- Server/client structures
- Creation of realistic graphics user interfaces for laboratory work
- Methods for controlling instruments from the Web or control server
- Protocols for capturing and transmitting audio and video signals

Our coverage will draw examples from a number of Web-based laboratories that have been created in the Department of Electrical and Computer Engineering at the National University of Singapore. To demonstrate what can possibly be done, we will now give an overview of these laboratories.

1.4.1 Web-Based Laboratories at National University of Singapore

Four of the Web-based laboratories that have been created and launched correspond to experiments on the design and implementation of control algorithms on a coupled-tank apparatus, the use of an oscilloscope to study an RC circuit, using an expensive spectrum analyzer to study the spectrum of frequency-modulated signals, and the control of a laboratory helicopter [20–24].

These laboratories are used in courses for both undergraduate and graduate students. While the class size ranges from tens to hundreds of students, the possibility to access and conduct experiments anytime and anywhere greatly enhances the flexibility of laboratory education and introduces students to a new paradigm of experimentation.

Specifically, even though the physical laboratories housing all the equipment are open and available only during scheduled hours, students are still able to log on to conduct experiments on a 24-hour basis. This is especially important for part-time evening graduate students with full-time jobs and greatly increases the educational impact of the already sizable investment in equipment and space without any security problem. Another side effect is that the equipment or laboratory also becomes available to users outside the university.

1.4.2 Coupled-Tank Experiment

Figure 1.1 and Figure 1.2 show a schematic block diagram of the coupled-tank apparatus and the interface for the associated Web-based laboratory, respectively.

The apparatus consists of two transparent tower-type tanks mounted on a reservoir that stores water. The head of water in the tanks can be read from a scale placed in front of the tank. Each tank is fitted with an outlet, which in turn is connected to a plastic hose for returning water to the reservoir. The water inflow rate of each tank is controlled by a pump individually, while the outflow rate of water returning to the reservoir is approximately proportional to the head of water in the tank. The levels of water in the tanks are monitored by two capacitance probes, each of which, along with some other additional circuits, provides an output signal proportional to the level of water in the corresponding tank.

The coupled-tank experiment is used for undergraduate and graduate teaching as well as for research. In the undergraduate course, the experiment is used as a vehicle for students to master concepts in the identification of the physical model for a common practical system using input–output data, as well as the design of a suitable PID controller (shown in Figure 1.2) and various fuzzy logic controllers, such as Takagi–Sugeno and Mamdani, for the system.

Due to the complexity in tuning the PID controller parameters, the membership functions, and the rule bases of the fuzzy controller, students have very little time to implement their controllers within the scheduled laboratory session of 3 hours. Through the virtual laboratory, however, each student is now able to carry out the experiment according to his or her own pace and time schedule. The manual control in the virtual laboratory also allows students to collect real-time coupled-tank input–output data for the identification of a realistic model. This is particularly useful since an accurate model would help in the design of a good closed-loop controller. Besides, students could also fine-tune the controller parameters and membership functions, and the resulting control performance could be visualized and compared since they are based upon the same laboratory platform.

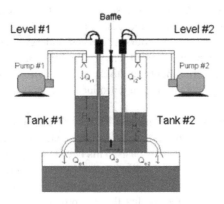

Figure 1.1. Coupled-tank apparatus.

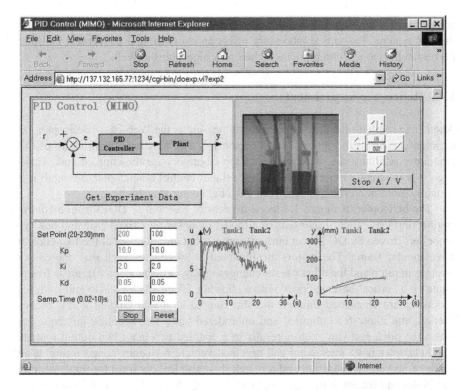

Figure 1.2. Web-based laboratory on the coupled-tank experiment.

A postgraduate course on optimal control systems also incorporates the virtual laboratory in its formal teaching. In this course, students are introduced to solving both classical optimal control system design problems, such as linear quadratic regulator (LQR) control and linear quadratic Gaussian (LQG) control, and advanced robust control problems, such as H_2 and H_∞ control. Since half the class consists of part-time students holding full-time employment in industry, classes are conducted in 3-hour sessions in the evenings once a week. Due to security, manpower, and other constraints, teaching laboratories are generally closed after working hours and it was almost impossible to schedule laboratory experiments or homework assignments on hardware implementations in the past. With the help of the virtual laboratory, which is available 24 hours a day, the course lecturer is now able to introduce a new teaching element on actual experimentation.

The virtual laboratory is used throughout the course homework assignments, in which students are required to solve an actual problem on the control of the flow levels in the coupled-tank system using techniques learned in the class and implement their designs on the actual system through the Internet. For the part-time students who can log on and use the system whenever they are free, the virtual laboratory provides highly flexible access to a real experiment. Feedback and comments from the students are generally very positive. Many students feel a great sense of achievement when they see that the controllers they have designed actually work in the real system. The virtual laboratory offers an excellent and convenient platform for researchers to test and implement their new algorithms as well.

1.4.3 Helicopter Experiment

Another example in the area of control engineering is the Web-based helicopter experiment as shown in Figure 1.3 and Figure 1.4. The function and structure of this laboratory is almost the same as that of the laboratory for the coupled-tank. However, it is inherently more difficult to model and control a helicopter, although it is certainly more interesting to be able to get a helicopter to stably fly.

The helicopter of Figure 1.3 has 2 degrees of freedom (2 DOF) from a control engineering viewpoint. It consists of a model mounted on a fixed base and has two propellers driven by DC (direct current) motors that are mounted at the two ends of a rectangular frame. The motors are mounted at 90 degrees such that one causes changes in pitch and the other causes changes in yaw. The helicopter frame is free to rotate on a vertical base equipped with a slip ring. Electrical signals to and from the helicopter are channeled through the slip ring to eliminate tangled wires, reduce friction, and allow for unlimited and unhindered yaw. The coupling in torque between the pitch and yaw motors results in a coupled two-input two-output system. The helicopter is an interesting and practical vehicle for control engineering at all levels of university education and research. It is an ideal platform for implementing and evaluating feedback strategies such as PID, LQ, fuzzy, H_2, and H_∞ control.

However, in addition to being rather expensive, the helicopter has very fast and powerful moving blades and extreme care has to be taken when experimenting with it. As shown in Figure 1.4, the Web-based laboratory developed around this system is therefore a good solution to ensure better and safer utilization of a scarce resource.

Figure 1.3. Helicopter system.

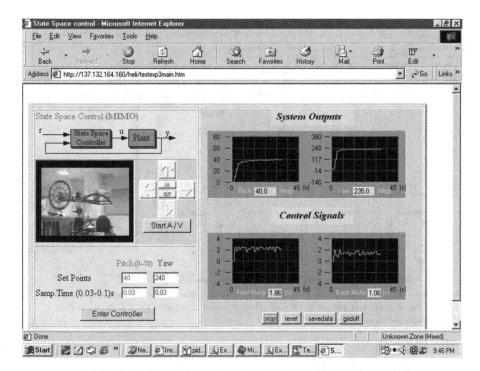

Figure 1.4. Web-based laboratory for the helicopter experiment.

1.4.4 Oscilloscope Experiment

In addition to matters of safety and the sharing of expensive equipment, the use of a Web-based laboratory is also very helpful in experimentation involving large classes. An example is the oscilloscope experiment shown in Figure 1.5.

The experiment aims to teach all the first-year engineering undergraduate students, which number about 1000 in the Faculty of Engineering at the National University of Singapore, the basic functions and controls of a dual-trace oscilloscope. The experiment complements lectures and tutorials on timing, amplitude, and phase measurements, as well as allowing students to master concepts on frequency and transient responses of a simple RC circuit.

The interface has been designed based on the front panels of the actual instruments in the laboratory. The display of the oscilloscope is captured by a video camera and shown on the interface in real time, while the instructions or experimental procedures are given at the bottom of the interface and can be scrolled. This Web-based experiment is particularly useful for students who are weak in the subject or from another discipline.

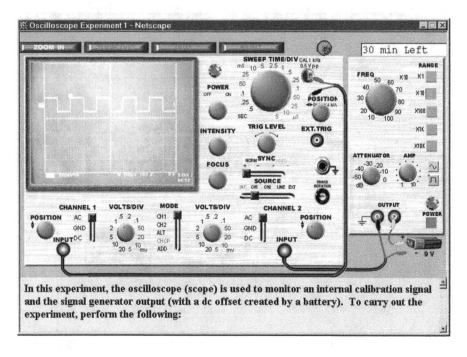

Figure 1.5. Web-based laboratory on the oscilloscope experiment.

1.4.5 Frequency Modulation Experiment

The frequency modulation experiment as shown in Figure 1.6 is similar to the oscilloscope experiment and is designed for a large undergraduate course on communications. However, an expensive spectrum analyzer is involved, and the Web-based laboratory enables students to access and share the use of such an instrument in a cost-effective manner.

This and the other instruments in the experiment are connected to server computers through the general-purpose interface bus (GPIB) in the laboratory. Remote users access these instruments by interacting with the user interface shown in Figure 1.6 on the client side.

However, to save bandwidth, visual feedback in the form of an image or video is not provided. Instead, all the graphical display on the client interface is reconstructed based on real-time data sent from the actual instruments through the Internet.

A version of this laboratory also has multicast capability. This allows other users to watch how the experiment is being conducted by the main user in control of all the instruments and can be taken as an example of collaborative learning.

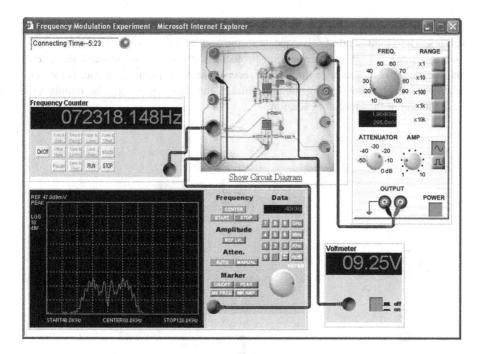

Figure 1.6. Web-based laboratory on the frequency modulation experiment.

1.4.6 Hardware Structure

The core of a Web-based laboratory is a cluster of general-purpose and/or specialized instruments interfaced to a set of personal computer systems connected to the Internet. As an example, Figure 1.7 shows the hardware structure for the laboratory on the coupled-tank experiment.

As illustrated, there are in general four subsystems in a Web-based laboratory: Web server, local controller, AV (audio/video) server, and client terminal. We will now give a brief description of these four subsystems.

Web Server

The Web server subsystem shown within the first circle of Figure 1.7 can be regarded as the heart of the whole system. It is through the Web server that a user will be able to access the Web-based laboratory, control the instruments, and obtain experimental results. In our Web-based laboratory, the Web server is implemented by using a PC running Red Hat Linux 7.0 with a Mysql database and Apache HTTP Server.

CGI (common gateway interface) and TCP (transmission control protocol) are selected as methods of communication between the client and the Web server and between the Web server and the local controller. CGI is an HTTP-based connection for setting up interaction between external applications and information or Web servers. The client sends CGI requests to the server and receives responses subsequently. Since HTTP is a per-session protocol, the connection between the client and the server is closed once the former receives an appropriate response. However, when the client is conducting the experiment, the connection must be maintained until the end of the laboratory session.

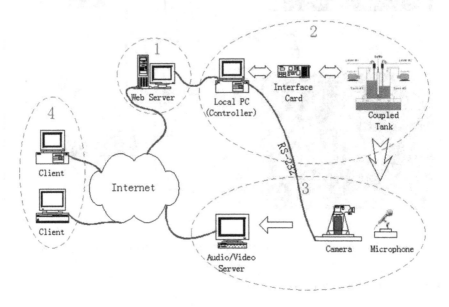

Figure 1.7. Hardware structure of a Web-based laboratory.

Local Controller

The local control server in the second circle of Figure 1.7 is realized by using a PC equipped with appropriate interface and networking cards. Depending on applications and instruments to be controlled, the interface card may be for data acquisition (DAQ), general-purpose interface bus (GPIB), digital signal processing (DSP), or other applications. In the coupled-tank experiment, the servo unit of the camera is controlled through an RS-232 interface so that zooming and changing of the viewing angle can be achieved.

In any implementation, it is quite possible for the functions of the Web server and local controller to be supported by a single computer as long as the latter has enough power. However, from the viewpoint of topology, it is better to treat them as two separate subsystems.

The local controller receives a command stream from the Web server through an established communication channel and translates the commands into control signals before they are fed to the interface cards. Local instruments connected to the interface cards may be apparatus used in the actual experiment as well as other equipment such as an oscilloscope, spectrum analyzer, signal generator, and frequency counter. In addition to sending control signals to the interface card, the local controller may also collect or retrieve information from the various instruments for downloading or updating the display on the remote client.

Audio/Video (AV) Server

The AV server subsystem in the third circle of Figure 1.7 has the task of providing the user with audio and video feedback on the happenings in the real laboratory. The subsystem may include monochrome and color cameras for video capture as well as microphones for picking up audio. The captured video and audio streams are processed and temporarily stored in the memory of the server before they are pushed to the client for downloading and playing.

As mentioned earlier, the control server has the responsibility of processing camera zooming and movement commands from the client. The main task of the AV server is thus streaming the audio and video data, which can be carried out by a variety of commercial software such as Microsoft NetMeeting and InetCAM.

Client

The client subsystem is actually embedded in the Web server. After logging onto the Web server, the user may browse the Web-based laboratory, look for general or detailed information on the nature and requirements of the experiment, and conduct the experiment. Due to its platform-independent nature and extensive network programming support, Java is chosen to implement the communication between the client and server.

The Java programs developed are compiled to give platform-independent machine code of the Java Virtual Machine, which can be executed by Java-enabled Web browsers such as Internet Explorer (IE) and NetScape. When the client downloads a Java applet from the Web server, the applet will be executed on the client to realize the client side in communicating with the server.

1.4.7 Software Structure

Figure 1.8 shows the software structure of the Web-based coupled tank laboratory. Basically, as in the hardware structure, four subsystems are involved: the Web client, Web server, control server and audio/video server. We will now briefly describe the first two subsystems, as the functions of the two other subsystems have already been discussed in the previous section.

Web Client

From a software and user-friendliness point of view, the Web client subsystem is very important, as this is the one that interfaces with the user directly and processes all his or her instructions. Experimental results in the form of data, images, audio, and video are also displayed via the Web client subsystem.

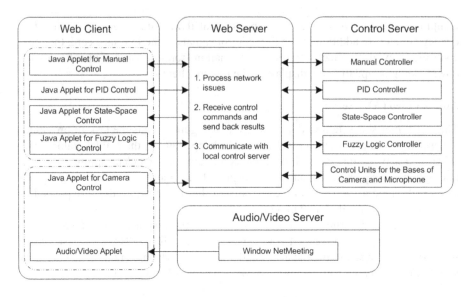

Figure 1.8. Software structure of a Web-based laboratory.

In the Web-based coupled-tank experiment, the Web client subsystem contains six Java applets. Four of these are for the manual, PID, general state-space, and fuzzy logic control of the coupled-tank apparatus. They communicate with the Web server and plot the relevant response curves using data obtained from the server.

Another Java applet handles camera control and is responsible for issues such as adjusting the zooming and position of the camera. The applet receives camera movement commands from the user interface and sends the command strings to the Web server. The latter in turn passes the commands to the control server, which then controls the servo unit or the base of the camera to make the appropriate movement.

The last applet is an audio/video one and is responsible for retrieving audio/video information from the audio/video server. The applet can be generated either by an ActiveX control object or Java Media Framework Player API. ActiveX controls are among the many types of components that use COM (component object model) technologies to provide interoperability with other types of COM components and services [25]. ActiveX controls correspond to the third version of OLE controls (OCX), and provide a number of enhancements specifically designed to facilitate the distribution of components over high-latency networks as well as integration of controls into Web browsers. The Java Media Player API, a portion of the Java Media Framework (JMF), allows Java programmers to easily embed audio and video within applets and applications. Both static and streaming multimedia supports from any valid URL are provided. JMF players may be controlled by other players to provide synchronous playback of multiple audio and video samples. The choice of ActiveX or JMF depends on the intended application. In the Web-based coupled-tank experiment, Microsoft NetMeeting is employed as the audio/video player and thus ActiveX is chosen as the API.

Web Server

The Web server uses LabVIEW to support network communication protocols, such as TCP and UDP, implemented in the form of virtual instruments' subVIs. In the Web-based coupled-tank experiment, LabVIEW uses the VIs as shown in Table 1.1 for communication through the Internet.

Table 1.1. VIs for communications in the coupled-tank experiment.

TCP Listen.vi	This VI waits for an incoming TCP connection request. It also returns a connection ID when the TCP connection is created.
TCP Read.vi	This VI receives a specified maximum number of bytes to read from the specified TCP connection.
TCP Write.vi	This VI writes a data string to the specified TCP connection.
TCP CloseConnection.vi	This VI is used to release the TCP connection.

The Web server's G programs receive information for the controllers and pass them on to the control server. The outputs of the control server are converted to analog voltages by the interfacing DAQ card and fed to the instrument. The output of the instrument is also sampled by the DAQ card periodically, and the sampled signals are sent to the client to draw the response curve.

1.5 Organization of the Book

To give a good understanding of the principles of the many systems involved in Web-based laboratories, and, more importantly, to show how a Web-based laboratory or similar application can be created, we divide this book into two parts: Part I – Basic Principles and Fundamentals; and Part II – Implementation of a Web-Based Laboratory.

Part I, on basic principles and fundamentals, is made up of eight chapters, Chapter 2 to Chapter 9. Chapter 10 on the implementation of the coupled-tank control system together with three appendices, give details on how a Web-based laboratory is implemented. The following gives a brief summary of the various topics that will be covered.

In Chapter 2, some networking topics, including client/server structure and network programming, are covered. These are essential for understanding the structure of Web-based laboratories. In particular, network programming issues such as protocols, port numbers, and sockets will be discussed. An innovative double client/

server structure will be introduced and its functions and benefits carefully studied. Besides the double client/server structure, a single client/server structure is also analyzed.

Chapters 3, 4, and 5 are for the creation of the client GUI (graphical user interface) in the Web-based laboratories. In Chapter 3, we emphasize the importance of creating vivid client GUIs and give some engineering background knowledge on the Web-based frequency modulation experiment. The fundamental programming methodology of OOP is briefly examined. In Chapter 4, we present detailed procedures for the creation of some fundamental component classes, including `imgButton`, `Knob`, `Connector`, and `DataDisplay` classes. In Chapter 5, we create the classes for the device canvas and the device. We use `SigGenCanvas` and `SigGen` classes as examples for the former and latter, respectively. `SigGenCanvas` is chosen as the example, as it contains all the classes we defined for the fundamental components in Chapter 4. Since `SigGenCanvas` is the blueprint of `SigGen`, we use the latter as the example for creating the classes for the device. The key ingredients of both `SigGenCanvas` and `SigGen` are thoroughly discussed in this chapter.

In Chapter 6, we discuss the most common interface cards used in Web-based laboratories: general-purpose interface bus (GPIB), data acquisition (DAQ), and digital signal processing (DSP) cards. The important features and benefits of these cards and their applications in Web-based laboratories are studied. We also discuss an important instrument control language, LabVIEW, which is used in most Web-based laboratories.

In Chapter 7, we study the topology of the audio/video service system. In such a system, two servers are required for audio/video and control. The former captures audio and video or image signals from the physical laboratory and then streams them to the client. The latter is for adjusting the manner or parameters for the capture of these signals. In the coupled-tank experiment, the main control is for the zooming and the movement of the camera.

In Chapter 8, we give a brief description of control theory and its applications in controlling the various instruments in some Web-based laboratories. The subject will be introduced with a presentation of some relevant mathematical models and control systems. Modeling of the plant, especially for the coupled-tank experiment, will then be discussed, followed by a discussion of some control algorithms and their implementations.

In Chapter 9, we address the topic of using multicast technology in the context of Web-based laboratories. The chapter introduces multicast and other related technologies, including multicast, time-to-live, and the Internet Group Management protocols. Also, an architecture is proposed for multicast Web-based laboratories. The implementation of the system, including user authentication, real-time transfer of data and command strings, is carefully studied.

Corresponding to Part II, Chapters 10 and Appendices A, B, and C give implementation details and some source code on the Web-based laboratories on the coupled-tank experiment.

2 Server and Client

2.1 Introduction

Despite its complexity, any Web-based network can be regarded as consisting of two logical parts, namely a client and a server. Generally speaking, servers are computers that provide service, while clients are computers that enjoy the service provided. Clients normally communicate with one server at a time. However, a server may handle multiple accesses simultaneously.

Network protocols are involved when a client is communicating with a server in an application. Figure 2.1 depicts the situation when this communication takes place on the Internet. As shown, the entire system can be regarded as consisting of four layers: application, transport, network, and hardware. The client and server in the application layer communicate using an application protocol (HTTP, FTP, Telnet, etc.), the transport layer uses TCP (transmission control protocol), and the network layer uses IP (Internet protocol). Even though the flow of information between the client and server actually goes down the protocol stack on one side, across the network, and up the protocol stack on the other side, these protocols are generally referred to as TCP/IP protocols, especially for applications on the Internet [25].

TCP/IP applications operate in the application layer of the network hierarchy and have two distinguishing features. Specifically, they are predominantly protocol-driven, and they are based on the architectural view that splits an application into a server and a client. Being protocol-driven, all TCP/IP applications behave in ways similar to that of communication protocols.

There are many readily available Web client applications, among which the most common ones are Microsoft Internet Explorer and Netscape Navigator. Both have been briefly described in Chapter 1. As for the Web server, numerous applications are also available, the best-known of which is perhaps Apache. Many general-purpose applications, such as LabVIEW and MATLAB, can also run as Web servers. In our Web-based laboratories, we run LabVIEW's inborn Internet toolkit as the

Web server, and use the LabVIEW G language as the main framework to build some important components of the system. One reason for using LabVIEW as the Web server is the fact that the variables in the server can be directly accessed by applications that are also coded in G. As an example, Figure 2.2 shows the HTTP server coded in G for the coupled-tank experiment.

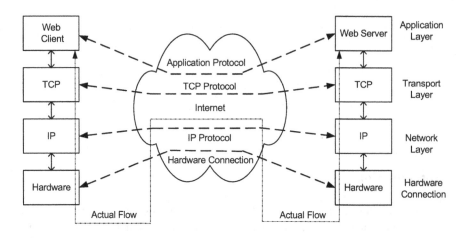

Figure 2.1. Server and client on the Internet.

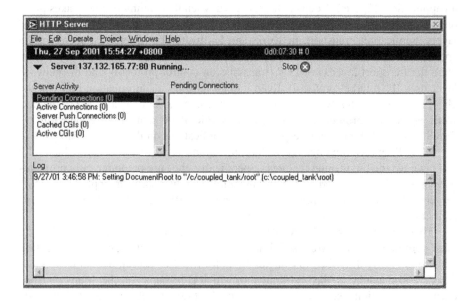

Figure 2.2. HTTP server for the coupled-tank experiment.

In this chapter, we will introduce some essential network principles and methodologies that are needed for understanding the structure of Web-based laboratories. The rest of the chapter is organized as follows. In Section 2.2, we describe some network programming concepts, including protocols, port numbers, and sockets. In Section 2.3, we will introduce and analyze an innovative double client/server structure that will be useful in Web-based laboratories. In Section 2.4, another client/server structure, the single client/server structure, is introduced and is briefly discussed.

2.2 Network Programming

2.2.1 Protocols

Most client/server applications use either TCP or UDP. These two protocols utilize either IP Version 4 (IPv4) or IP Version 6 (IPv6) of the network-layer protocol IP.

User Datagram Protocol – UDP

UDP is a simple transport-layer protocol [26]. The application writes a datagram, encapsulated as either an IPv4 datagram or an IPv6 datagram, to a UDP socket. This is then sent to the destination. However, under UDP, there is no guarantee that the datagram will reach its final destination. The problem with network programming using UDP is thus its lack of reliability. If one needs to be certain that a datagram reaches its destination, a lot more features have to be built into the application, including acknowledgments from the other end, timeouts, and so on.

Each UDP datagram has a length and can be considered as a record. If the datagram reaches its final destination, the length of the datagram is passed to the receiving application. This is in contrast to TCP, which is a byte-stream protocol and has no record length.

UDP provides a simple connectionless service, and there is no need to establish any long-term relationship between a UDP client and a server. A UDP client can create a socket and send a datagram to a given server and then immediately send another datagram on the same socket to a different server. Similarly, a UDP server can receive several datagrams in a row on a single UDP socket, each from a different client.

Transmission Control Protocol – TCP

Similar to UDP, TCP resides in the transport layer [26], positioned above IP but below the upper layers and their applications, as shown in Figure 2.1. There are, however, some notable differences between UDP and TCP.

First, the TCP protocol provides reliability. When data are sent to the other end using TCP, a return acknowledgment is required. If the acknowledgment is not received within a certain interval, TCP automatically retransmits the data and waits for a longer time frame. After a few retransmissions, TCP will give up, with the total amount of time spent trying to send data typically ranging from 4 to 10 minutes. TCP makes use of algorithms to estimate the round-trip time (RTT) between a client and server dynamically and uses this to determine the waiting time needed for an acknowledgment. This is important, as the RTT on a LAN can be in milliseconds while that across the Internet may be in seconds. Under TCP, a current estimated RTT of 1 second between a client and server may, due to variations in the network traffic, become 2 seconds if measured 30 seconds later on the same connection.

The second feature that distinguishes TCP from UDP is that the former provides a mechanism for ordering the data bytes sent. TCP sequences the data by associating a sequence number with every byte that it sends. For example, suppose an application writes 2048 bytes to a TCP socket, causing TCP to send two segments, with the first containing data with sequence numbers 1–1024 and the second containing data with sequence numbers 1025–2048. Here, the term segment is used to refer to the unit of data that TCP passes to IP, and its length is 1024 for this case. If the two segments arrive out of order, perhaps due to different transmission paths, the receiving TCP will reorder the two segments based on their sequence numbers before passing the data to the receiving application. In the event that the sender thought that a segment was lost and made a retransmission, duplicate segments may be received and the receiving TCP will discard the duplicate automatically.

TCP also provides some flow control mechanisms by telling its peer exactly how many bytes of data it is willing to accept from the peer. This is called the advertised window. At any time, the window is the amount of room currently available in the receiving buffer. The intention is to guarantee that the sender does not overflow the buffer in the receiver. The window changes dynamically over time. When data are received from the sender, the window size decreases. When data are read by the receiving application, the window size increases. It is possible for the window to reach 0, at which time the receiving buffer for the specific TCP socket is full and one must wait for the application to read the data from the buffer before any more data can be taken from the peer. On the contrary, UDP provides no flow-control mechanism. It is quite possible for a fast UDP sender to transmit datagrams at a rate that is too fast for the UDP receiver.

Finally, a TCP connection is full-duplex, while a UDP connection is not. With a TCP connection, an application can send and receive data in both directions simultaneously. This means that TCP must keep track of information such as sequence numbers and window sizes for each direction of the data flow.

Internet Protocol – IP

The Internet protocol (IP) is the primary protocol of the network layers and an integral part of TCP/IP. Although the word "Internet" appears in the name of the protocol, it is not restricted to use within the Internet. Specifically, while all machines on the Internet use or understand IP, IP can also be used on dedicated networks that have no relation to the Internet. IP defines a protocol and not a connection. It is a very good choice for any network that needs an efficient protocol for machine-to-machine communications.

The main task of IP is to provide addresses of datagrams for sending between computers and to manage the fragmentation process of these datagrams. The protocol includes a formal definition of the layout of a datagram in terms of the data to be carried and a header comprising information about the datagram. IP is also responsible for the routing of a datagram, determining where the latter will be sent, and devising alternate routes in case of problems.

Another important task of IP is to provide a connectionless and unreliable datagram service. IP makes a best effort to deliver an IP datagram to the specified destination. On this count, it is somewhat similar to UDP, even though they are entirely different protocols residing in different layers.

Figure 2.3 shows the format of an IP header [26]. Currently, two versions of IP protocols, IPv4 and IPv6, are available. Most applications use IPv4 nowadays, with the Internet and most local area networks (LANs) not giving support to IPv6 at present. The latter is compatible with IPv4 and is also called as IPng, an abbreviation for IP next generation. We will introduce IPv4 here with a description of the key components of the Ipv4 header given below.

- **Version**

  This is a 4-bit field that contains the IP version number of the protocol. The version number is required by the receiving IP software to properly decode the rest of the header, which may change with each new release of the IP standards. For IPv4, this value is 4.

- **Header Length**

  The header length is the length of the entire header, including any options, in 32-bit words. The maximum value of this 4-bit field is 15, giving a maximum IP header length of 60 bytes. Hence, with the fixed portion of the header occupying 20 bytes, the header may contain another 40 bytes of optional information.

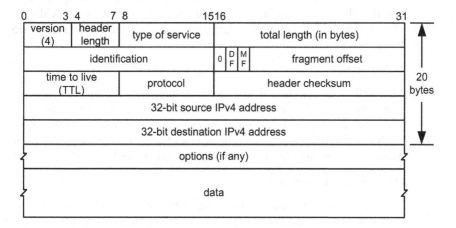

Figure 2.3. Format of an IPv4 header.

- **Type of Service**

  As shown in Figure 2.4, this 8-bit type-of-service (TOS) field consists of a 3-bit precedence field (which is ignored), 4 bits specifying the type of service, and an unused bit that must be 0.

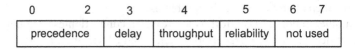

Figure 2.4. Layout of type of service.

  The first 3 bits (precedence) indicate the datagram's precedence, with a value from 0 (normal) through 7 (network control). The higher the number, the more important the datagram is, and, in theory at least, the faster the datagram should be routed to its destination. However, most implementations of TCP/IP and practically all hardware that uses TCP/IP ignore this field, treating all datagrams with the same priority.

  The next three bits are 1-bit flags that control the delay, throughput, and reliability of the datagram. A bit set to 0 means normal. A bit set to 1 implies low delay, high throughput, and high reliability for the respective flags. The last two bits of the field are not used. Most of these bits are ignored by current IP implementations, and all datagrams are treated with the same delay, throughput, and reliability settings.

- **Total Length**

  This 16-bit total length field gives the total length in bytes of the IP datagram, including the IPv4 header. The amount of data in the datagram is given by this field minus four times the header length. This field is required because some datalinks (for example, Ethernet) pad the frame to some minimum length, and it is possible for the size of a valid IP datagram to be less than the datalink minimum. Since the size of the total length field is 16 bits, the maximum length of a datagram (including the header) is 65,535 bytes.

- **Identification**

  This 16-bit identification field is set to a different value for each IP datagram and is used for fragmentation and reassembly. The purpose is to ensure that the fragments of one message are not intermixed with others. Each chunk of data received by the IP layer from a higher protocol layer is assigned one of these identification numbers when the data arrive.

- **DF, MF, and Fragment Offset**

  The DF bit corresponds to "don't fragment," the MF bit corresponds to "more fragment," and the 13-bit fragment offset indicates the offset of the current fragment. All these are used in fragmentation and reassembly.

- **Time to Live**

  The 8-bit time-to-live (TTL) field is set by the sender and then decremented by one by each router that forwards the datagram. The datagram is discarded by the router that decreases the value to 0. This limits the lifetime of any IP datagram to 255 hops. A common default for this field is 64.

  If the TTL field reaches 0, the datagram must be discarded by the current node and a message will be sent back to the source. The latter can then resend the datagram. The rules governing the TTL field are designed to prevent IP packets from endlessly circulating through networks.

- **Protocol**

  The 8-bit protocol field specifies the type of data contained in the IP datagram. The possible data types are specified by the Network Information Center (NIC), which governs the Internet. There are currently about 50 defined protocols, each with an assigned transport protocol number. Typical values are 1 (ICMPv4), 2 (IGMPv4), 6 (TCP), and 17 (UDP).

- **Header Checksum**

  A 16-bit header checksum is calculated for the entire IP header (including the options field). The standard Internet checksum algorithm, based on 16-bit ones-complement addition, is used. Since the time-to-live (TTL) field is decremented at each node, the checksum also changes with every machine the datagram passes through.

- **Source and Destination IPv4 Addresses**

  These fields contain the 32-bit IP addresses of the sending and destination devices. These fields are established when the datagram is created and are not altered during the routing process.

- **Options**

  As mentioned earlier, the size of this field is limited to 40 bytes. There are ten different options defined for IPv4: (1) NOP (no operation); (2) EOL (end of list); (3) LSRR (loose source and record route); (4) SSRR (strict source and record route); (5) timestamp; (6) record route; (7) basic security; (8) extended security; (9) stream identifier (this option is obsolete); and (10) router alert.

2.2.2 IP Address

The 32-bit address in IPv4 is usually written in the form of four decimal numbers separated by decimal points. This is the so-called dotted-decimal notation, and each decimal number corresponds to one of the four bytes in the 32-bit address. The first of the four decimals identifies the address class.

As shown in Figure 2.5, there are generally five classes of IPv4 addresses: A, B, C, D, and E. The first three classes, classes A, B, and C, are the common unicasting addresses employed in Internet applications. Class D consists of addresses for multicasting purposes, while Class E contains addresses reserved for future use.

Historically, an organization would be assigned either a class A, B, or C network ID, and it could do whatever it wanted with the host ID portion of the address. However, addresses are now considered classless, and the distinction between classes A, B, and C, as well as the implied network ID and host ID, can be ignored. Instead, whenever an IPv4 network address is assigned to an organization, a 32-bit network address and a corresponding 32-bit mask are given. Bits of 1 in the mask cover the network address, while bits of 0 in the mask cover the host address. For example, the IP address assigned for our VLAB server is "137.132.165.78," with the mask being "255.255.255.0."

2.2.3 Port Numbers

At any given time, there may be many processes or applications that use TCP or UDP. Both TCP and UDP use 16-bit port numbers as means to differentiate the interaction with different processes.

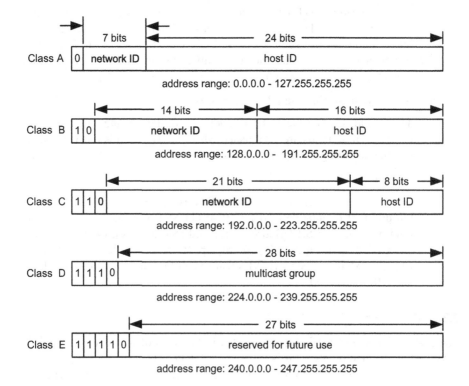

Figure 2.5. Classes of IPv4 addresses.

When a client wants to contact a server, the client must identify the server with which it wants to communicate [26]. Both TCP and UDP define a group of well-known ports to identify well-known services. For example, every TCP/IP implementation that supports FTP assigns the well-known port of 21 to the FTP server. TFTP servers, using the trivial file transfer protocol, are assigned the UDP port of 69. The clients, on the other hand, use ephemeral ports; that is, short-lived ports. These port numbers are normally assigned automatically to the client. Clients normally do not bother about the values of the ephemeral ports as long as they are unique on the client host.

The assignment of the various port numbers for network services is carried out by the Internet Assigned Numbers Authority (IANA). In general, the port numbers are divided into the following three ranges [27]:

- **Well-Known Ports**

  Ports from 0 to 1023. These port numbers are controlled and assigned by the IANA. Whenever possible, the same port should be assigned to a given service for both TCP and UDP.

- **Registered Ports**

  Ports from 1024 to 49151. These are not controlled by the IANA but are listed for the convenience of the community. If possible, the same port should be assigned to a given service for both TCP and UDP.

- **Dynamic or Private Ports**

  Ports 49152 through 65535. These are ephemeral ports and are not controlled by IANA.

2.2.4 Socket Pairs

On the Internet, the term network programming usually means TCP/IP programming, as almost all Internet applications are based on TCP/IP. This is also the case for our Web-based laboratories, which are TCP/IP and client/server based. In this subsection, we will discuss TCP/IP programming in the context of Web-based laboratories.

When a TCP connection is established, the connection will be in place until one of the two parties involved in the communication releases it. Hence, TCP is the ideal communication protocol for implementing Web-based control of instruments that may require frequent adjustments. Figure 2.6 shows the communication between a client and a server under TCP.

Before any communication is established, a socket pair must be created. The socket pair for a TCP connection is the 4-tuple that defines the two endpoints of the connection: the local IP address, the local TCP port, the remote IP address, and the remote TCP port. A socket pair uniquely identifies every TCP connection on the Internet. The IP address and port number that identify an endpoint make up a socket. We can also extend the concept of a socket pair to UDP, even though UDP is connectionless.

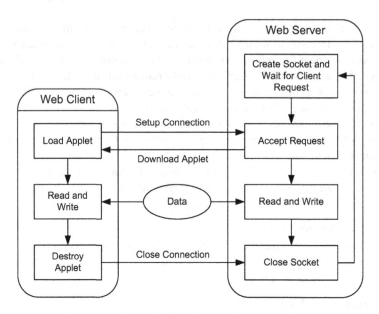

Figure 2-6. Server/Client interaction using TCP/IP.

We will use the notation { *.*, *.* } to indicate a 4-tuple socket pair, where each "*.*" denotes an IP address and port number. For example, the first "*" may be for the server vlab.ee.nus.edu.sg with an IP address of 137.132.165.78, while the second "*" may be for the HTTP service that it provides at port number 80.

Client applications must obtain, or bind, a port to establish a socket connection. Because the client initiates the communication with the server, such a port number could conveniently be assigned at runtime and is generally a dynamically allocated number above 1024. Since no two applications can bind the same port on the same machine simultaneously, a socket uniquely identifies a communication link.

Suppose that a client with an IP address 137.132.164.29 has established a connection with the server vlab.ee.nus.edu.sg. To identify the connection, the client assigns the ephemeral port 4000 for the process. Then, the 4-tuple for the server is

    {137.132.165.78.80, 137.132.164.29.4000},

while that for the client is in the reverse order, that is,

    {137.132.164.29.4000, 137.132.165.78.80}.

For TCP/IP programming, there is a well-defined socket API (application programming interface) that dictates how an application uses TCP/IP. The TCP/IP API is portable (it works across all operating systems and hardware that support TCP/IP), language-independent (it does not depend on the language used for writing the application), and relatively uncomplicated.

2.3 Double Client/Server Structure

Figure 2.7 shows a client/server structure that is suitable for use in Web-based laboratories. Since the Web server and the controller are implemented as two entities in the form of two client/server pairs, this topology will be referred to as a double server/client structure. The Web-based laboratory for the frequency modulation experiment is created based on this structure, where the first client/server pair corresponds to the client and Web server and the second pair corresponds to the Web server and controller.

Data flow in the structure is as follows. The Java applet that runs on the client side sends a request for connecting to the Web server. The server program, transit.c, in turn sends a connection request to the controller as well as accepting the request from the client. The Controller.vi on the controller accepts the request and thus establishes an indirect channel from the client to the controller. Obviously, Controller.vi is also responsible for executing programs for controlling the instruments.

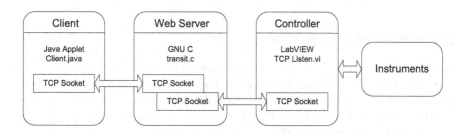

Figure 2.7. Double client/server structure.

2.3.1 Client

Java supports network programming extensively, and it is convenient to implement a client using Java with TCP sockets. When a user downloads a Java applet from the Web server, the applet will run on the client machine and represents the client side of the connection. The applet may make use of the Socket class in Java to facilitate a TCP client socket. Some important steps to implement a TCP client under Java are as follows.

1. Creating a socket.
    ```
    sock = new Socket(InetAddress address,int port);
    ```
    The first argument specifies the Internet address of the server for establishing the connection, while the second port specifies the port number of the server.

2. Retrieving input streams associated with the socket.

```
datain = new DataInputStream(new
    BufferedInputStream(sock.getInputStream()));
```

3. Retrieving output streams associated with the socket.

```
dataout = new DataOutputStream(new
    BufferedOutputStream(sock.getOutputStream()));
```

4. Reading from `datain` or writing to `dataout` with various read/write methods implemented in the `DataInputStream` or `DataOutput-Stream` class. For example,

    - `int read(byte[] b)`
    - `string readUTF()`
    - `void write(byte[] b, int off, int len)`
    - `void writeUTF(String str)`

5. Closing the socket.

```
synchronized void close();
```

2.3.2 Server Entity in the Web Server

The Web server performs two roles. To the client, it is a server. To the controller, it is a client. In our Web-based laboratory, the Web server is realized under the Linux platform, where GNU C, with a well-defined application programming interface (API) for TCP/IP, is used to develop the relevant communication programs. The essential data structures of the API are listed in Figure 2.8.

To establish a server entity, the following procedures are needed:

- Creating a socket
- Binding an address
- Specifying the queue
- Waiting for a connection
- Transferring data

Creating a Socket

The API below allows one to create a socket with a simple function call whenever necessary.

```
socket(family, type, protocol)
```

To inform the operating system of the type of socket to assign and how information can be decoded, the function has arguments on the family of the protocol to be used, the communication type, and the specific protocol to use.

```
                            Data Structure
 1   struct hostent
 2   {
 3      char     *h_name;                /* official name of host */
 4      char     **h_aliases;            /* alias list */
 5      int      h_addrtype;             /* host address type */
 6      int      h_length;               /* length of address */
 7      char     **h_addr_list;          /* list of addresses */
 8   }

 9   struct in_addr
10   {
11      unsigned long int s_addr;        /* 32 bit IP address*/
12   }

13   struct sockaddr_in
14   {
15      short int  sin_family;           /* Address family*/
16      unsigned short int sin_port;     /* Port number*/
17      struct in_addr sin_addr;         /* Internet address*/
18      unsigned char sin_zero[8];       /* Same size as sockaddr */
19   }
```

Figure 2.8. Data structures for TCP/IP programming.

Binding an Address

Since a socket can be created without binding to an address, there must be a function call to complete this process and establish a full connection. The socket function does not supply information on the local port number and the destination port. The bind function can be called to provide the local port number for the connection and has the format:

```
        bind(socket, local_address, address_length)
```

where socket is the integer number of the socket to which the bind is to be completed; local_address is the local address to which the bind is performed; and address_length is an integer that gives the length of the address in bytes.

Specifying the Queue

A server application has to create a socket by using the function socket(), bind it to a port by using the function bind(), and then wait for incoming requests for data. The function listen() handles issues that may occur by establishing a queue for incoming connection requests to prevent bottlenecks and collisions. For example, a request may arrive before the previous one is completely handled, or two requests may arrive simultaneously. The listen() function establishes a buffer to queue incoming requests, thereby avoiding losses. The function allows the socket to accept incoming connection requests and then has these sent to the queue for future processing. The format of the function is

```
listen(socket, queue_length)
```

where `queue_length` is the size of the incoming buffer. If the buffer still has room, incoming requests for connections are added to the buffer and the application will deal with them in the order of reception. If the buffer is full, the connection request is rejected.

Waiting for a Connection

After the server has used the `listen()` function to set up the incoming connection request queue, the `accept()` function can be used to wait for a real connection. The format of the function is

```
accept(socket, address, length)
```

where `socket` is the socket of interest; `address` is a pointer to a structure of type `sockaddr_in`; and `length` is a pointer to an integer showing the length of the address.

Transferring Data

There are five functions within the socket API for sending data through a socket. They are `send()`, `sendto()`, `sendmsg()`, `write()`, and `writev()`. All of them send data from the application to TCP through a buffer created by the application and then pass the entire buffer to TCP.

Since there are five functions to send data through a socket, there are correspondingly five functions to receive data; that is, `read()`, `readv()`, `recv()`, `recvfrom()`, and `recvmsg()`. All of them will accept incoming data from a socket and pass the data into a reception buffer. The receiving buffer can then be transferred from TCP to the application.

2.3.3 Client Entity in the Web Server

Correspondingly, to set up a client, the following procedures are needed:

- Creating a socket
- Connecting to the server
- Transferring data

Creating a Socket

This is similar to that for the server entity.

Connecting to the Server

Once a local socket address and port number have been assigned, the destination socket can be connected. To get connected, the destination socket must be added to complete the connection. To establish a connection to a remote socket, the function connect() can be called. The format of the function is

connect(socket, destination_address, address_length),

where socket is the integer number of the socket, destination_address is the socket address for the destination address, and address_length is the length of the destination address in bytes.

Transferring Data

This is similar to that for the server entity.

2.3.4 Controller

LabVIEW supports network communication protocols, such as TCP and UDP, in the form of VIs. In our experiment, a link between the client and the instrument controller is needed for data to be transmitted continuously. A LabVIEW G program running on the controller works as a TCP server. It waits for a request from the client side and in turn acknowledges the setting up of the connection.

Figure 2.9 shows the Controller.vi for the frequency modulation experiment. The VI receives command strings from the Web server, analyzes the command, and calls other sub-VIs to control the instruments. LabVIEW uses the following VIs to communicate with other peers over the Internet. The key components of which are explained as follows.

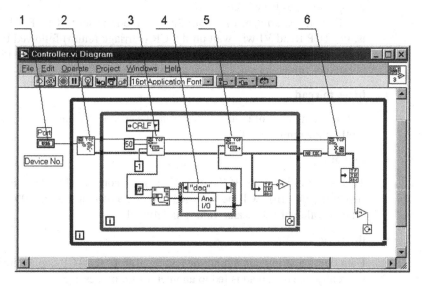

Figure 2.9. Controller.vi for the frequency modulation experiment.

1. Port number. This is the TCP port number to which data will be sent. In the current application, the number is 2055.

2. TCP Listen VI. This VI creates a listener and waits for the accepted TCP connection at the specified port.

3. TCP Read VI. This VI requests a certain maximum number of bytes on the specified TCP connection and returns the resulting in data. This VI can be further specified as follows.

   - **mode (standard)**

     This specifies the behavior of the read operation. Four options are available:
     Standard – Waits until all bytes requested have arrived or time runs out and then returns the number of bytes that have been received so far. If less than the requested number of bytes arrive, a timeout error is reported.
     Buffered – Waits until all bytes requested have arrived or time runs out and then returns the number of bytes requested or none. If less than the requested number of bytes arrive, it reports a timeout error.
     CRLF – Waits until a CR (carriage return) followed by an LF (line feed) have been received within the number of bytes requested or time runs out and then returns the bytes read up to and including the CR and LF or nothing. If a CR and LF are not found, it reports a time-out error.
     Immediate – Waits until a byte is received or time runs out and then returns the number of bytes received so far. It reports a timeout error if no bytes have been received.
     For the experiment of Figure 2.9, the mode is set to CRLF. That is, the TCP Read VI will wait until a CR (carriage return) followed by an LF (line feed) have been received within the number of bytes requested or time runs out.

   - **bytes to read**

     This is the number of bytes to read from the specified connection. Currently, the number is 50.

   - **timeout**

     This is in milliseconds. If the operation is not completed in the specified time, an error will be returned. The default value is 25,000. A timeout value of −1 means waiting indefinitely.

   - **data out**

     Data out is a string containing the data read from the TCP connection. Currently, the data read is fed to another VI for processing.

4. Case selection. The command string from the TCP Read VI is parsed and fed to other more specialized VI for further processing. In Figure 2.9, the Ana.I/O VI is called to control the DAQ card.

5. TCP Write VI. This writes specified string data into the specified TCP connection.

6. TCP Close Connection VI. This VI closes the connection associated with the connection ID. After completing a TCP communication, the connection should be closed.

2.4 Single Client/Server Structure

The main feature of the double client/server structure is that there are two separate computers working as Web server and controller. This structure allows the Web server to work as a general proxy for many Web-based laboratories, with the advantage that the controller need not be connected to the Internet. In addition, the Web server and the controller can be more specialized in undertaking their individual tasks, and the whole system has a clearer and more transparent hardware and software structure. The shortcoming of the double client/server structure is that two computers are needed for the entire system, although, at present, PC-based servers have costs that may be negligible compared with some instrument and overhead costs. Still, the maintenance of the system may be slightly more difficult to carry out, especially when the two servers run on different operating systems.

Hence, in less intensive applications when it is not necessary to employ two servers, we can combine the two servers into one. In this situation, the same computer performs as both the Web server and controller, and the topology corresponds to a single client/server structure as shown in Figure 2.10. Apart from the laboratory for the frequency modulation experiment, all our other Web-based laboratories are created using such a structure.

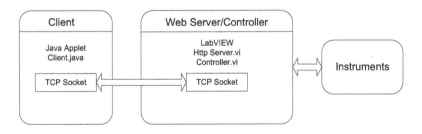

Figure 2.10. Single client/server structure.

3 Client GUI Design

3.1 Introduction

The user interface of a remote laboratory should be as realistic as possible to give users an impression that they are actually operating on the physically existing instruments. Also, a user-friendly interface will enable the user to conduct the experiments conveniently and efficiently. The design and creation of vivid control and parameter adjustment components such as buttons, knobs, and cables are thus essential in any Web-based laboratory.

Typically, these movable components are positioned on top of an instrument panel or an appropriate laboratory setup or background. On the panel, buttons can be pressed or released, knobs can be turned, and plugs and cables can be plugged in or dragged to connect or disconnect relevant input or output terminals in the laboratory experiment. As examples, some instrument panels for the frequency modulation and oscilloscope experiments are illustrated in Figures 3.1 and 3.2, respectively.

The client graphical user interface (GUI), which includes the instrument panel and other information such as experimental procedures and real-time experimental data, may be implemented using Java, JavaScript, and HTML technologies, most of which are supported by popular Web browsers such as Microsoft Internet Explorer and Netscape Navigator.

Java applets embedded in HTML pages can be used to construct the main interface of the experiment. Java is a natural choice on the client side because of its flexibility in GUI design, convenient network programming capability, and platform independence. Platform independence, the last feature, is most significant since it allows the same applet program to run on client machines with different platforms. To use Java, the codes must be compiled into applets and embedded into the HTML file.

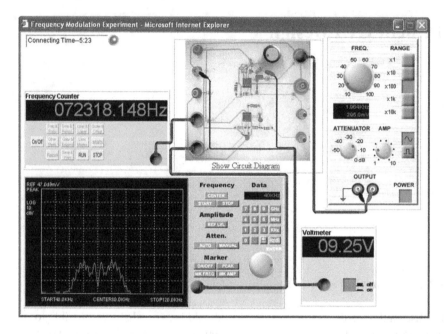

Figure 3.1. Instrument panels for the frequency modulation experiment.

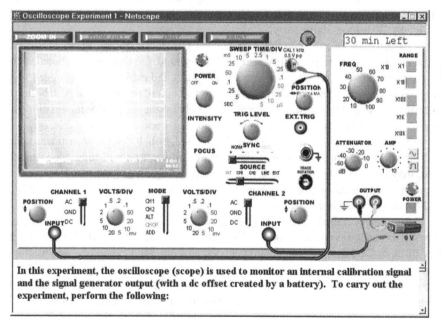

Figure 3.2. Instrument panel for the oscilloscope experiment.

Unlike Java, JavaScript is a scripting language, which is a subset of programming languages. JavaScript code can be included directly in HTML documents and can be easily modified. Typically, scripting languages are software extensions or operating system extensions, unlike true programming languages that can create compiled self-contained applications. PERL, VBScript, and JavaScript are examples of scripting languages, while Java, C, C++, and Pascal are examples of true programming languages. Scripting languages are in general less powerful but also easier to learn. A higher-level language such as Java, for instance, has a very steep learning curve and requires substantial involvement to master. JavaScript is actually descended from Java, but it was developed by Netscape as a means of bringing the simplicity of scripting language to a wider audience.

To create and realize a realistic instrument panel, it is necessary to mix codes in Java, JavaScript, and HTML together. Although the processes or functions written in JavaScript can always be rewritten in Java, the former may be preferred in some places for the sake of simplicity and efficiency in development.

In the following sections and the next two chapters, we will describe in detail, step-by-step, how a user-friendly and vivid panel can be created from scratch. In our discussion, we will use the GUIs of the frequency modulation and oscilloscope experiments as examples.

3.2 Frequency Modulation Experiment

Before we proceed, we will present some background knowledge on the instruments in the frequency modulation experiment that will be relevant to the design of the GUI and the instrument panels on the client. Essentially, the experiment makes use of a spectrum analyzer and some other instruments so that the user can investigate the spectrum of a frequency-modulated signal generated from a circuit board.

3.2.1 Circuit Board

Figure 3.3 shows the circuit diagram of the circuit board used for generating the frequency-modulated signal in the experiment. The circuit to the left of the dashed line is the frequency modulator, while that to the right corresponds to a second-order low-pass filter.

On the client GUI under the Internet Explorer browser, the circuit board is realized as shown in Figure 3.4. Note that a picture of the actual circuit board in the laboratory is used. The important terminals or components, including the input and output terminals, a test point, and a variable resistor, are marked by dashed circles in the figure.

The input terminal and socket in circle 1 corresponds to the input or point 1 in Figure 3.3. The knob in circle 2 is the variable resistor R_v in Figure 3.3. The terminal in circle 3 is a test point and corresponds to point 3 of Figure 3.3. The terminal in circle 4 is the ground terminal. By measuring the voltage difference between terminals 3 and 4, the voltage at pin 5 of the voltage-controlled oscillator LM566 can be found. The sockets under both circles 5 and 6 correspond to point 5 of Figure 3.3. Through socket 5, the output signal can be fed to a frequency counter to be measured. Through socket 6, the same signal can be sent directly to a spectrum analyzer to be analyzed.

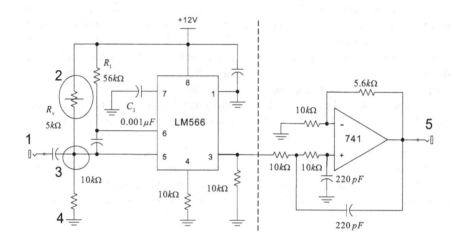

Figure 3.3. Circuit diagram for the frequency modulation experiment.

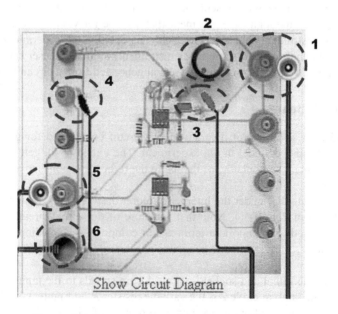

Figure 3.4. Instrument panel for the circuit board.

3.2.2 Spectrum Analyzer

Figure 3.5 shows the HP 8590L spectrum analyzer [28] used in the frequency modulation experiment. It is a full-featured analyzer that can operate from 9 kHz to 1.8 GHz with an amplitude range of –115 dB to +30 dB. Regardless of whether it is manually or remotely operated, the analyzer has more than 200 functions, including marker types such as marker delta, marker peak search, and up to four on-screen markers. With the option of a GPIB interface, the instrument can be controlled by a computer.

On the Internet Explorer GUI, the spectrum analyzer is realized as shown in Figure 3.6. Since the actual instrument has many features but only a few important ones are relevant for the experiment, a simplified front panel is provided in the GUI. Another reason for having such a design is that the users or students will not be overwhelmed by the complexity of the instrument and yet will be able to get a good, realistic feeling of using a real, expensive spectrum analyzer. In terms of feasibility, it is in fact quite straightforward for the Web-based instrument to have exactly the same function as the real equipment if necessary. The controls and components on the instrument panel of the spectrum analyzer are described below [28].

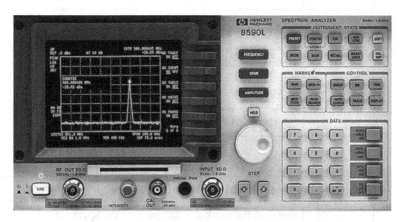

Figure 3.5. HP 8590L spectrum analyzer.

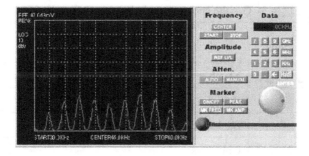

Figure 3.6. Instrument panel for the spectrum analyzer.

- **Buttons**

There are five groups of buttons on the panel:

○   Frequency Buttons

CENTER	Activate the center-frequency function to set the frequency at the center of the display.
START	Set the start frequency or that corresponding to the left-most position of the display.
STOP	Set the stop frequency or that corresponding to the right-most position of the display.

○   Amplitude Button

REF LVL	Set the reference level, which corresponds to the power in dBm at the top topmost position of the display.

○   Attenuation Buttons

AUTO	Couple the attenuation to the reference level. The spectrum analyzer will attenuate the input signal power accordingly.
MANUAL	Set the input attenuation in 10 dB increments.

○   Marker Buttons

ON/OFF	Turn the marker on or off.
PEAK	Position the marker at the peak of the spectrum.
MK FREQ	Specify the frequency of the active marker.
MK AMP	Get the spectrum value at the marker position.

○   Data Buttons

0 to 9	Number keys.
.	Decimal point.
⌫	Backspace or negative sign.
GHz to Hz/dB	Unit keys.

The data buttons allow the entry of exact values, which may include a decimal point, for many of the spectrum analyzer functions. All numerical entries must be terminated with a unit key, which will activate the instrument to accept the values and make corresponding changes in the operation of the instrument.

- **Knob**

  The knob allows changes to be made to parameters such as the center frequency, reference level, and marker position in an incremental continuous or discrete manner. Clockwise rotation of this control corresponds to an increase in value. To change values in a continuous manner, the extent of the change or resolution is determined by the range of the function selected. The speed at which the knob is turned, however, does not affect the rate at which values are changed. Through the GUI on the client side, the turning of the knob is achieved by dragging the mouse pointer when it is positioned next to the red dot of the control.

3.2.3 Frequency Counter

Figures 3.7 and 3.8 show the frequency counter used in the experiment and the corresponding GUI version under the Internet Explorer browser, respectively. The instrument counter is capable of measuring frequencies up to 225 MHz [29]. Frequency and time-interval resolutions are 10 digits in one second and 500 picoseconds, respectively. Programmable control is performed via GPIB, and this provides the user with a speed of 200 measurements per second.

In the experiment, this instrument is used to measure the frequency of the carrier signal for the purpose of calibrating the voltage-controlled oscillator (VCO) before the latter is used for frequency modulating an input message signal.

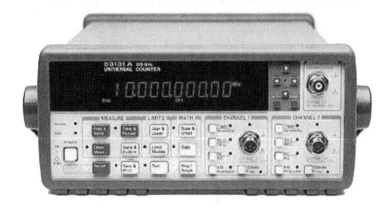

Figure 3.7. HP 53131A universal counter.

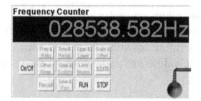

Figure 3.8. Instrument panel for the frequency counter.

3.2.4 Signal Generator

The signal generator for producing the input message signal and its corresponding Internet Explorer GUI version are shown in Figures 3.9 and 3.10, respectively. The instrument is a versatile arbitrary waveform generator, can operate over the frequency range from 1 mHz to 10 MHz, and is capable of giving a 1 mV to 10 V peak-to-peak output into a 50 Ω load [30]. In the experiment, the instrument is remotely operated via the IEEE 488.2 bus and is SCPI-compatible.

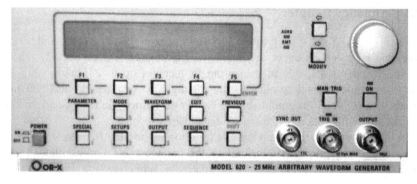

Figure 3.9. OR-X Model 620 arbitrary waveform generator.

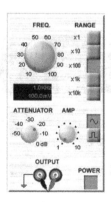

Figure 3.10. Instrument panel for the signal generator.

3.2.5 Voltmeter

The last instrument used in the experiment is a standard remote-controlled voltmeter for measuring the voltage of the VCO on the circuit board. The instrument is controlled and its reading is captured through the IEEE 488.2 bus. In the GUI under Internet Explorer, it is simply realized as shown in Figure 3.11. Basically, once the power button is on, the voltage applied to its input will be continuously measured and displayed.

Figure 3.11. Instrument panel for the voltmeter.

3.3 Java and OOP

3.3.1 Java Applet

The instrument panels described above are created using Java applets. In general, Java can be used to create either a stand-alone application or an applet [31]. The former does not need to be embedded in an HTML document and can be run without using any browser.

In our Web-based laboratories, most of the Java programs are for the creation of applets. Put simply, an applet is a part of a Web page, just like an image or a line of text in a document. Thus, similar to how a browser looks after the display of an image in an HTML document, a Java-enabled browser is needed to locate and run an applet. When a Java-capable Web browser loads an HTML document, the Java applet is also loaded and executed. Using applets, one can perform tasks such as having animated graphics, games, or utilities executed from a Web page downloaded from the Internet.

The development of Web-based laboratories will involve many languages, such as Java, JavaScript, VBScript, Perl, MATLAB, and LabVIEW. However, Java is perhaps the most important in dealing with situations, especially the user interface, on the Internet.

To create a Java program, a text editor can be used to create a Java language source code file. After saving the source code with a .java file extension, the saved file can then be compiled into its byte-code format, creating another file with a .class extension. It is the .class file that the interpreter loads and executes. Because the byte-code files are fully portable between operating systems, they can be executed on any system that has a Java interpreter.

3.3.2 Class

The creation of classes in the context of OOP (object-oriented programming) is crucial in the development of Web-based laboratories. However, before we describe in detail how this can be done for the client GUI in the next two chapters, we will first present here some basic concepts and principles on classes.

Under OOP, a class is essentially a template for an object. An example is the common data type integer, or int, which is predefined in Java and practically all other programming languages. When the need arises for a new class to be created, however, the characteristics of the class must be specified. Specifically, a class associated with the display of a button can be defined by using the class keyword along with an appropriate class name, as follows:

```
class imgButton
    {
    }
```

Despite having an empty body, these few lines actually create a complete class. If they are saved in a file called imgButton.java, compilation to a .class file can be carried out and execution will be possible, even though nothing useful will result.

Nevertheless, one can still create an object powerButtt from the defined example class. To do this, we can use either

```
ImgButton powerButtt = new imgButton();
```

or

```
ImgButton powerButtt;
```

The ImgButton is empty and useless. Both data fields and methods will have to be specified for the class if it is to serve any purpose. The declaration of four integer fields for storing the size of any button created from the class imgButton can be achieved as shown in the following example:

```
class imgButton
    {
        int left, top, width, height;
    }
```

As specified, the data fields are by default accessible only by methods in the same class. However, these can be changed by using the public, protected, and private keywords. A public data field can be accessed by any part of the program, inside or outside of the class in which the field is defined. A protected data field can only be accessed from within the class or from within a derived class or subclass. A private data field is not accessible even for a derived class.

In addition to adding relevant data fields, appropriate methods or functions must also be provided to operate on the fields if the defined class is to serve any specific purpose. Of all the methods, the most special one is the constructor. This is a method with the same name as the class and enables an object to initialize itself as it is created.

Figure 3.11 shows the constructor of the imgButton class. The constructor assigns input values to the data fields left and top and initiates the button image, including its pushed-down and released-up status. As shown, the constructor starts with the public keyword. This is necessary and important so that an object belonging to this class can be created anywhere in the program. When an object is created, its constructor is actually called. After the public keyword and the name of the constructor or class, the constructor's arguments are specified in parentheses. When an imgButton object is created, these arguments must be supplied. For example, a new button may be created by using

```
nButt = new imgButton(ButtUpName,ButtDownName,140,290);
```

which will pass all four arguments to the constructor for processing.

The creation of other methods is similar to that for the constructor. Also, as for data fields, an appropriate type of access must be provided. Specifically, methods callable from outside the class should be defined as public, methods callable only from the class and its derived classes should be defined as protected, and methods callable only from within the class should be declared as private.

ImgButton: Constructor

```
public imgButton(String s_upImg, String s_downImg, int x, int y)
  {
      left = x;
      top = y;

      try{
          InitImage(new URL(s_upImg), new URL(s_downImg));
          }
      catch(MalformedURLException e)
          {
          System.out.println("imgButton.class: MalformedURL");
          }
  }
```

Figure 3.11. Constructor of the imgButton class.

3.3.3 Class Creation

Like other OOP languages, one can create a new class from an existing class in Java through the principle of inheritance. As an example, using the `extends` keyword, we can create a new `imgButton` subclass from the `Component` superclass by using the following:

```
public class imgButton extends Component
```

The `Component` class is one that has been created in Java for the convenience of programmers. There are numerous basic classes such as this in Java, a common feature of which is that they contain all the basic functionality one may need for various purposes.

The creation of a new subclass enables one to inherit all the data fields and methods that have been created for the superclass without the need to develop new codes. In addition, one can also specify new data fields and methods for the new class that will be special or new or not supplied by the superclass. Also, it is possible to override or specify a new version of a method that forms part of the superclass.

4 Components

4.1 Introduction

In Chapter 3, the frequency modulation experiment was used as an example for describing how the client GUI and instrument panel can be vividly designed. Some brief background information on the programming methodology that can be used to create components for constructing the GUI was also presented.

In general, the construction and realization of the GUI and instrument panels require the creation of many Java classes, some simple and some complicated, for a variety of purposes and components. As will be described shortly, this diverse set of classes can be divided roughly into a few tiers, as shown in Figure 4.1. Note that the figure shows the relationships between different tiers, with the arrows denoting inheritance. A description of the four tiers follows.

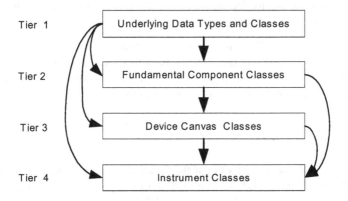

Figure 4.1. Class tiers.

- **Underlying Data Types and Classes**

  This tier contains the basic data types and classes that are available in Java [31]. Common basic data types are `byte`, `short`, `int`, `long`, `float`, `double`, `char`, and `boolean`, while some frequently used classes are `Applet`, `Component`, and `Canvas`.

- **Classes for Fundamental Components**

  Derived from the classes in tier 1, this tier contains all the fundamental component classes and serves as the foundation for building instrument panels. Some of the classes in this tier that have been created for our Web-based laboratories are `imgButton`, `Knob`, `Connector`, and `dataDisplay`, which are templates for buttons, knobs, connectors, and display windows, respectively.

- **Classes for Device Canvases**

  A device canvas class is basically a coarse panel template for an instrument or device and is obtained from the grouping of some appropriate fundamental components that have been created. In our experiments, device canvas classes include `SigGenCanvas`, `SpecAnaCanvas`, and `CircuitBoardCanvas`, which are blueprints for the signal generator, spectrum analyzer, and circuit board, respectively.

- **Classes for Instruments**

  An instrument class is the final class that gives a virtual template for an instrument. Derived from the device canvas and other classes, it has the capability to draw an instrument panel and deal with other related processing such as connecting signals, pushing buttons, turning knobs, and so on. Instances or objects created by this class can be embedded in an HTML file and executed on the client side. In the next chapter, we will take the `SigGen` class, the template for a signal generator, as an example to demonstrate how an instrument class can be derived from other classes.

In this chapter, we will be discussing the creation of `imgButton`, `Knob`, and other fundamental component classes. Note that since Java comes with a class called `Button`, we use `imgButton` as the name of our own button class. Classes in the third and fourth tiers will be discussed in the next chapter.

4.2 ImgButton Class

Figures 4.2, 4.3 and 4.4 give a listing of the Java code for the `imgButton` class. For ease of understanding, the code is separated into three parts, each of which is given in the respective figure. Specifically, Figure 4.2 defines the class and its constructor, Figure 4.3 defines the `initButton()` method, and Figure 4.4 defines other methods.

```
                        imgButton Class

1   import java.awt.*; import java.net.*;
2   public class imgButton extends Component
3   {
4     int left, top, width, height;
5     boolean status = false;
                //false: not pushed, true: pushed
6     Image upImage, downImage;
7     boolean changed = true;
                //whether the button status is changed

8   public imgButton(String s_upImg,
                    String s_downImg, int x, int y)
9   {
10    left = x;
11    top = y;
12    try{
13      InitImage(new URL(s_upImg), new URL(s_downImg));
14      }
15    catch(MalformedURLException e)
16        {
17      System.out.println("imgButton.class: MalformedURL");
18        }
19  }
```

Figure 4.2. imgButton class: definition and constructor.

4.2.1 Class Definition and Constructor

The Java code for the definition and constructor of the imgButton class for the purpose of creating buttons in our Web-based laboratories is listed in Figure 4.2. The purpose of the various important lines is described below.

1   Tell Java that the program uses the awt and net packages.

2   Derive the imgButton class from the Component class in Java. In Java, a component is an object that has a graphical representation, is displayable on the screen, and can interact with the user. Examples of components are the buttons, checkboxes, and scrollbars of a typical graphical user interface. The Component class is the abstract superclass of the nonmenu-related Abstract Window Toolkit (awt) components. The class can also be extended directly to create a lightweight component, a component that is not associated with a native opaque window.

4   Declare int variables left, top, width, and height. These give the left and top positions as well as width and height of the button.

5   Declare a `boolean` variable `status`. A `true status` means that the button has been pushed down.

6   Declare `image` objects `upImage` and `downImage`. These are used for the images of the button, with the former corresponding to a released-up button and the latter to a pushed-down one.

7   Declare a `boolean` variable `changed` for determining whether the status of the button has changed.

8   Define the constructor. The constructor has four arguments: `String s_upImg`, `String s_downImg`, `int x`, `int y`. The arguments `s_upImg` and `s_downImg` are used to retrieve the URL addresses of the released-up and pushed-down images, while `x` and `y` give the coordinates of the top left position of the button.

10–11   Initialize the variables with the constructor arguments.

12–14   Call the `initImage()` method to initialize the button's images.

15–18   Catch and handle exceptions.

19   End of definition and constructor.

4.2.2 `initImage()` Method

Figure 4.3 lists the code for the `initImage()` method, which is used to initialize the images of the button. The following give details for the important lines.

20   Define the `initImage()` method. The return type is `void`, which implies that the method does not return any value. The method has two URL arguments: `URL URLupImg` and `URL URLdownImg`. The `URL` class provides methods for one to query URL objects. By using its accessory methods, one can obtain the protocol, host name, port number, and filename of a URL.

22   Declare `MediaTracker` object `tracker`. The `MediaTracker` class is a utility class for tracking the status of a number of media objects, which may include audio clips and images. To use a media tracker, one creates a `MediaTracker` object and calls its `addImage()` method for each image to be tracked. In addition, each image may be assigned a unique identifier. Controlling the order in fetching images, this identifier can also be used to identify unique subsets of the images that can be waited on independently. Images with a lower ID are loaded in preference to those with a higher ID.

24–25   Download `URLupImg` and `URLdownImg`, and then pass it to `upImage` and `downImage`.

```
                    imgButton Class (continued)
20    public void InitImage(URL URLupImg, URL URLdownImg)
21    {
22        MediaTracker tracker;

23        try{
24            upImage = getToolkit().getImage(URLupImg);
25            downImage = getToolkit().getImage(URLdownImg);
26            tracker = new MediaTracker(this);
27            tracker.addImage(upImage,0);
28            tracker.addImage(downImage,1);
29            tracker.waitForAll();
30            }
31        catch(InterruptedException e)
32            {
33                e.printStackTrace();
34            }

35        width = upImage.getWidth(this);
36        height = upImage.getHeight(this);
37    }
```

Figure 4.3. imgButton class: initImage() method.

26   Initialize tracker by using the current instance.

27   Call addImage() method to add upImage for tracking and assign it an ID number of 0, signifying the highest priority for fetching the image.

28   Call addImage() method to add downImage for tracking and assign it an ID number of 1, signifying the second highest-priority for fetching the image.

29   Wait for happenings over the tracked objects and take corresponding actions.

31–34 Catch and handle exceptions.

35–36 Pass the height and width of the image to associated variables.

4.2.3 Other Methods

Some explanations of the codes listed in Figure 4.4 for defining other methods are given below:

38–42 Define method set(). The purpose of this method is to set the status of the button to the input argument. If the former is different from the latter, the variable changed is set to true.

```
┌─────────────────────────────────────────────────────┐
│              imgButton Class (continued)              │
├─────────────────────────────────────────────────────┤
│ 38 public void Set(boolean b)                         │
│ 39   {                                                │
│ 40       changed = (b != status);                     │
│ 41       status = b;                                  │
│ 42   }                                                │
│                                                       │
│ 43 public boolean isDown()                            │
│ 44   {                                                │
│ 45       return status;                               │
│ 46   }                                                │
│                                                       │
│ 47 public boolean isUp()                              │
│ 48   {                                                │
│ 49       return (! status);                           │
│ 50   }                                                │
│                                                       │
│ 51   }    //end of the class                          │
└─────────────────────────────────────────────────────┘
```

Figure 4.4. `imgButton` class: other methods.

43–46   Define method `isDown()`. Return `True` if `status` is `true` or the button is currently pushed down.

47–50   Define method `isUp()`. Return `True` if `status` is `false` or the button is currently in the released or up position.

51   End of definition of the `imgButton` class.

4.3 Knob Class

The `Knob` class is similar to the `imgButton` class, and the code for defining it is also made up of three parts: definition of the class and constructor; definition of the `initImage()` method; and definition of other methods.

However, the two objects are inherently slightly different and behave differently. Specifically, a button can only be on or off, while a knob may have values over a continuous range that can be expressed in terms of its angle. Also, a mouse click would change the status of a button, while one has to drag the knob using the mouse to turn or change its position.

4.3.1 Class Definition and Constructor

Figure 4.5 lists the code for defining the `Knob` class and gives its constructor. An Important explanation of the code follows:

```
                          Knob Class

   1   import java.awt.*; import java.net.*;

   2   public class Knob extends Component
   3     {
   4       Point Central;
   5       int Radius;
   6       Dimension knobDimension;
   7       Dimension indicatorDimension;
   8       Image knobImage;
   9       Image indicatorImage;
  10       int numOfPos = 0;
  11       int currentPos = -1;
  12       int Positions[];
  13       float Angle = 0;
  14       float startAngle = 0;
  15       float endAngle = 0;
  16       boolean Moved = false;
  17       public Knob(String s_knob, String s_indicator, int r)
  18         {
  19           Radius = r;
  20           try{
  21             InitImage(new URL(s_knob), new URL(s_indicator));
  22             }
  23           catch(MalformedURLException e)
  24             {
  25               System.out.println("Knob.class: MalformedURL");
  26             }
  27         }
```

Figure 4.5. Knob class: class definition and constructor.

1 Tell Java that the program uses the awt and net packages.

2 Derive the Knob class from the Component class.

4 Declare Point object Central. The Point class deals with the *x* and *y* coordinates of a specific point. Here, the object Central gives the central position of the knob in terms of its *x* and *y* coordinates.

5 Declare int variable Radius for storing the radius of the knob.

6–9 Declare Dimension objects knobDimension and indicatorDimension and Image objects knobImage and indicatorImage. As shown in Figure 4.6, a knob actually consists of two images: the knob canvas and the knob indicator. When the knob is turned, the indicator is made to move along with the mouse while the canvas remains in the same fixed position. This will result in a visual effect that the knob is being turned.

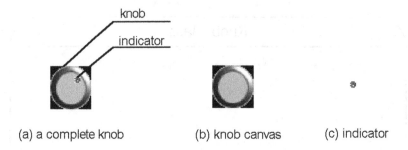

(a) a complete knob   (b) knob canvas   (c) indicator

Figure 4.6. A knob is constructed with a canvas and an indicator.

10–12   Declare `int` variables for the position of the knob and its processing. In certain realizations, a knob may represent a value that is continuous, as when it is used to denote a variable resistor. However, in applications such as the one illustrated in Figure 4.7, where the realization corresponds to the "SWEEP TIME/DIV" knob in an oscilloscope panel, the value that the knob can take is discrete in nature. For this and other practical reasons, the knob can be implemented in a discrete manner by using a variable `numOf-Pos` to denote the number of positions available for the indicator or knob, an array `Positions[]` to indicate the available discrete angles in degree (from –180 to 180) for all the positions, and a variable `currentPos` to give an index to this array for the current position.

13–15   Declare `int` variables for transforming or mapping the internal discrete knob position and the actual visual angle of the indicator.

Figure 4.7. A knob that may take on any value in a discrete set.

16   Declare a `boolean` variable `Moved`, which is used to determine whether the knob has been turned. If it has, the panel needs to be repainted.

17   Define the constructor. The constructor has three arguments: `String s_knob`, `String s_indicator` and `int r`. The arguments `s_knob` and `s_downImg` are used to retrieve the URL addresses of the images of the knob canvas and the indicator, respectively. `r` is the radius of the knob.

19   Pass the constructor argument `r` to the class variable `Radius`, initializing the knob's radius.

20–22   Call method `initImage()` to load the images of the knob canvas and indicator.

23–26   Catch and handle exceptions.

27   End of definition of the constructor.

4.3.2 `initImage()` Method

Figure 4.8 lists the code for the definition of the `initImage()` method for the Knob class. This definition is almost the same as that for the `imgButton` class and will not be discussed further.

```
                    Knob Class (continued)

28   public void InitImage(URL URLknob, URL URLindicator)
29   {
30     MediaTracker tracker;
31     try{
32         knobImage = getToolkit().getImage(URLknob);
33         indicatorImage = getToolkit().getImage(URLindicator);
34         tracker = new MediaTracker(this);
35         tracker.addImage(knobImage,0);
36         tracker.addImage(indicatorImage,1);
37         tracker.waitForAll();
38         }
39     catch(InterruptedException e)
40         {
41         e.printStackTrace();
42         }
43     knobDimension = new Dimension(knobImage.getWidth(this),
                                     knobImage.getHeight(this));
44     indicatorDimension =
                  new Dimension(indicatorImage.getWidth(this),
45                              indicatorImage.getHeight(this));
46   }
```

Figure 4.8. Knob class: `initImage()` method.

4.3.3 Other Methods

Figure 4.9 lists the code for defining the standardAngle() method. This method normalizes a float into the range of –180 to 180 and is included for convenience in subsequent processing. Figure 4.10 lists the code for the definition of the setAngle() method. The method sets the current angle and the movement status of the knob. A detailed explanation is given below.

122   The float argument a is normalized into the range of –180 to 180.

123   Check whether the normalized a is a valid angle.

125   If a is valid, it is assigned to the class variable Angle.

126   At the same time, the boolean variable Moved is set to true, indicating that the knob has been successfully dragged.

Knob Class (continued)

```
47 public static float standardAngle(float a)
48   {
49     a = a%360; //make 'a' in the range of -180 to 180
50     if (a>180)
51       {
52         a -= 360;
53       }
54     if (a<=-180)
55       {
56         a += 360;
57       }
58     return a;
59   }
```

Figure 4.9. Knob class: standardAngle() method.

Knob Class (continued)

```
120   public void setAngle(float a)
121   {
122     a = standardAngle(a);
123     if (! outOfBoundary(a))
124       {
125           Angle = a;
126           Moved = true;
127       }
128   }
```

Figure 4.10. Knob class: setAngle() method.

Figure 4.11 lists the code for the definitions of the setStartAngle() and setEndAngle() methods. As shown, these two methods are quite simple and serve to set the starting and ending angles of the knob.

Lastly, Figure 4.12 lists the setPosition() method, which is used to approximate the float value given by Angle to the nearest available discrete value defined for the knob. This method finds out such a value and sets the value at the knob's current position.

Knob Class (continued)

```
129  public void setStartAngle(float a)
130  {
131    a = standardAngle(a);
132    startAngle = a;
133  }

134  public void setEndAngle(float a)
135  {
136    a = standardAngle(a);
137    endAngle = a;
138  }
```

Figure 4.11. Knob class: setStartAngle() and setEndAngle() methods.

4.4 Connector Class

A connector is an important component that helps to establish an electrical connection between two instruments or circuits. As examples, we will need to connect the output of the signal generator to the modulation circuit if we want to modulate the former using FM, and we have to connect the output of the modulation circuit board to the input terminal of the spectrum analyzer if we want to see the spectrum of the modulated signal. As illustrated in the dashed ovals in Figure 4.13, frequently used connectors in Web-based laboratories are crocodile clips, coaxial plug-in probes, and so on.

The Connector class bears more resemblance to the imgButton than the Knob class. It has two possible statuses: connected or disconnected. As for the two other classes, however, the definition of the Connector class can also be divided roughly into three sections.

4.4.1 Class Definition and Constructor

Figure 4.14 lists the code for defining the Connector class and its constructor. The following gives some details on the important lines.

```
                        Knob Class (continued)

139   public void setPosition()
140   {
141     //set the angle to the nearest position, if
                               positions are available
142       int i;
143       int index=0;
144       float min = 360;
145       float temp;

146        //find index
147        if (numOfPos>0)
148        {
149         for (i=0;i<numOfPos;i++)
150         {
151            temp = Math.abs(Positions[i]-Angle)%360;
152            if (temp>180)
153            {
154              temp = 360-temp;
155            }
156            if (temp< min)
157            {
158              min = temp;
159              index = i;
160            }
161         }
162         setAngle((float)Positions[index]);
163         currentPos = index;
164        }
165   }

166   } //end of class
```

Figure 4.12. Knob class: `setPosition()` method.

1 Tell Java that the program uses the `awt` and `net` packages.

2 Derive the `Knob` class from the `Component` class.

4 Declare `int` variables `left`, `top`, `width`, and `height`. These denote the left and top positions as well as the width and height of the connector, respectively.

5 Declare a `boolean` variable `status`. A `true status` means that the connector is connected to the associated test point, terminal, or socket.

6 Declare `Image` objects `connectImage` and `disconnectImage` to be used for the images of the connector. As shown in the dashed rectangles of Figures 4.15 and 4.16, there are different images for the disconnected (off) and connected (on) statuses.

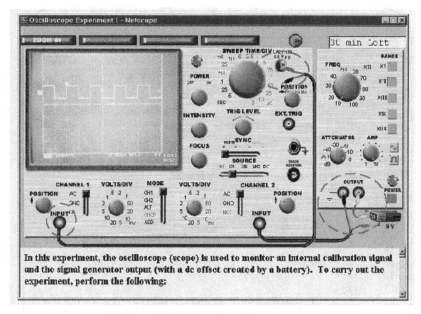

Figure 4.13. Samples of connector.

7   Declare a `boolean` variable `changed`. Once the status of the connector is changed (that is, the connector has been plugged into or pulled out of the socket), `changed` is set to `true`.

8–9   Declare `int` variables `connectArea_left`, `connectArea_top`, `connectArea_right`, and `connectArea_bottom`. These are used to define the active area for making a connection. As shown in Figure 4.16, when the plug is dragged over the dashed rectangle, the connector will be taken to have been plugged into the socket and a connection will be established.

10–11   Like the four variables above, the variables declared here are used to define the active area for a disconnection. As shown in Figure 4.15, when the plug is dragged over the dashed rectangle, the connector will be taken to have been pulled out of the socket and the connection will be broken.

12   Declare `int` variable `moveMode` to denote the movement mode of the connector. There are four possible modes: 0 – from left to right; 1 – from right to left; 2 – from down to up; and 3 – from up to down.

13   Define the constructor. The constructor has four arguments: `String s_connectImg`, `String s_disconnectImg`, `int x`, `int y`. The arguments `s_connectImg` and `s_disconnectImg` are used to retrieve the URL addresses of the connection and disconnection images; `x` and `y` give the coordinates of the top left position of the connector.

Connector Class

```
1   import java.awt.*; import java.net.*;

2   public class Connector extends Component
3   {
4    int left, top, width, height;
5    boolean status = false;
6    Image connectImage, disconnectImage;
7    boolean changed = false;
8    int connectArea_left, connectArea_top,
9       connectArea_right, connectArea_bottom;
10   int disconnectArea_left, disconnectArea_top,
11      disconnectArea_right, disconnectArea_bottom;
12   int moveMode = 0;

13   public Connector(String s_connectImg,
                     String s_disconnectImg, int x, int y)
14   {
15    left = x;
16    top = y;
17    try{
18        InitImage(new URL(s_connectImg),
                   new URL(s_disconnectImg));
19        }
20    catch(MalformedURLException e)
21        {
22      System.out.println("Connector.class: MalformedURL");
23        }
24   }
```

Figure 4.14. `Connector` class: class definition and constructor.

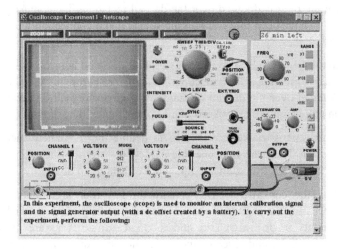

Figure 4.15. Connecter status: disconnected or off.

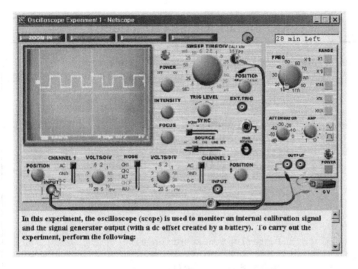

Figure 4.16. Connector status: connected or on.

15–16   Initialize the variables with the constructor arguments.

17–19   Call the `initImage()` method to initialize the connector images.

20–23   Catch and handle exceptions.

24   End of definition and constructor.

4.4.2 `initImage()` Method

Figure 4.17 lists the code for the definition of the `initImage()` method for the `Connector` class. This is quite similar to that for the `imgButton` class, and a detailed explanation can be found there.

4.4.3 Other Methods

Figure 4.18 lists the code for the definition of the `Set()` and `isConnected()` methods for the `Connector` class. Basically, the former sets the status of the connector to the input argument and changes the variable `changed` to `true` if this results in an actual change in status. The latter simply returns the status or indicates whether the connector is connected.

Figure 4.19 gives the codes for the definition of the `setMouseActive-Area()` method. The first half of the code sets the active area for making connection (within the dashed rectangle in Figure 4.16), while the second half sets the active area for disconnection (within the dashed rectangle in Figure 4.15). If the values of the arguments are valid, they are passed to the class variables.

```
              Connector Class (continued)

25    public void InitImage(URL URLconnectImg,
                            URL URLdisconnectImg)
26    {
27      MediaTracker tracker;
28      try{
29          connectImage =
                getToolkit().getImage(URLconnectImg);
30          disconnectImage =
                getToolkit().getImage(URLdisconnectImg);
31          tracker = new MediaTracker(this);
32          tracker.addImage(connectImage,0);
33          tracker.addImage(disconnectImage,1);
34          tracker.waitForAll();
35          }
36      catch(InterruptedException e)
37          {
38            e.printStackTrace();
39          }
40      width = connectImage.getWidth(this);
41      height = connectImage.getHeight(this);
42    }
```

Figure 4.17. Connector class: initImage() method.

```
              Connector Class (continued)

43    public void Set(boolean b)
44      {
45          changed = (b != status);
46          status = b;
47      }

48    public boolean isConnected()
49      {
50          return status;
51      }
```

Figure 4.18. Connector class: Set() method and isConnected() method.

```
                    Connector Class (continued)

52   public void setMouseActiveArea(int x1, int y1, int x2,
53                    int y2, int x3, int y3, int x4, int y4)
54   {

55    if (x1>=0 && x1<x2 && x2<=width ){
56       connectArea_left = x1;
57       connectArea_right = x2; }
58    else{System.out.println("invalid value");}

59    if (y1>=0 && y1<y2 && y2<=height ){
60       connectArea_top = y1;
61       connectArea_bottom = y2; }
62    else{System.out.println("invalid value");}

63    if (x3>=0 && x3<x4 && x4<=width ){
64       disconnectArea_left = x3;
65       disconnectArea_right = x4; }
66    else{System.out.println("invalid value");}

67    if (y3>=0 && y3<y4 && y4<=height ){
68       disconnectArea_top = y3;
69       disconnectArea_bottom = y4;}
70    else{System.out.println("invalid value");}
71    }

72   } //end of class
```

Figure 4.19. `Connector` class: `setMouseActiveArea()` method.

4.5 `DataDisplay` Class

In most Web-based laboratory applications, the real-time display of digital data is necessary to reflect changes in signals or readings measured by instruments in the physical laboratory. Figure 4.20 shows an example where the vivid display of data in an instrument panel makes conducting an experiment in a Web-based laboratory a realistic experience.

Figure 4.20. A simple example of the display of digital data.

By using Java and OOP, it is not difficult to implement inviting digital data displays. In our Web-based laboratories, we have created a dataDisplay class for this purpose.

4.5.1 Class Definition and Constructor

Figure 4.21 lists the code for the definition of the class and constructor.

1 Tell Java that the program uses the awt package.

4 Declare the int variables left, top, width, height, and fontSize. The first four variables denote the left and top positions as well as width and height of the display, respectively. The last variable, fontSize, gives the font size for the display.

5 Declare the String object displayString, which contains the data string to be displayed.

6 Declare the boolean variable changed. If the data being displayed are changed, the variable is set to true.

```
                      dataDisplay Class

 1   import java.awt.*;

 2   class dataDisplay
 3   {
 4     int left, top, width, height, fontSize;
 5     String displayString;
 6     boolean changed;
 7     boolean newData;
 8     Color bgColor, strColor;

 9     public dataDisplay(int x, int y, int w, int h, int fs)
10     {
11       left = x;
12       top = y;
13       width =w;
14       height = h;
15       fontSize = fs;
16       changed = false;
17       newData = false;
18       bgColor = Color.black;
19       strColor = Color.green;
20       displayString = "";
21     }
```

Figure 4-21. dataDisplay class: class definition and constructor.

7 Declare the `boolean` variable `newData`. On the arrival of a new data string, the variable `newData` will be set to `true` and the display will be cleared.

8 Declare the `Color` objects `bgColor` and `strColor`. The former deals with the background color of the display, while the latter is used to set the color of the display font.

9–21 Define the constructor. The constructor initializes the settings for the data display. By default, the background color and font color are set to black and green, respectively.

4.5.2 Other Methods

Figure 4.22 lists the code for the definition of the `clearDisplay()`, `setDisplayString()`, and `getDisplayString()` methods.

The `clearDisplay()` method clears the content of the display and sets the variable `changed` to `true`. The `setDisplayString()` method is for passing a new data string to be displayed, while the `getDisplayString()` method returns the data string currently being displayed.

```
                    dataDisplay Class (continued)

22    public void clearDisplay()
23    {
24        displayString = "";
25        changed = true;
26    }

27    public void setDisplayString(String s)
28    {
29        if (displayString != s)
30        {
31            displayString = s;
32            changed = true;
33        }
34    }

35    public String getDisplayString()
36    {
37        return displayString;
38    }
39 }
```

Figure 4.22. `dataDisplay` class: other methods.

5 Panels

5.1 Introduction

In the previous chapter, we created some Java classes for a few frequently used fundamental components. Belonging to the first and second tiers in the class tier of Figure 4.1, these classes form the foundation for more complicated classes. In this chapter, we will continue this process to discuss the creation of classes in the third and fourth class tiers: classes for the device canvases and for devices. This will eventually lead to the creation of vivid and complicated GUIs for Web-based laboratories.

5.2 Classes for Device Canvases

As any well-designed Web-based laboratory will involve the use of many device canvas classes, it will not be possible for each of these to be discussed. Instead, the discussion in this chapter will be focused on that for the signal generator, which is a good representation of the other classes.

As shown inside the dashed rectangle in Figure 5.1, the signal generator makes use of all the fundamental component classes that were created in the last chapter: `imgButton`, `Knob`, `Connector` and `dataDisplay`. We will now show how they can be used in the creation of the `SigGenCanvas` class for this instrument.

5.2.1 Class Definition and Variables

Figure 5.2 lists the code for defining the class and the related variables.

1–4 Tell Java that the program uses the `awt`, `awt.event`, `applet` and `net` packages.

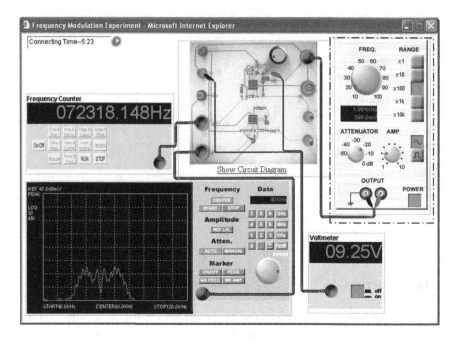

Figure 5.1. Signal generator.

SigGenCanvas Class

```
1    import java.awt.*;
2    import java.awt.event.*;
3    import java.applet.*;
4    import java.net.*;

5    class SigGenCanvas extends Canvas
6    {
7      Knob freqKnob, attenKnob, ampKnob;
8      imgButton rangeButt[];
9      imgButton squareWaveButt, sineWaveButt, powerButt;
10     Connector groundConn, outputConn;
11     Image panelImg;
12     int w,h;
13     float frequency, amplitude, attenuateFactor;
14     int freqRange;
15     dataDisplay freqDisplay, ampDisplay;
16     Client client;
17     CircuitBoard cb;
```

Figure 5.2. SigGenCanvas class: definition and variables.

5 Derive the SigGenCanvas class from the Canvas class. A Canvas object corresponds to a blank rectangular area of the screen onto which an application can draw or from which an application can trap input events from the user. An application must subclass the Canvas class in order to obtain useful functionality such as creating a custom component. Also, the paint method must be overridden in order to perform custom graphical processing on the canvas.

7 Declare Knob objects freqKnob, attenKnob, and ampKnob. As shown in Figure 5.1, these are used for the FREQ, ATTENUATOR, and AMP knobs of the instrument, respectively.

8–9 Declare imgButton objects for the eight buttons of the signal generator. The array rangeButt[] is for the five range buttons, squareWave-Butt is for the square waveform button, sineWaveButt is for the sinusoidal waveform button, and powerButt is for the power button.

10 Declare Connector objects groundConn and outputConn. These objects are for the two crocodile clips for making connections to the two input terminals of the instrument.

15 Declare dataDisplay objects freqDisplay and ampDisplay for displaying the values of the selected frequency and amplitude of the output signal from the signal generator.

16–17 Declare objects on network connection and the circuit board.

5.2.2 Constructor

Figures 5.3 and 5.4 list the code for defining the constructor for SigGenCanvas.

18 Define the constructor, with the argument path giving the URL path for the images.

21–22 Initialize the background of the signal generator by calling the InitImage() method.

23–24 Set default values for amplitude, attentuateFactor, and freqRange. All the variables are initialized to 1. The default settings conform to those for the actual signal generator in the laboratory.

26–33 Create knobs. Note that, as described in Chapter 4, a knob consists of two components: a background and an indicator.

34–53 Initialize the frequency, attenuation, and amplitude knobs. The center point, starting angle, ending angle, and current angle are set to default values.

SigGenCanvas Class (continued)

```
18  public SigGenCanvas(String path)
19  {
20    int i;

21    InitImage(path);
22    setSize(w, h);

23    amplitude = 1;
24    attenuateFactor = 1;
25    freqRange = 1;

26    //create knobs
27    String dotImgName = path + "dot.gif";
28    String freqKnobImgName = path + "biggreyknob.gif";
29    String attenKnobImgName = path + "smallgreyknob.gif";
30    String ampKnobImgName = attenKnobImgName;

31    freqKnob = new Knob(freqKnobImgName, dotImgName, 25);
32    attenKnob = new Knob(attenKnobImgName, dotImgName, 12);
33    ampKnob = new Knob(ampKnobImgName, dotImgName, 12);

34    //initialize frequency knob
35    freqKnob.Central = new Point(60,75);
36    freqKnob.setStartAngle(-120);
37    freqKnob.setEndAngle(-60);
38    freqKnob.setAngle(freqKnob.startAngle);

39    //initialize attenuate knob
40    attenKnob.Central = new Point(40, 215);
41    attenKnob.numOfPos = 6;
42    attenKnob.Positions = new int[6];
43    for (i=0;i<6;i++)
44      {
45        attenKnob.Positions[i] = 180-i*45;
46      }
47    attenKnob.setAngle(attenKnob.Positions[5]);
48    attenKnob.currentPos = 5;

49    //initialize amptitude knob
50    ampKnob.Central = new Point(110, 215);
51    ampKnob.setStartAngle(-120);
52    ampKnob.setEndAngle(-60);
53    ampKnob.setAngle(ampKnob.startAngle);
```

Figure 5.3. SigGenCanvas class: constructor.

SigGenCanvas Class (continued)

```
54   String ButtUpName = path + "range_up.gif";
55   String ButtDownName = path + "range_down.gif";
56   String sineWaveButtUpName = path + "sinewave_up.gif";
57   String sineWaveButtDownName = path + "sinewave_down.gif";
58   String squareWaveButtUpName = path + "squarewave_up.gif";
59   String squareWaveButtDownName=path+"squarewave_down.gif";
60   rangeButt = new imgButton[5];
61   for (i=0;i<5;i++)
62   {
63      rangeButt[i] = new imgButton(ButtUpName, ButtDownName,
                                              145, 30+i*25);
64   }
65   sineWaveButt = new imgButton(sineWaveButtUpName,
66                       sineWaveButtDownName, 145, 180);
67   squareWaveButt = new imgButton(squareWaveButtUpName,
68                       squareWaveButtDownName, 145, 205);
69   powerButt=new imgButton(ButtUpName,ButtDownName,140,290);
70   rangeButt[0].Set(true);
71   sineWaveButt.Set(true);
72   String groundDisconnImgName=path+"BlackEndDisconn.gif";
73   String groundConnImgName = path + "BlackEndConn.gif";
74   String outputDisconnImgName = path + "RedEndDisconn.gif";
75   String outputConnImgName = path + "RedEndConn.gif";
76   groundConn = new Connector(groundConnImgName,
77                       groundDisconnImgName, 44, 288);
78   outputConn = new Connector(outputConnImgName,
79                       outputDisconnImgName, 74, 288);
80   groundConn.setMouseActiveArea(10,0,25,25,0,15,25,30);
81   groundConn.moveMode = 2;  //down-->up
82   outputConn.setMouseActiveArea(0,0,15,25,0,15,25,30);
83   outputConn.moveMode = 2;  //down-->up
84   freqDisplay = new dataDisplay(10, 125, 70, 15, 10);
85   ampDisplay = new dataDisplay(10, 140, 70, 15, 10);

86 }
```

Figure 5.4. SigGenCanvas class: constructor – continued.

54–71   Create and initialize imgButton objects.

72–83   Create and initialize Connector objects.

84–85   Create and initialize dataDisplay objects.

86   End of definition of constructor.

5.2.3 initImage() and Other Display Methods

The definition of initImage() for SigGenCanvas is the same as that for the fundamental component classes in the previous chapter and will not be further discussed here. For other methods used for display processing and formatting, Figure 5.5 lists the code for the float2Hz() method, which converts a float that represents a frequency in Hz into a string with an appropriate unit from Hz, kHz, MHz, and GHz.

Note that the algorithm makes use of methods in the Math class. As an example, Math.abs(freq) is used to call the abs() method under the Math class to find the absolute value of the input freq. Also, the method public double round(double a, int digits) has been used to round down a double float a so that it has digits in significant decimal digits.

Figure 5.6 lists the code for defining the showFreq() and showAmp() methods for the purpose of displaying the frequency and amplitude of the output.

```
                        SigGenCanvas Class (continued)
118    public String float2Hz(float freq)
119    {
120       //convert float value to Hz, KHz, MHz or GHz
121       String result;
122       freq = (float)round(freq, 4);
123       if (Math.abs(freq)>=1e9)
124       {
125          freq /= 1e9;
126          result = Float.toString(freq) + "GHz";
127       }
128       else if (Math.abs(freq)>=1e6)
129       {
130          freq /= 1e6;
131          result = Float.toString(freq) + "MHz";
132       }
133       else if (Math.abs(freq)>=1e3)
134       {
135          freq /= 1e3;
136          result = Float.toString(freq) + "KHz";
137       }
138       else
139       {
140          result = Float.toString(freq) + "Hz";
141       }
142       return result;
143    }
```

Figure 5.5. SigGenCanvas class: float2Hz() method.

```
                    SigGenCanvas Class (continued)

175    public void showFreq()
176    {
177      if (powerButt.isDown())
178        {
179    freqDisplay.setDisplayString(float2Hz(frequency));
180        }
181    }

182    public void showAmp()
183      {
184      if (powerButt.isDown())
185        {
186          float a = amplitude*attenuateFactor;
187          a = (float)round(a, 3);
188          if (a < 1)
189            {
190              ampDisplay.setDisplayString(
                          Float.toString(a*1000) + "mV");
191            }
192        else
193          {
194              ampDisplay.setDisplayString(
                          Float.toString(a) + "V");
195          }
196        }
197      }
```

Figure 5.6. SigGenCanvas class: showFreq() and showAmp() methods.

175–181   Define the showFreq() method. If the signal generator is turned on, the frequency of the output signal is displayed. The method float-2Hz() is called to format the string to be displayed in the appropriate unit.

182–197   Define the showAmp() method. When the signal generator is turned on, the amplitude of the output signal is displayed. The amplitude is rounded to three significant digits before it is displayed. Also, if the value is less than 1V, it is displayed in mV.

5.2.4 Methods for Client Server Communications

Figure 5.7 lists the code for methods associated with network connection. Through these methods, manipulations on the client GUI panel can be sent to the server and cause corresponding changes in the actual instrument in the laboratory. A brief discussion of client/server systems can be found in Chapter 2.

```
                    SigGenCanvas Class (continued)

205    public void sendAmplitude()
206    {
207     if (powerButt.isDown() && cableConnected())
208      {
209         client.DataExchange("sg#amp#"
                   +Float.toString(amplitude*attenuateFactor));
210      }
211    }

212    public void sendWaveform()
213    {
214     if (powerButt.isDown() && cableConnected())
215      {
216         if (sineWaveButt.isDown())
217          {
218             client.DataExchange("sg#wav#sin");
219          }
220         else
221          {
222             client.DataExchange("sg#wav#squ");
223          }
224      }
225    }

226    public void sendAll()
227    {
228     sendFrequency();
229     sendAmplitude();
230     sendWaveform();
231    }
```

Figure 5.7. SigGenCanvas class: methods for client/server communications.

205   Define the sendAmplitude() method for sending the selected output
      amplitude to the server.

207   First check if the power button is pushed down and the signal cable is
      connected.

209   If they are, the selected signal amplitude will be transformed from a float
      to a string by using Float.toString(). The resulting string is then
      prefixed by sg to indicate signal generator and amp to indicate ampli-
      tude, resulting in a formatted command. Eventually, the Client.Data-
      Exchange() method is called to send the command to the server.

212–225 Define the sendWaveform() method that sends a command string to
      the server for selecting the type of waveform to be generated.

5.2.5 Methods for Instrument Handling

Figure 5.8 gives the code for methods that interact with the user in the handling of the various controls of the instrument. In general, the procedure to handle a control knob or button on the instrument is as follows: (1) format the input user-selected value of the control from float to a style that can be displayed; (2) display the value on the appropriate digital data display window; and (3) send the value to the server to make corresponding changes in the actual instrument.

```
                    SigGenCanvas Class (continued)

232     public void setFrequency()
233     {
234         frequency = mapFrequency();
235         showFreq();
236         sendFrequency();
237         repaint();
238     }

239     public void setAmplitude()
240     {
241         amplitude = mapAmplitude();
242         showAmp();
243         sendAmplitude();
244         repaint();
245     }

246     public void setAttenuate()
247     {
248         attenuateFactor = mapAttenFactor();
249         showAmp();
250         sendAmplitude();
251         repaint();
252     }

253     public void setWaveform()
254     {
255         sendWaveform();
256     }
```

Figure 5.8. SigGenCanvas class: methods for handling instruments.

5.2.6 Methods for Switching the Instrument on and Off

Figure 5.9 gives the code for the displayOn() and displayOff() methods. The former turns on the digital displays for the frequency and amplitude, while the latter turns off the displays.

```
                    SigGenCanvas Class (continued)

292    public void displayOn()
293    {
294        frequency = mapFrequency();
295        showFreq();
296        amplitude = mapAmplitude();
297        attenuateFactor = mapAttenFactor();
298        showAmp();
299    }

300    public void displayOff()
301    {
302        freqDisplay.clearDisplay();
303        ampDisplay.clearDisplay();
304    }
```

Figure 5.9. SigGenCanvas class: displayOn()/displayOff() methods.

Figure 5.10 lists the code for the outputOn() and outputOff() methods. Like the methods in Figure 5.7, these involve network connection and instrument control. In outputOn(), if the power button is turned on and the two crocodile clips are connected to the output terminals, the signal generator in the laboratory is electrically turned on by sending a relevant command through the Internet. In outputOff(), a similar command is sent to electronically turn off the signal generator and its output.

```
                    SigGenCanvas Class (continued)

305    public void outputOn()
306    {
307        if (powerButt.isDown() && cableConnected())
308        {
309            client.DataExchange("sg#on#");
310            sendAll();
311        }
312    }

313    public void outputOff()
314    {
315        client.DataExchange("sg#off#");
316    }
```

Figure 5-10. SigGenCanvas class: outputOn() and outputOff() methods.

Figure 5.11 gives the codes for the `powerOnOff()` method. The purpose of the method is simply to turn the output and digital display on whenever the power button is pushed down or in the on position, and vice versa. The method makes use of the other methods discussed in this subsection and then calls the overridden method `repaint()` to repaint the panel.

SigGenCanvas Class (continued)

```
317    public void powerOnOff()
318    {
319        powerButt.Set(!powerButt.status);
320        if (powerButt.isDown())
321        {
322            outputOn();
323            displayOn();
324        }
325        else
326        {
327            outputOff();
328            displayOff();
329        }
330        repaint();
331    }
```

Figure 5.11. `SigGenCanvas` class: `powerOnOff()` method.

5.2.7 Methods for Connectors

Figure 5.12 lists the code for methods that involve the connectors.

332–337 Define the `Connect()` method. The method sets the status of the connector to `true` and turns on the signal generator output.

338–343 Define the `Disconnect()` method. This is the reverse of the `Connect()` method. It sets the status of the connector to `false` and turns off the output.

344–348 Define the `cableConnected()` method. The method returns the overall connection status of the cable. The cable is taken to be connecting the signal generator to the input of the circuit board successfully if the ground terminal `groundConn`, output terminal `outputConn`, and input terminal on the circuit board `VmInConn` are connected appropriately.

```
                  SigGenCanvas Class (continued)

     332    public void Connect(Connector c)
     333    {
     334       c.Set(true);
     335       outputOn();
     336       repaint();
     337    }

     338    public void Disconnect(Connector c)
     339    {
     340       c.Set(false);
     341       outputOff();
     342       repaint();
     343    }

     344    public boolean cableConnected()
     345    {
     346       return(groundConn.isConnected()
                  && outputConn.isConnected()
     347          && cb.cbc.VmInConn.isConnected());
     348    }
```

Figure 5.12. `SigGenCanvas` class: methods for connectors.

5.2.8 `update()` and `paint()` Methods

Figures 5.13 and 5.14 give the codes for the `update()` and `paint()` methods. These two methods refresh the panel once some components or controls are moved or changed.

In `update()`, when a control is changed, only that control is refreshed. The other controls or components are left untouched. In `paint()`, all the controls or components on the panel are refreshed. This difference allows the two methods to be effectively used in different scenarios.

In both `update()` and `paint()`, a variety of generic `draw*()` methods are used to draw the relevant components. As an illustration, the codes for the `drawKnob()` and `drawImgImage()` methods are presented in Figure 5.15.

5.3 Classes for Devices

The creation of the device canvas `SigGenCanvas` class was discussed in Section 5.2, with a detailed description of the main variables and methods presented in Subsections 5.2.1–5.2.8. Although the entire program is lengthy and complicated, the use of OOP and an appropriate class structure reduces the complexity to something more manageable.

```
                   SigGenCanvas Class (continued)

349     public void update(Graphics g)
350     {
351     //To avoid flashing, only redraw the moved knob.
352     //Other knobs/panel background won't be redrawn.
353      int i;

354      if (freqKnob.Moved)
355      {
356          drawKnob(g, freqKnob);
357          freqKnob.Moved = false;
358      }

        ...

369      for (i=0;i<5;i++)
370      {
371          if (rangeButt[i].changed)
372          {
373              drawImgButton(g, rangeButt[i]);
374              rangeButt[i].changed = false;
375          }
376      }
        ...

418     }
```

Figure 5.13. SigGenCanvas class: update() method.

```
                   SigGenCanvas Class (continued)

419     public void paint(Graphics g)
420     {
421      int i;

422      g.drawImage(panelImg, 0, 0, this);

423      drawKnob(g, freqKnob);
424      drawKnob(g, attenKnob);
425      drawKnob(g, ampKnob);

426      for (i=0;i<5;i++)
427      {
428          drawImgButton(g, rangeButt[i]);
429      }
430      drawImgButton(g, sineWaveButt);
431      drawImgButton(g, squareWaveButt);
432      drawImgButton(g, powerButt);
433      drawConnector(g, groundConn);
434      drawConnector(g, outputConn);
435      drawDataDisplay(g, freqDisplay);
436      drawDataDisplay(g, ampDisplay);
437     }
```

Figure 5.14. SigGenCanvas class: paint() method.

```
           SigGenCanvas Class (continued)
438   public void drawKnob(Graphics g, Knob k)
439   {
440     int x0 = k.Central.x ;
441     int y0 = k.Central.y ;
442     g.drawImage(k.knobImage,
                    x0 - k.knobDimension.width/2,
443                 y0 - k.knobDimension.height/2, this);
444     double temp = Math.PI*k.Angle/180;
445     int x = (int)Math.rint(x0+k.Radius*Math.cos(temp));
446     int y = (int)Math.rint(y0-k.Radius*Math.sin(temp));
447     g.drawImage(k.indicatorImage,
                    x-k.indicatorDimension.width/2,
448                 y-k.indicatorDimension.height/2, this);
449   }

450   public void drawImgButton(Graphics g, imgButton ib)
451   {
452     if (ib.status)
453     {
454       g.drawImage(ib.downImage, ib.left, ib.top, this);
455     }
456     else
457     {
458       g.drawImage(ib.upImage, ib.left, ib.top, this);
459     }
460   }
```

Figure 5.15. `SigGenCanvas` class: `drawKnob()` and `drawImgButton()` methods.

In this section, the `SigGenCanvas` class, which lies in the third tier of the class structure of Figure 4.1, will be used as an example to aid in the creation of a fourth tier class for the template of an instrument. In particular, it will be used as the blueprint to create the `SigGen` class for a signal generator.

5.3.1 Class Definition and Variables

Figure 5.16 gives the code for defining `SigGen` and the main variables involved.

1–4   Tell Java to use the `awt`, `awt.event`, `applet`, and `net` packages.

5–6   Derive the `SigGen` class from the `Applet` class. In the definition clause, the keyword `implement is` used to specify the interfaces to be implemented. The use of `implements` is basically a mechanism for a class to adhere to the behavior protocols defined by certain interfaces. A class can implement more than one interface, and, for this case, two interfaces, `MouseListener` and `MouseMotionListener`, are implemented

8   Instantiate the `SigGenCanvas` object `sgc`. This object is the main constituent of the class.

```
                          SigGen Class
     1   import java.awt.*;
     2   import java.awt.event.*;
     3   import java.applet.*;
     4   import java.net.*;

     5   public class SigGen extends Applet implements
     6         MouseListener,MouseMotionListener
     7   {
     8     SigGenCanvas sgc;
     9     int obj = 0;
    10     int x0,y0;
    11     int r;
    12     Knob movingKnob;
    13     Connector movingConnector;
    14     float mouseangle, newangle;
    15     int start_x, start_y;
    16     Monitor mon;
    17     boolean runtag = true;
```

Figure 5.16. SigGen class: class definition and variables.

9   Declare int variable obj, which is used to denote the current focused object. Value 0 means there is no focused object at present.

10–11   Declare int variables x0, y0, and r. The first two variables give the center point of the moving knob, while the last one gives its radius at present.

12–13   Declare moving objects movingKnob and movingConnector, which give the current moving knob and connector.

14   Declare float variables mouseangle and newangle, which are used in calculations involving the angle of the knob.

15   Declare int variables start_x and start_y. These two variables are used for the connector.

5.3.2 Overriding the init() Method

In general, the life cycle of an applet consists of five stages: (1) initialization; (2) starting; (3) painting; (4) stopping; and (5) destruction. To achieve certain specific objectives in an application, the corresponding default method for the applet can be overridden.

An applet enters the initialization stage when it is created and loaded. Figure 5.17 shows the code for overriding the init() method in the creation of a signal generator.

```
                  SigGen Class (continued)

18   public void init()
19   {
20     String path = getCodeBase().toString();

21     sgc = new SigGenCanvas(path);
22     sgc.addMouseListener(this);
23     sgc.addMouseMotionListener(this);
24     setLayout(new BorderLayout());
25     add("Center", sgc);

26     //get other applets in the same HTML page
27     while (sgc.client==null)
28       {
29         sgc.client = (Client)
                  (getAppletContext().getApplet("client"));

30
31       }
32     while (sgc.cb==null)
33       {
34          sgc.cb = (CircuitBoard)
                 (getAppletContext().getApplet("CircuitBoard"));

35
36       }
37       sgc.outputOff();
38     }
```

Figure 5.17. SigGen class: overriding the init() method.

20   Retrieve the code base of the class. Whenever an applet needs to load some data from a file that is specified with a relative URL, the applet usually uses either the code base or the document base to form the complete URL. The code base, returned by the Applet getCodeBase method, is a URL that specifies the directory from which the classes of the applet were loaded.

21   Create an instance for SigGenCanvas.

22–23   Add a mouse listener and mouse motion listener to the object sgc. This enables the object to respond to mouse events.

24–25   Set the object layout. Layout managers are special objects that determine how elements of an applet are organized in the display of the applet. When an applet is created, default layout managers are automatically created and assigned to determine where controls will appear. However, one can also create different layout managers to give a better-looking applet. There are five layout managers: FlowLayout, GridLayout, BorderLayout, CardLayout, and GridBagLayout. Each of these layout managers is represented by a class of the same name. To create a layout manager for an applet, an instance of the appropriate layout class has to be created first. The setLayout() method can then be called to tell Java the layout object to be used. Line 24 creates the BorderLayout manager, which enables the positioning of components using the directions north, south, east, west, and center. In Line 25, the sgc object is added to the center of the applet.

27–31 Find the client applet from all the applets that will be used in the GUI of the frequency modulation experiment. Note that, besides the applet for the signal generator (SigGen.class), there are also independent applets for the client (Client.class), circuit board (CircuitBoard.class), frequency counter (FreqCounter.class), spectrum analyzer (SpecAna.class), and voltmeter (VoltMeter.class). Although these applets are independent, communication between them can be carried out by invoking the relevant methods. Specifically, one applet can access another one by using the getApplet method.

32–36 Find the CircuitBoard applet.

37 Turn off the output of the signal generator.

5.3.3 Methods for Detecting the Mouse over Controls

Figure 5.18 lists the code for the isKnob() method, which returns the status on whether the mouse is over a knob.

42–43 Retrieve the current position of the mouse.

44–45 Retrieve the center point of the knob.

46 Retrieve the radius of the knob.

47–54 Determine whether the mouse is over the knob. As shown in Figure 5.19, the formula used corresponds to finding whether the arrow point of the mouse lies inside the knob.

Similarly, Figures 5.20 and 5.21 give the codes for the isImgButton() and isConnector() methods, respectively. The former determines whether the mouse is over a button, while the latter is for finding out if the mouse is over the effective area of a connector. Note that the code for the latter is slightly more complicated, as a connector has two different statuses and has different connected and disconnected areas.

Finally, Figure 5.22 shows the code for defining the whichObject() method, which checks whether the mouse is over any control knobs, buttons, or connectors. Making use of isKnob(), isImgButton(), and isConnector(), the method assigns an identification number (ID) for the component found. The list of IDs for the various controls is given in Table 5.1.

SigGen Class (continued)

```
39    public boolean isKnob(Knob k, MouseEvent e)
40    {
41        int x,y,x1,y1,r;
42        x = e.getX();
43        y = e.getY();
44        x1 = k.Central.x;
45        y1 = k.Central.y;
46        r = k.knobDimension.width/2;
47        if ((x-x1)*(x-x1)+(y-y1)*(y-y1) < r*r)
48        {
49            return true;
50        }
51        else
52        {
53            return false;
54        }
55    }
```

Figure 5.18. SigGen class: isKnob() method.

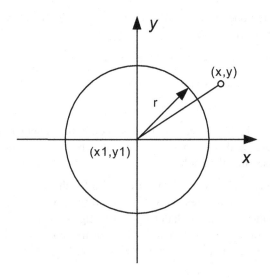

Figure 5.19. Detecting whether the mouse is over a knob.

```
                    SigGen Class (continued)

56  public boolean isImgButton(imgButton ib, MouseEvent e)
57  {
58    int x,y;
59    x = e.getX();
60    y = e.getY();
61    if (x>=ib.left && x<=ib.left+ib.width
                       && y>=ib.top && y<=ib.top+ib.height)
62    {
63        return true;
64    }
65    else
66    {
67        return false;
68    }
69  }
```

Figure 5.20. SigGen class: isImgButton() method.

```
                    SigGen Class (continued)

70  public boolean isConnector(Connector c, MouseEvent e)
71  {
72    int x,y,left,top,right,bottom;
73    x = e.getX();
74    y = e.getY();
75    if (c.status)
76    {
77      left = c.left + c.connectArea_left;
78      top = c.top + c.connectArea_top;
79      right = c.left + c.connectArea_right;
80      bottom = c.top + c.connectArea_bottom;
81    }
82    else
83    {
84      left = c.left + c.disconnectArea_left;
85      top = c.top + c.disconnectArea_top;
86      right = c.left + c.disconnectArea_right;
87      bottom = c.top + c.disconnectArea_bottom;
88    }
89    if (x>=left && x<=right && y>=top && y<=bottom)
90    {
91        return true;
92    }
93    else
94    {
95        return false;
96    }
97  }
```

Figure 5.21. SigGen class: isConnector() method.

```
                    SigGen Class (continued)
98   public int whichObject(MouseEvent e)
99   {
100    int i;
101    if (isKnob(sgc.freqKnob, e)) return 1;
102    if (isKnob(sgc.attenKnob, e)) return 2;
103    if (isKnob(sgc.ampKnob, e)) return 3;
104    for (i=0;i<5;i++)
105    {
106      if (isImgButton(sgc.rangeButt[i],e)) return (11+i);
107    }
108    if (isImgButton(sgc.sineWaveButt, e)) return 16;
109    if (isImgButton(sgc.squareWaveButt,  e)) return 17;
110    if (isImgButton(sgc.powerButt, e)) return 18;
111    if (isConnector(sgc.groundConn, e)) return 21;
112    if (isConnector(sgc.outputConn, e)) return 22;
113    return 0;
114  }
```

Figure 5.22. SigGen class: whichObject() method.

Table 5.1. ID assignment.

Component	ID
No event	0
Frequency knob (sgc.freqKnob)	1
Attenuation knob (sgc.attenKnob)	2
Amplitude knob (sgc.ampKnob)	3
Range buttons 1–5 (sgc.rangeButt[i])	11–15
Sine wave button (sgc.sineWaveButt)	16
Square wave button (sgc.squareWaveButt)	17
Power button (sgc.powerButt)	18
Ground connector (sgc.groundConn)	21
Output connector (sgc.outputConn)	22

5.3.4 Methods for Mouse Movement and Dragging

Figure 5.23 gives the code for the changeCursor() method. The purpose of this method is for the mouse cursor to be shown in the usual form of an arrow icon (DE-FAULT_CURSOR) if it is not over any control and for it to be shown as a hand icon (HAND_CURSOR) when it is moved over a control button, knob, or connector. This change in the icon is a very user-friendly way to inform the client user whenever the mouse is moved over a control that can be adjusted.

```
                    SigGen Class (continued)
115   public void changeCursor(MouseEvent e)
116   {
117     obj = whichObject(e);
118     if (obj != 0)
119       {
120         setCursor(Cursor.getPredefinedCursor(Cursor.
                                      HAND_CURSOR));
121       }
122     else
123       {
124         setCursor(Cursor.getPredefinedCursor(Cursor.
                                      DEFAULT_CURSOR));
125       }
126   }
```

Figure 5.23. SigGen class: changeCursort() method.

Figure 5.24 gives the codes for the startDrag() and endDrag() methods. These methods together handle the turning of knobs by the user through dragging the mouse. The startDrag() method keeps track of the current angle of the knob in float format, while the endDrag() method handles the processing when the dragging is released by calling the appropriate method to update the display and change the setting of the physical instrument.

Similarly, Figure 5.25 presents the codes for the StartMove() and end-Move() methods for handling the processing associated with connectors.

156–161 Record the position when the mouse starts to move.

165–166 Retrieve the position when the mouse stops.

167 Check the move mode for the connector. This mode, as mentioned before, may be one of four types: 0 – from left to right; 1 – from right to left; 2 – from down to up; and 3 – from up to down. Basically, the direction specified by the mode is used so that if the mouse moves in that direction, the connector will be taken to be connected. If the movement is

in the opposite direction, a disconnection operation will be taken to have happened. As an example, with a move mode of 0 and a mouse movement from left to right, a plug will be taken to have been inserted into a socket. On the other hand, if the movement is from right to left, the plug will be taken to have been pulled out of the socket.

SigGen Class (continued)

```
127   public void startDrag(Knob k, MouseEvent e)
128   {
129      int x,y;
130      r = k.knobDimension.width/2;
131      x0 = k.Central.x;
132      y0 = k.Central.y;
133      x = e.getX();
134      y = e.getY();
135      mouseangle = (float)(Math.atan2(y0-y,
                                       x-x0)/Math.PI*180);
136      movingKnob = k;
137   }

138   public void endDrag(MouseEvent e)
139   {
140      if (obj>=1 && obj<=3)
141      {
142         if (movingKnob.numOfPos>0)
143         {
144            sgc.setKnobPos(movingKnob);
145         }
146         switch (obj)
147         {
148            case 1: sgc.setFrequency(); break;
149            case 2: sgc.setAttenuate(); break;
150            case 3: sgc.setAmplitude(); break;
151            default:
152         }
153         obj = 0;
154      }
155   }
```

Figure 5.24. SigGen class: startDrag() and endDrag() methods.

169   For the case when the connection has a move mode of 0.

171–172   The mouse moves from right to left. Thus, the connector is disconnected.

176–178   The mouse moves from left to right. Thus, the connector is connected.

```
                    SigGen Class (continued)

156   public void startMove(Connector c, MouseEvent e)
157   {
158      start_x = e.getX();
159      start_y = e.getY();
160      movingConnector = c;
161   }

162   public void endMove(MouseEvent e)
163   {
164      int x,y;
165      x = e.getX();
166      y = e.getY();
167      switch (movingConnector.moveMode)
168      {
169        case 0:
170        if (movingConnector.status){
171            if (x < start_x){
172                sgc.Disconnect(movingConnector);
173            }
174        }
175        else{
176            if (x > start_x){
177                sgc.Connect(movingConnector);
178            }
179        };
180        break;

181        case 1:
              ...
217        default: ;
218      }
219      obj = 0;
220   }
```

Figure 5.25. SigGen class: startMove() and endMove() methods.

Figure 5.26 shows the code for the moveIt() method, which is used to handles events when a knob is turned by using the mouse in a dragging action.

224 Carry out processing only if obj, which gives the object of interest, is
    equal to 1 (frequency knob), 2 (attenuation knob), or 3 (amplitude knob).

228–231 If the mouse is outside the knob, the movement will be taken to be fin-
    ished and the endDrag() method is called.

232–237 Otherwise, the movement continues.

```
                    SigGen Class (continued)
221   public void moveIt(MouseEvent e)
222   {
223    int x,y;
224    if (obj>=1 && obj<=3)
225    {
226       x = e.getX();
227       y = e.getY();
228       if ((x-x0)*(x-x0)+(y-y0)*(y-y0)>r*r)
229       {
230          endDrag(e);
231       }
232       else
233       {
234          newangle=(float)(Math.atan2(y0-y,
                             x-x0)/Math.PI*180);
235          sgc.setKnobAngle(movingKnob,
                 movingKnob.Angle + newangle-mouseangle);
236          mouseangle=newangle;
237       }
238    }
239   }
```

Figure 5.26. SigGen class: moveIt() method.

5.3.5 Methods for Mouse Events

A mouse may generate seven types of event messages that an applet can capture. Although the Applet class supplied has default methods for responding to these events, special handling of these events is often necessary in Web-based laboratories. This can be achieved by overriding the default methods. The following list gives down the important mouse event messages [31].

MOUSE_PRESS

This is generated when the user presses the mouse button. It is handled by the mousePressed() method.

MOUSE_RELEASE

This is produced when the user releases the left mouse button and is handled by the mouseReleased() method.

MOUSE_CLICK

This is generated when the user presses the mouse button and releases it quickly. It is handled by the mouseClicked() method.

MOUSE_MOVE

This is produced when the user moves the mouse pointer on the screen. It is handled by the mouseMoved() method.

MOUSE_DRAG

This is generated when the user moves the mouse pointer while holding down the left mouse button. It is handled by the mouseDragged() method.

MOUSE_ENTER

This is produced when the mouse pointer enters an area owned by an applet or component. It is handled by the mouseEntered() method.

As an example, Figures 5.27 and 5.28 give the code for overriding the default mouse event handling methods.

240–265 Handle MOUSE_PRESS events. From the type of object or control over which the mouse is pressed, this method takes the user action to be that corresponding to the beginning of either turning a knob, moving a connector, or pressing a button. The appropriate processing method is then called.

```
                    SigGen Class (continued)

240   public void mousePressed(MouseEvent e)
241   {
242     switch (obj)
243       {
244        case 1:  startDrag(sgc.freqKnob, e); break;
245        case 2:  startDrag(sgc.attenKnob, e); break;
246        case 3:  startDrag(sgc.ampKnob, e); break;
247        case 21: startMove(sgc.groundConn, e); break;
248        case 22: startMove(sgc.outputConn, e); break;
249        default:
250          { //buttons
251           if (obj>=11 && obj<=15)
252             {
253                sgc.changeRange(obj);
254             }
255           if (obj==16 || obj==17)
256             {
257                sgc.changeWaveform(obj);
258             }
259           if (obj==18)
260             {
261                sgc.powerOnOff();
262             }
263          };
264       }
265   }
```

Figure 5.27. SigGen class: mouse*() method.

```
                    SigGen Class (continued)

266  public void mouseReleased(MouseEvent e)
267  {
268    if (obj>=1 && obj<=3)
269    {
270       endDrag(e);
271    }
272    if (obj>=21 && obj<=22)
273    {
274       endMove(e);
275    }
276  }

277  public void mouseExited(MouseEvent e)
278  {
279  }

280  public void mouseEntered(MouseEvent e)
281  {
282  }

283  public void mouseClicked(MouseEvent e)
284  {
285  }

286  public void mouseMoved(MouseEvent e)
287  {
288    changeCursor(e);
289  }

290  public void mouseDragged(MouseEvent e)
291  {
292    moveIt(e);
293  }
```

Figure 5.28. SigGen class: mouse*() method – continued.

266–276   Handle MOUSE_RELEASE events. From the object or control type, this
          method regards the action to be that associated with the end of turning a
          knob or moving a connector. It then calls the relevant processing method.

286–289   Handle MOUSE_MOVE events. When the mouse enters an area that corre-
          sponds to a control that the user can operate or adjust, the mouse cursor
          is changed to inform the user that suitable action may be taken.

290–293   Handle MOUSE_DRAG events.

6 Interface Cards

6.1 Introduction

Conventional stand-alone instruments and commercial products, such as washers, refrigerators, and water heaters, to name a few, have dominated the market for many years. They are now facing fierce competition from PC-based instruments that have plug-in interface cards. PC-based instruments are up-compatible with the stand-alone instruments and thus they can be controlled either by hand or by control units such as a computer. In contrast to conventional equipment and products, PC-based instruments introduce almost no overhead because important hardware components are already available in the host PC. The production of PC-based instruments is extremely cost-efficient because casing, power supply, memory, operating elements, displays, and a large part of the firmware are not required. Also, due to low storage cost and flexibility in developing new customer-specific features, a PC-based instrument can be adapted to changing market situations much more easily. Important development steps can be ignored so that the time to market of such products is unbeatable.

Key components of PC-based instruments are the interface cards, through which can the stand-alone instruments communicate with the computer. Figure 6.1 shows the cards used in the Web-based laboratories. As shown, we make use of three types of interface cards:

- Data acquisition card (DAQ)
- General-purpose interface bus card (GPIB)
- Digital signal processing card (DSP)

In this chapter, we will research how these interface cards and their controls are used in creating Web-based laboratories. Features of the cards and the manipulation languages for the cards are analyzed one by one. The rest of the chapter is organized as follows. In Section 6.2, a significant instrument control language, LabVIEW, is introduced. In Section 6.3, the general-purpose interface bus (GPIB) card is described. In Section 6.4, the data acquisition (DAQ) card is exploited, together with running examples. In Section 6.5, the digital signal processing (DSP) card is briefly introduced.

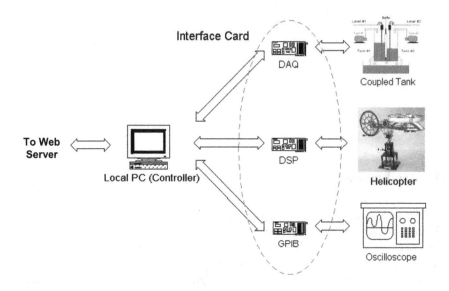

Figure 6.1. Interface cards connecting instruments to a PC.

6.2 LabVIEW

We proceed to give a brief description of an important language used in creating Web-based laboratories. LabVIEW is a virtual graphical programming language and a general-purpose program suitable for measurement and control purposes [12–13, 32]. Like other programming systems, such as Java, C, BASIC, and PASCAL, LabVIEW is fully-featured. However, LabVIEW is also different from these programming languages. Programming is carried out in block diagram form rather than by using text-based codes. All the codes in LabVIEW are constructed and saved in graphical structures. A diagrammatic view shows how the data flows through the program. One can then visualize data flows in the programs.

As a general-purpose program development application, LabVIEW also has convenient debugging tools. A programmer can set breakpoints and animate the execution to see how data flows through the program. He or she can also single-step through the program to make program debugging and program development easier. Although LabVIEW itself does not contain text-based codes, it can conveniently call text-based functions or subroutines programmed by other languages such as C, C++, and MATLAB.

The G language is the formal name of the graphical programming language and is the heart of LabVIEW. G includes extensive libraries of functions for many programming tasks. It also includes libraries for data acquisition, GPIB and serial instrument control, data analysis, data presentation, and data storage. Programs written using G are also called virtual instruments (VIs) because their appearance and operation can imitate actual instruments. A VI consists of an interactive user interface, a dataflow diagram that serves as the source code, and icon connections that set up the VI so that it can be called from VIs of higher level. More specifically, the VI consists of three parts: front panel, block diagram, and subprogram [32].

6.2.1 Front Panel

The interactive user interface of a VI is called the front panel because it simulates the panel of a physical instrument, which can contain knobs, push buttons, graphs, other controls, and indicators. The controls simulate instrument input devices and supply data to the block diagram of the VI, and indicators simulate instrument output devices that display data acquired or generated by the block diagram of the VI. Figure 6.2 shows the front panel of a VI.

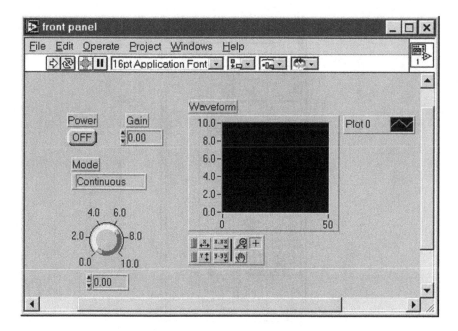

Figure 6.2. Front panel of a VI.

Data can be entered into the front panel by using a mouse or keyboard, and the results can be viewed on the computer screen. Users can also add controls and indicators to the front panel by selecting them from the floating control palette (See Figure 6.3). In addition, each control or indicator has a pop-up menu, which can be used to change various attributes and functions.

6.2.2 Block Diagram

The VI receives instructions from a block diagram constructed in G. The block diagram is a pictorial solution to a programming problem. It is also the source code for the VI. Programmers can switch from the front panel to the block diagram by selecting from the menu.

The diagram window holds the block diagram of the VI, which is the graphical source code of a VI. Users can construct a block diagram by wiring together objects that send or receive data, perform specific functions, and control the flow of execution. Figure 6.4 shows a simple VI that computes the sum and the difference of two numbers. The corresponding front panel is shown in Figure 6.5. When a control or indicator is placed on the front panel, a corresponding terminal appears on the block diagram. One cannot delete a terminal that belongs to a control or indicator unless the control or the indicator itself is deleted from the front panel.

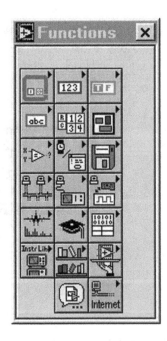

Figure 6.3. Control palette.

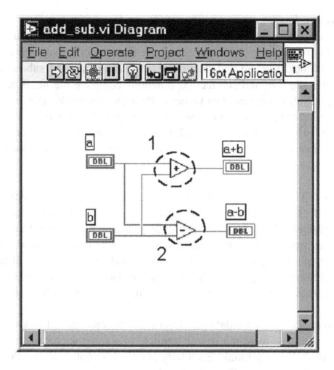

Figure 6.4. A simple VI: addition and subtraction (block diagram).

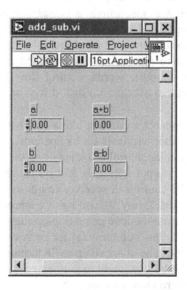

Figure 6.5. A simple VI: addition and subtraction (front panel).

The addition function ("1" of Figure 6.4) and the subtraction function ("2" of Figure 6.4) also generate terminals, which can be treated as entry and exit ports. Data entered into the controls (a and b) exit the front panel through the control terminals on the block diagram and then enter the addition and the subtraction functions. After the addition and subtraction functions complete the necessary internal calculations, they produce new data values at their exit terminals. The resulting data flow to the indicator terminals and reenter the front panel, where they are displayed. Terminals that produce data are referred to as data source terminals, and terminals that receive data are data sink terminals. The following are some key terminologies in the G program.

- Nodes: The nodes in the G program are program execution elements analogous to statements, operators, functions, and subroutines in conventional programming languages. The addition and subtraction functions in Figure 6.4 are one type of node. Another type of node is the structure. Structures are graphical representations of the loop and case statements of traditional programming languages. The G language also has special nodes for linking to external text-based code and for evaluating text-based formulas.

- Wires: The wires are data paths between the sources and sink terminals. It is not allowed to wire a source terminal to another source or to wire a sink terminal to another sink. Each wire is of a different style or color, depending on the value that flows through the wire.

- Dataflow: The dataflow is the principle that governs the G program's executions. In dataflow mode, a node executes only when all data inputs arrive; the node supplies data to all of its output terminals when it finishes execution. This execution mode is different from conventional control flow programming, where instructions are executed in the sequence in which they are written. In other words, control flow execution is instruction-driven, while dataflow execution is data-driven or data-dependent.

- Connector: The connector is much like a parameter list of a function call, whereas the connector terminals act like parameters. Each terminal is associated with a particular control or indicator on the front panel. A connector receives data at its input terminals and passes them onto a sub-VI code through the sub-VI controls or receives results at its output terminals from the sub-VI indicators. Every VI also has a connector, which is available at Show Connector from the icon panel pop-up menu on the front panel. The connector generally has one terminal for each control or indicator on the front panel, and it can be assigned up to 28 terminals. If one anticipates future changes to the VI that might require a new input or output, one should leave some extra terminals unconnected.

6.2.3 Subprogram

When an icon of a VI is placed in the diagram of another VI, it becomes a sub-VI, which is equivalent to a subroutine in the G program. The controls and indicators of a sub-VI receive data from and return data to the diagram that calls sub-VI. Every VI has a default icon displayed in the icon panel in the upper right corner of the front panel and block diagram windows.

6.3 General-Purpose Interface Bus

The general-purpose interface bus (GPIB) was developed by Hewlett Packard in the late 1960s and early 1970s. The IEEE standardized it in 1975, after which it became the IEEE 488 Standard. The terms GPIB, HP-IB, and IEEE 488 are synonymous [33]. The original purpose of the bus was to provide simultaneous computer control for test and measurement instruments. However, it is quite versatile and is now widely used for computer-to-computer communication and control communication. The ANSI/IEEE Standard 488.2-1992 extends IEEE 488.1 by defining a bus communication protocol, a common set of data codes and formats, and a generic set of common device commands.

The GPIB used in creating Web-based laboratories is a digital, 24-conductor parallel bus. It consists of eight data lines, five management lines (ATN, EOI, IFC, REN, and SRQ), three handshake lines, and eight ground lines. It uses an 8-bit parallel, byte-serial, asynchronous data transfer scheme, which means that whole bytes are sequentially hand-shaken across the bus at a speed that the slowest participant in the transfer determines. Because the unit of data on the GPIB is a byte (8 bits), the messages transferred are frequently encoded as ASCII character strings.

6.3.1 Data Transfer Signals

The GPIB has three different methods to signal the end of a data transfer: hardware line, end of string, and byte count.

- Hardware Line: This is the most preferred method. In this mode, the GPIB includes a hardware line (EOI) that can be asserted with the last data byte.

- End of String: In this method, a specific end-of-string (EOS) character is placed at the end of the data string itself. Some instruments use this method instead of, or in addition to, the EOI line assertion.

- Byte Count: In this method, the listener counts the hand-shaken bytes and stops reading when the listener reaches a byte count limit. The method is often used as a default termination method because the transfer stops on the result of the logical OR of EOI and EOS (if used) in conjunction with the byte count.

6.3.2 Network Topology

Every device, including the computer interface board, must have a unique GPIB address ranging from 0 to 30. Address 0 is normally assigned to the GPIB interface board itself. The instruments on the GPIB can use addresses from 1 through 30. To transfer commands or data to the instrument, the controller addresses one talker and one or more listeners. The data strings are then hand-shaken across the bus from the talker to the listener(s). Devices are linked in a linear topology, a star topology, or a combination of the two. Figure 6.6 and Figure 6.7 show the linear and star configurations, respectively.

To achieve high data transfer rate for which the GPIB was designed, the following restrictions are normally required.

- A maximum separation of 4 meters between any two devices and an average separation of 2 meters over the entire bus.

- A maximum total cable length of 20 meters.

- No more than 15 device loads each bus, with no less than two-thirds powered on.

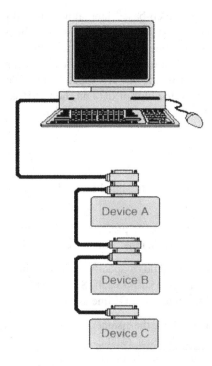

Figure 6.6. Linear configuration of the GPIB.

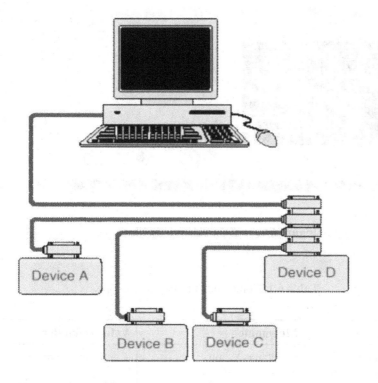

Figure 6.7. Star configuration of the GPIB.

6.3.3 Examples of GPIB Instruments

In creating our Web-based laboratories for both the oscilloscope and the frequency modulation experiments, some GPIB-based instruments are employed. In the former, there are two GPIB-based instruments: a GPIB-based digital oscilloscope and a GPIB-based digital signal generator. We will now discuss how these two instruments can be controlled.

Digital Oscilloscope

Figure 6.8 shows the Tektronix digital oscilloscope used in the Web-based laboratory. The oscilloscope is GPIB-based and is a very good tool for acquiring, displaying, and measuring waveforms. The commands for controlling the digital oscilloscope are given in Table 6.1. As shown, the commands include selecting the specified channel, turning off the specified channel, changing the coupling resource, setting the time per division for the main time base, and other functions.

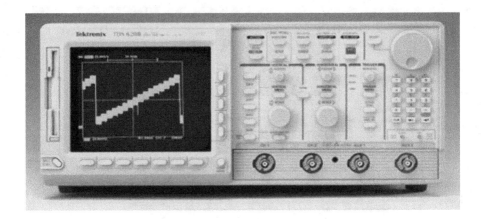

Figure 6.8. Tektronix digital oscilloscope.

Table 6.1. Commands for the oscilloscope.

Action	Mnemonic	Value Delimiter
To turn on the display of a channel	select: ch\<X\> on	X = channel number
To turn off the display of a channel	select: ch\<X\> off	X = channel number
To set the vertical gain of a channel	ch\<X\>: SCALE \<NR3\>	X = channel number \<NR3\>= gain (in volts per division)
To set the vertical position of a channel	ch\<X\>: Position \<NR3\>	X = channel number \<NR3\> = desired position
To set the time per division	HORizontal: SCALE \<NR3\>	\<NR3\> = time per division
To position the waveform horizontally on the display	HORizontal: Position \<NR3\>	\<NR3\>= the desired position
To establish AC | DC | GND coupling on the specified channel	ch\<X\>: coupling AC ch\<X\>: coupling DC ch\<X\>: coupling GND	X = channel number AC = ac coupling DC = dc coupling GND = ground

Digital Signal Generator

Details of the signal generator have been introduced in the last few chapters, where we described its functions and created a class for the instrument. From the discussion leading to the generation of a complete SigGen class, we have presented the logic and techniques for creating panels for the GUI in Web-based laboratories. Here, we will be concerned with the hardware control of the actual signal generator, which has the following capabilities.

- Multi-waveform generation: sine, square, and triangle.
- Complete GPIB programmability.
- 7 ns transition time for pulse and square wave.

The commands for controlling the signal generator are shown in Table 6.2. The functions include setting the frequency and amplitude, selecting different waveforms, enabling or disabling output, as well as others.

Table 6.2. Commands for the signal generator.

Action	Mnemonic	Value Delimiter
To set frequency	FRQ	MZ = millihertz HZ = hertz KHZ = kilohertz MHZ = megahertz
To set amplitude	AMP	MV = millivolts V = volts
To select sine waveform	W1	
To select square waveform	W3	
To enable output	D0	
To disable output	D1	

6.3.4 Controlling GPIB Instruments

It is convenient to control GPIB-based instruments using the LabVIEW G language. The block diagrams of the program for controlling the oscilloscope are shown in Figures 6.9 to 6.13. The whole flowchart consists of five stages (five sequences) from 0 through 4. Each figure displays the program for one stage. The program does not use any text-based codes. It uses only nodes and wires.

Oscilloscope Control Program: Sequence 0

Figure 6.9 shows Sequence 0 of the oscilloscope control program. As mentioned earlier, the execution order of a G program is different from that of a text-based program, where codes are executed in the order that they are written. In the graphic-based G program, codes are executed along with the data flow. To strictly fix the execution order, one has to place the codes in the frames of the sequence structure, which is a way of obtaining control flow when data dependencies are not sufficient.

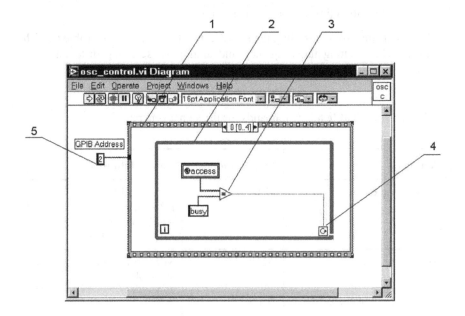

Figure 6.9. Oscilloscope control program: Sequence 0.

A sequence structure executes all the frames in the order that they are placed in the structure. Only when the last frame completes its execution do data leave the structure. The content inside the film-like rectangle "1" of Figure 6.9 is the graphical code for frame 0. The functions of the key components of the program are as follows:

- Item 1 corresponds to a sequence structure (frame 0), which consists of five frames ([0...4]).

- Item 2 is a while loop, which executes its subdiagram, the content inside the loop structure, until the value passed to the conditional terminal becomes false.

- Items 3 and 4 define a comparison subdiagram, where 3 is a comparison block that compares the two inputs and 4 is the termination condition of the while loop. The whole subdiagram for the while loop is equivalent to the following pseudocode:

```
do
{
    execute subdiagram; /* empty in this case */
}
while(access == "busy")
```

- Item 5 gives a constant variable for the GPIB address for the oscilloscope. In this case, the GPIB address of the oscilloscope is 2.

Oscilloscope Control Program: Sequence 1

Figure 6.10 shows the first sequence of the oscilloscope control program. The subdiagram is simply equivalent to the pseudocode:

```
access= "busy";
```

where access is a global string variable and busy is a constant string.

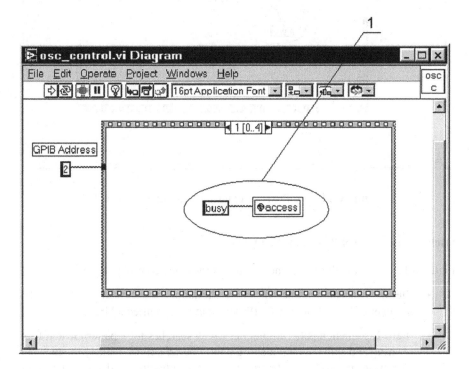

Figure 6.10. Oscilloscope control program: Sequence 1.

Oscilloscope Control Program: Sequence 2

Figure 6.11 shows the second sequence of the oscilloscope control program. In this subdiagram, the command string is written to the device with a specified GPIB address.

- Item 1 contains a command string to be written to the GPIB address.

- Item 2 is the conventional GPIB write function provided by LabVIEW. It writes data to the device identified by the input address.

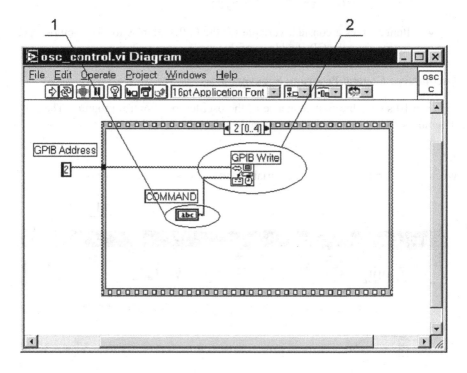

Figure 6.11. Oscilloscope control program: Sequence 2.

Oscilloscope Control Program: Sequence 3

Figure 6.12 shows the third sequence of the oscilloscope control program.

- Item 1 is a conventional GPIB read function, which reads DATA COUNT number of bytes from the GPIB device at the specified address.

- Item 2 is a match pattern function, which searches for a pattern match from a string and splits the input string into three substrings, namely the matched substring, the pattern substring before the substring, and the pattern substring after the substring.

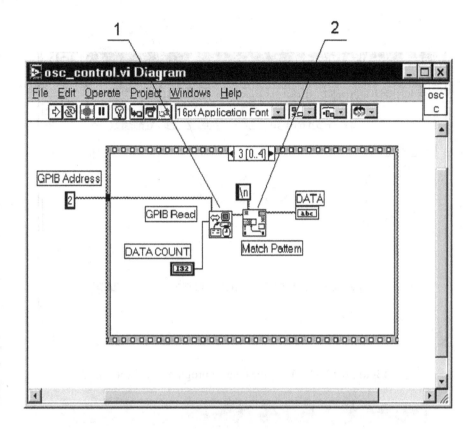

Figure 6.12. Oscilloscope control program: Sequence 3.

Oscilloscope Control Program: Sequence 4

Figure 6.13 shows Sequence 4 of the oscilloscope control program. It is the last stage of the sequence. The subdiagram is simply equivalent to the following pseudo-code:

```
access= "free";
```

For ease of reference, the front panel of the oscilloscope control program is shown in Figure 6.14. Except for the global variable access, the other variables that appear in the diagram are also listed in the front panel. At the same time, only through the front panel can one add or delete variables or objects of types such as numeric, boolean, string, tables, and graphs. The global variable access is associated with another VI, global1.vi in Figure 6.13. In the G language, users can group global variables in one or more VIs and use these variables anywhere in any part of the program.

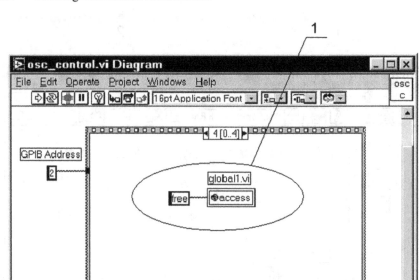

Figure 6.13. Oscilloscope control program: Sequence 4.

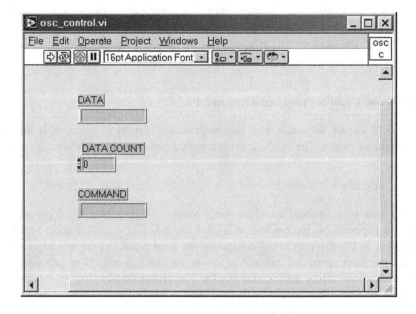

Figure 6.14. Oscilloscope control program: front panel.

6.4 Data Acquisition Card

Although GPIB-based devices have become quite popular nowadays, the combination of PCs and Data acquisition (DAQ) cards is also widely used. When a PC communicates with a device through a DAQ card, the PC may be sampling data from the device through an analog to digital (A/D) channel, performing some calculations, and then sending out a control signal to the device through a digital to analog (D/A) channel.

The advantage of using DAQ cards over the GPIB interface is that for a GPIB-based device, the device itself must be equipped with a processing unit to process events concerned with the GPIB protocol, whereas for a DAQ-based device, this processing is done by the PC.

On the other hand, the DAQ-based device must have transducers that convert various kinds of continuous physical signals to digital signals. Typical transducers include thermocouples, strain gauges, microphones, potentiometers, or any other device that supplies a voltage within the input range of the DAQ board. In general, signal conditioning is necessary for the amplification of low-level signals, filtering of unwanted frequency components, or linearizing of nonlinear signals such as those from thermocouples. Figure 6.15 shows a typical DAQ system.

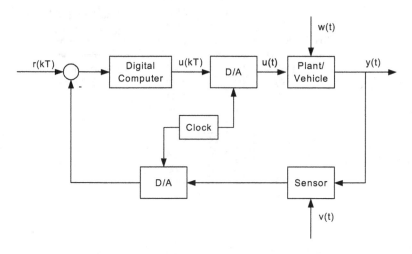

Figure 6.15. A typical DAQ system.

In the coupled-tank experiment, two analog channels are needed to control the two pumps of the tanks. At the same time, the output voltages from two sensors, which reflect the water levels of the two tanks, have to be read.

A Lab-PC-1200 board, from National Instruments, has been chosen for the experiment [34, 35]. The board is a low-cost, high-performance analog, digital, and timing board for PCs. It has two analog output channels, eight analog input channels, a 12-bit successive approximation ADC (analog to digital converter), 24 lines of TTL-compatible digital I/O, and three 16-bit counter/timers for timing I/O.

Also, the board is completely switchless and jumperless. It allows DMA, interrupts, and base I/O addresses to be assigned by the system to avoid resource conflicts with other boards in the system. This board is designed for high-performance data acquisition and control for applications in laboratory testing, production testing, and industrial process monitoring and control. Figure 6.16 shows the pin assignments of the Lab-PC-1200 I/O connector [35].

6.4.1 Drivers

The use of DAQ-based systems is normally accompanied by a set of driver software, which spares the user from complicated hardware-related interface configurations and handling such as those dealing with special protocols and other software layers. Specifically, drivers are at the following three levels.

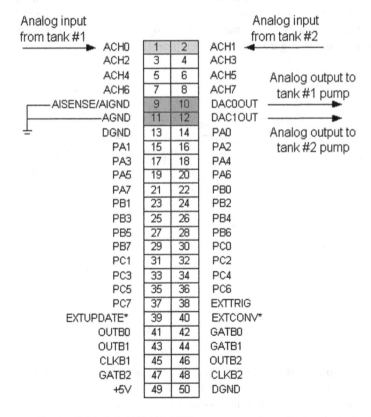

Figure 6.16. Lab-PC-1200 I/O connector pin assignments.

- Hardware Level: This gives support at the lowest level, including that for connections, signal conditioning, acquisition plug-in cards (A/D multifunction types), and RS-485, RS-232, parallel, and other communication ports on the PC.

- NI-DAQ Driver Software: This gives support at the medium level and serves as the connecting link between the hardware level and the application software at the top level.

- Application Software. This language-independent top level allows development environments such as LabVIEW, LabWindows/VCI, Visual Basic, Excel VBA, and C++ to access the hardware level effectively.

6.4.2 Controlling Card

There are two basic ways to develop applications with DAQ hardware and software components. The first method is to make use of the data acquisition libraries of LabVIEW, while the second method is to exploit the DAQ wizards [35]. Since we make use of the first scheme, we will now briefly outline the main components of the libraries.

- LabVIEW Data Acquisition Library. The library is divided into several main groups, which are again divided into several subgroups.

- Analog Input Library: This library contains functions for A/D conversion, which ranges from single-point measurement to continuous multiple-point acquisition with sampling rate ranging from MHz to the PCI bus speed.

- Analog Output Library: This library is similar to that of the previous group and contains functions for the D/A converter card.

- Digital I/O Library: The Digital I/O library allows the programmer to set, reset and read input and output ports in any port width. The programmer can freely define the inputs and outputs.

Reading Data from the DAQ Card

Figure 6.17 gives an illustration of how a signal can be read from the DAQ card using LabVIEW. In the figure, data are read from the specified channel (0) of the specified device (0). Key components and functions are described as follows.

- Item 1 corresponds to the device number of the specified DAQ card. In our coupled-tank experiment, there is only one DAQ card on the control server and thus the device number is set to 1 by default. For a PC with multiple DAQ cards installed, a sequential identification number starting from 1 will be assigned for the cards.

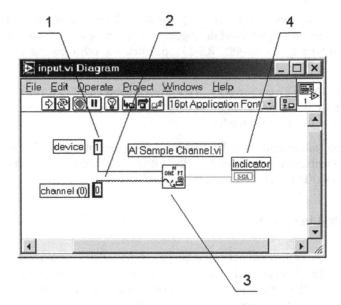

Figure 6.17. A DAQ control example: `input.vi`.

- Item 2 specifies an input channel number. A DAQ card generally has several D/A and A/D channels, analog input channels and/or analog output channels. It is up to the user to specify a channel number to be used.

- Item 3 is an "easy analog input VI" that performs some simple analog input operations. It reads the signal from the specified channel of the specified device. Such VIs can be run from the front panel or be used as subVIs in basic applications.

- Item 4 reads the result of the input signal. The result must be fed to other nodes for further processing.

Outputting Signal to the DAQ Card

Figure 6.18 shows an example of how control signals can be sent to the DAQ card using LabVIEW. As shown, the control signal is sent to the specified channel (0) of the specified device (0). Detailed functions are as follows.

- Item 1 is the device number of the DAQ card, which is 1 for this example.

- Item 2 specifies an output channel number (0 for this example).

- Item 3 is an "easy analog output VI" that performs some simple analog output operations. It sends a control signal to the specified channel of the specified device.

- Item 4 specifies a float value that will be sent to the DAQ card.

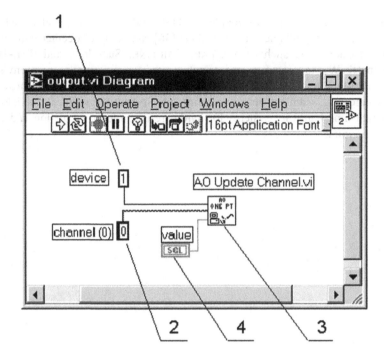

Figure 6.18. A DAQ control example: `output.vi`.

6.5 Digital Signal Processing Card

Digital signal processing (DSP) is currently a very hot topic with numerous applications. Since the implementation of Web-based laboratories may also require the use of some DSP technologies, we will now give a very brief introduction to this topic.

To control a plant whose bandwidth is relatively low, a normal PC can serve both as an HTTP server and local controller with a reasonably good performance. For example, we have implemented four different control algorithms, namely manual, PID, state-space, and fuzzy-logic control, on the coupled-tank apparatus with a sampling period of 20 ms. However, to control a sensitive plant, such as a helicopter, a much shorter sampling period is needed. In such a situation, a single PC will not meet the processing requirements. A DSP card, which has its own processing unit, turns out to be a natural solution for solving such a problem.

In reality, DSP technology is used in a wide variety of applications such as communication, digital TV, radar, audio, sensor, fax, multimedia processing and process control. Although it is difficult to give a precise definition of DSP, most of the available DSP cards have some common features: (1) they involve significant mathematical operations such as for multiplying and adding signals; (2) they deal with real-time signals; and (3) they need to produce a response within a certain time.

The dSPACE card is a good example of a DSP card and has many advanced features. The dSPACE Real-Time Interface (RTI) [36] can be used together with many popular software tools, such as MATLAB, SIMULINK, Stateflow, and Real-Time Workshop (RTW), to construct an integrated, ready-to-use development environment for real-time applications. For control engineering, the dSPACE RTI provides an automatic and seamless implementation of SIMULINK graphical models on dSPACE real-time hardware systems for hardware-in-the-loop simulation and controller prototyping.

7 Audio and Video

7.1 Audio/Video Server

Audio and video play an important role in the performance of a Web-based laboratory [20, 22]. Through the latter, the user can see changes in the actual experiment. From the former, the user can hear the sounds of plants and apparatus. In a word, users can get a real feeling of the experiment conducted and monitor the actual happenings of the devices controlled through an audio and video feedback system.

Figure 7.1 shows the topology of the audio/video system for the Web-based coupled-tank experiment. Two servers are utilized to provide the audio/video service: an audio/video server and a control server. The former collects sound and image signals from the coupled-tank hardware and then transfers them to the client. The latter operates on the control unit, through which the user (the client) can adjust the visual angle of the camera. In the coupled-tank experiment, the camera can be zoomed in and out, and the viewpoint can be moved up, down, left, and right. Through these adjustments, the remote user will be able to have a thorough examination of the operating devices.

In this chapter, we will discuss the audio and video aspects of the audio/video service. The related protocols for audio/video communication, together with the associated audio/video application, are studied in detail. In addition, the unit for controlling the camera's viewpoint and the structure of the control software are investigated.

7.1.1 H.323 Protocol

To understand the communication mechanism associated with the audio and video signals, one should have some background knowledge of the H.323 protocol, which is a set of protocols for voice, video, and data conferencing over packet-based networks. The current recommendation (Version 2.0) of H.323 has been ratified by Study Group 16 (SG16) of the Telecommunications Sector of the International Telecommunication Union (ITU-T) [37, 38].

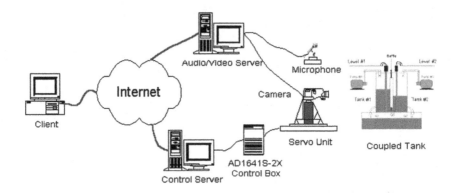

Figure 7.1. Topology of an audio/video service system.

The H.323 protocol stack is designed to operate above the transport layer of the underlying network. It can be used on top of any packet-based network transport (Ethernet, TCP/UDP/IP, ATM, Frame Relay, and others) to provide real-time multimedia communication. H.323 uses the Internet protocol (IP) for internetwork conferencing.

H.323 corresponds to one of several videoconferencing recommendations issued by ITU-T. The other recommendations in the series include H.310 for conferencing over broadband ISDN (B-ISDN), H.320 for conferencing over narrowband ISDN, H.321 for conferencing over ATM, H.322 for conferencing over LANs that provide a guaranteed quality of service, and H.324 for conferencing over public switched telephone networks (PSTN). The H.323 standard is designed to allow clients on H.323 networks to communicate with clients on other videoconferencing networks.

H.323 is a broad and flexible recommendation. As a minimum, H.323 specifies protocols for real-time point-to-point audio communication between two terminals on a packet-based network that do not provide a guaranteed quality of service. The scope of H.323, however, is much broader and encompasses internetwork multipoint conferencing among terminals that support not only audio but also video and data communication. The scopes of Recommendation H.323 are summarized as follows [37].

- Point-to-point and multipoint conferencing support

   H.323 conferences may be set up between two or more clients without any specialized multipoint control software or hardware. However, when a multipoint control unit (MCU) is used, H.323 supports a flexible topology for multipoint conferences. A multipoint conference may be centralized, where new participants can join all the others in the conference. This is the so-called hub-and-spoke topology. On the other hand, a multipoint conference may be decentralized, where new participants can elect to join one or more participants in the conference but not all. This approach will produce a flexible tree topology.

- Internetwork interoperability

  H.323 clients are interoperable with switched-circuit network (SCN) conferencing clients such as those based on Recommendations H.320 (ISDN), H.321 (ATM), and H.324 (PSTN/Wireless).

- Heterogeneous client capabilities

  An H.323 client must support audio communication. Video and data support is optional. This heterogeneity and flexibility do not make the clients incompatible.

- Audio and video codecs (code-decodes)

  H.323 specifies a required audio and video codec. However, there is no restriction on the use of other codecs and two clients can agree on any codec that is supported by both of them.

- Management and accounting support

  H.323 calls can be restricted on a network based on the number of calls already in progress, bandwidth limitations, or time restrictions. Using these policies, the network manager can manage H.323 traffic. Furthermore, H.323 provides accounting facilities that can be used for billing purposes.

- Security

  H.323 provides authentication, integrity, privacy, and nonrepudiation support.

- Supplementary services

  Recommendation H.323 recognizes the huge potential for applications based on IP telephony and multimedia. It provides a basic framework for the development of such services. In Version 2.0 of H.323, two services, call transfer and call forwarding, have been specified.

7.1.2 H.323 Architecture

Recommendation H.323 specifies components, protocols, and procedures for real-time point-to-point and multipoint multimedia communication over packet-based networks. It also sets interoperability guidelines for communication between H.323-enabled networks and the H.32X-based family of conferencing standards [37, 38].

In a typical H.323 implementation, four logical entities or components are required – terminals, gateways, gatekeepers, and multipoint control units (MCU) – among which terminals, gateways, and MCUs are collectively known as endpoints. Even though an H.323-enabled network can be established with only terminals, the other components are essential for providing greater practical usefulness of the services.

Terminal

A terminal, or client, is an endpoint where H.323 data streams and signaling originate and terminate. It may be a multimedia PC with an H.323 compliant stack or a stand-alone device such as a USB (universal serial bus) IP telephone. A terminal must support audio communication, while video and data communication support is optional.

Gateway

A gateway is an optional component in an H.323-enabled network. However, when communication between different networks is required, a gateway is needed at the interface. Through the provision of gateways in H.323, it is possible for H.323 terminals to interoperate with other H.32X-compliant conferencing terminals. For example, it is possible for an H.323 terminal to set up a conference with terminals based on H.320 or H.324 through an appropriate gateway. A gateway provides data format translation, control signaling translation, audio and video codec translation, and call setup and termination functionality on both sides of the network. Depending on the type of network to which translation is required, a gateway may support H.310, H.320, H.321, H.322, or H.324 endpoints.

Gatekeeper

A gatekeeper is a very useful, but optional, component of an H.323-enabled network. Gatekeepers are needed to ensure reliable, commercially feasible communications. A gatekeeper is often referred to as the brain of the H.323-enabled network because of the central management and control services it provides. When a gatekeeper exists, all endpoints (terminals, gateways, and MCU) must be registered with it. Registered endpoints' control messages are routed through the gatekeeper. The gatekeeper and the endpoints it administers form a management zone.

A gatekeeper provides several services to endpoints in its zone, which include:

- **Address translation:** A gatekeeper maintains a database for translation between aliases, such as international phone numbers and network addresses.

- **Admission and access control of endpoints:** This control can be based on bandwidth availability, limitations on the number of simultaneous H.323 calls, or the registration privileges of endpoints.

- **Bandwidth management:** Network administrators have the capability of managing network bandwidth by specifying limitations on the number of simultaneous calls and by limiting the authorization of specific terminals to place calls at specified times.

- **Routing capability:** A gatekeeper can route all calls originating or terminating in its zone. This capability provides numerous advantages. First, the accounting information of calls can be maintained for billing and security purposes. Second, a gatekeeper can reroute a call to an appropriate gateway based on bandwidth availability. Third, rerouting can be used to develop advanced services such as mobile addressing, call forwarding, and voice mail diversion.

Multipoint Control Unit

A multipoint control unit (MCU) enables conferencing between three or more endpoints. It consists of a mandatory multipoint controller (MC) and zero or more multipoint processors (MP). Although the MCU is a separate logical unit, it may be combined into a terminal, gateway, or gatekeeper. The MCU is an optional component of an H.323-enabled network [38].

The multipoint controller provides a centralized location for multipoint call setup. Call and control signaling are routed through the MC so that endpoint capabilities can be determined and communication parameters negotiated. An MC may also be used in a point-to-point call, which can later be extended into a multipoint conference. Another useful job of the MC is to determine whether to unicast or multicast the audio and video streams depending on the capability of the underlying network and the topology of the multipoint conference. The multipoint processor handles the mixing, switching, and processing of the audio, video, and data streams among the conference endpoints.

The MCU is required in a centralized multipoint conference in which each terminal establishes a point-to-point connection with the MCU. The MCU determines the capabilities of each terminal and sends each a mixed media stream. In the decentralized model of multipoint conferencing, an MC ensures communication compatibility but the media streams are multicast and the mixing is performed at each terminal.

7.2 Microsoft NetMeeting

Microsoft NetMeeting is a typical audiovisual application that uses the H.323 standard [39]. With NetMeeting, the audio and video captured by the microphone and camera can be sent to the client side and played. NetMeeting includes support for the H.323 audio and video conferencing standard and the T.120 data conferencing standard. NetMeeting can be used to place calls to and receive calls from products that are H.323 and T.120 compatible. With appropriate equipment and services from third parties, NetMeeting can place a call to a telephone using an H.323 gateway. NetMeeting can also place calls to H.323 multipoint conferencing units and participate in multipoint audio and video conferences.

NetMeeting works best with a fast Internet connection, such as a 56 kilobits per second (kbps) or faster modem or a LAN. 800×600 resolution or higher can be used for the best viewing results. Users can also use a compact mode for audio conferencing without any video information. However, in the Web-based laboratories, since both audio and video are required, NetMeeting should not be run under the compact mode. To run NetMeeting, the client PC must have a 32-bit TCP/IP stack and Windows sockets interface. NetMeeting has been tested with the 32-bit TCP/IP and Windows sockets built into Windows 95, Windows 98, Windows NT, and Windows XP.

A sound card, speakers, and a microphone are required to use the audio features of NetMeeting. To send video with NetMeeting, one needs either a video capture card and camera or a video camera that connects through a PC parallel (printer) or USB port. It is not possible to send video on some computers with a processor slower than a Pentium.

7.2.1 Server and Client Setup

In the Web-based laboratory, NetMeeting runs on both the client and the server sides. On the server side, NetMeeting works as an audio/video server. It is always waiting for a connection request. Once a proper call is detected, it will try to establish a connection with the client to collect audio and image signals and then send them to the receiving NetMeeting client. On the client side, NetMeeting will try to dial the server initially. Once the call is accepted, it will continuously receive the relevant signals and display them on the panel.

Server

The program should be configured to receive calls immediately without any user intervention on the server side. To realize this, the waiting mode must be set to Automatically Accept Calls, as shown in Figure 7.2. Also, NetMeeting should be configured to send out live audio and video at the start of each call. Figure 7.3 shows a scenario when NetMeeting waits for a call as well as when a call is in progress.

Client

On the client side, we employ ActiveX control to deal with NetMeeting issues. ActiveX control is part of the Windows NetMeeting Resource Kit that can be invoked and controlled using VBScript. ActiveX can also embed live audio and video on Web pages so that a user can activate NetMeeting easily.

Figure 7.2. Setup of NetMeeting.

(a) Waiting for a call

(b) Call in progress

Figure 7.3. NetMeeting on an audio/video server.

As an example, in Figure 7.4, NetMeeting can be activated simply by clicking the Start A/V button. Once this is activated, the client will automatically dial Net-Meeting residing on the audio/video server to establish a stable network connection. Similarly, NetMeeting can be closed by clicking the Stop A/V button (Figure 7.5).

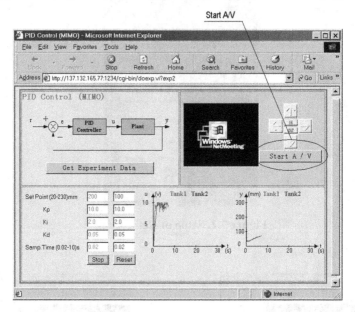

Figure 7.4. Panel of the coupled-tank experiment: NetMeeting not activated.

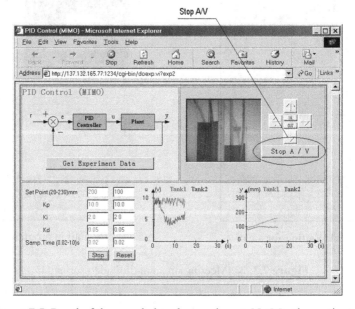

Figure 7.5. Panel of the coupled-tank experiment: NetMeeting activated.

7.2.2 ActiveX Control

ActiveX controls are amongst the many types of components that use Component Object Model (COM) technologies to provide interoperability with other types of COM components and services [25]. ActiveX controls are the third version of OLE controls (OCX), providing a number of enhancements specifically designed to facilitate the distribution of components over high-latency networks and to provide the integration of controls into Web browsers.

ActiveX controls allow users to customize Internet Explorer's interaction with third-party products and industry media standards. Microsoft's ActiveX control API (application programming interface) also attempts to address the concerns of programmers, providing a high degree of flexibility and cross-platform support. For most users, integrating ActiveX controls is transparent because they open up and become active whenever Internet Explorer is opened. Furthermore, users may not see ActiveX controls at work because most ActiveX controls are not activated unless a Web page that initiates them is opened.

In the coupled tank experiment, an ActiveX control object is created to handle NetMeeting issues. The definition of this object is shown in Figure 7.6. The main points are emphasized as follows.

```
                        ActiveX Control
1   <object>
2     <embed name="NetMeeting"
3        classid="CLSID:3E9BAF2D-7A79-11d2-9334-0000F875AE17"
4        type="application/oleobject"
5        param_mode="RemoteNoPause"
6        width="220" height="156">
7     </embed>
8   </object>
```

Figure 7.6. ActiveX control: object definition.

1. ActiveX controls are embedded in HTML documents through use of the HTML <OBJECT> tag and </OBJECT> tag. The attributes of the <OBJECT> tag determine the ActiveX control (or other Web object) used, as well as its size and alignment on the Web page.

2. The ActiveX control is set to embedded mode by the <EMBED> tag. When an ActiveX control is installed and initiated by a Web page, it manifests itself in one of the three potential forms: embedded, full-screen, or hidden. An embedded ActiveX control appears as a visible, rectangular window integrated into a Web page. This window may not appear any different from

a window created by a graphical object, such as from an embedded GIF or JPEG image. The main difference between the previous windows supported by Internet Explorer and those created by ActiveX controls is that ActiveX control windows support a much wider range of interactivity and movement, and thereby remain live instead of static. In addition to mouse clicks, embedded ActiveX controls can also read and take note of mouse location, mouse movement, keyboard input, and input from virtually any other input device. In this way, an ActiveX control can support the full range of user events required to produce sophisticated applications.

3.   The NAME attribute is used to give the ActiveX control a name that can be used within the Web browser (or other application) environment. This is the easiest way for the parameters of the ActiveX control to be accessed and manipulated by other elements running within the Web browser (usually VBScript or JavaScript applications).

4.   The CLASSID attribute gives the identification code for the ActiveX control being used. It is what Internet Explorer will use to load the correct ActiveX control code module from the user PC, and its value is set for each control by the control's author. The code for the ActiveX NetMeeting control, as displayed in Figure 7.6, is CLSID:3E9BAF2D-7A79-11d2-9334-0000F875AE17.

5.   The TYPE attribute defines the MIME type of the ActiveX control. In general, this will be application/oleobject. For other object types embedded in an HTML document using the <OBJECT> tag, the value of this attribute will be different.

6.   The clause param_mode = "RemoteNoPause" informs Internet Explorer that only the video portion of the window will display the image received and no Start/Stop Video button is displayed.

VBScript Functions

To use an ActiveX control object, functions must be defined to call the object's methods. The ideal language to accomplish this task is VBScript [25]. Like JavaScript, VBScript allows one to embed commands into an HTML document. When a user of a compatible Web browser downloads the page, VBScript commands are loaded by the Web browser along with the rest of the document and are run in response to any of a series of events. VBScripts do not need to be compiled into an executable form.

Figure 7.7 shows the code for the definitions of two functions: connection() and disconnection(). As their names suggest, the two functions are for carrying connection and disconnection operations to the server. In the code listed in Figure 7.6, we use NetMeeting as the name of the ActiveX control object. We can thus use this name to refer to the object in other places. It is easy to see find from the code that the clause

```
Netmeeting.CallTo("137.132.165.178");
```

will try to call the audio/video server 137.132.165.178 and establishes connection with the NetMeeting on the server side, while the clause

```
Netmeeting.LeaveConference();
```

will break the connection and close the session.

```
                    ActiveX Control (continued)

1   <SCRIPT LANGUAGE="VBScript" TYPE="text/vbscript">

2       Function connection()
3           Netmeeting.CallTo("137.132.165.178")
4       end Function

5       Function disconnection()
6           Netmeeting.LeaveConference()
7       end Function

8   </SCRIPT>
```

Figure 7.7. ActiveX control: VBScript.

Calling VBScript Functions from JavaScript

To call the VBScript functions, we can use either VBScript or JavaScript. Since a major part of the Web-based laboratory is implemented using JavaScript, we adopt JavaScript here with Figure 7.8 giving the corresponding code. Explanation of the code follows.

   1   JavaScript code begins.

   2   Define a variable onshow and set its initial value to false, which implies that the NetMeeting object is initially not active.

3–17   Define the function callnetmeeting(). The function handles the events caused by clicking the Start A/V button (Figure 7.4) or Stop A/V button (Figure 7.5).

  18   JavaScript code ends.

ActiveX Control (continued)

```
1   <SCRIPT LANGUAGE="JavaScript">
2     onshow=false
3     function callnetmeeting()
4       {
5        if(!onshow)
6          {
7           connection();
8           document.forms["call"].button.value="Stop A / V";
9           onshow=true;
10         }
11        else
12         {
13          disconnection();
14          document.forms["call"].button.value="Start A / V";
15          onshow=false;
16         }
17       }
18   </SCRIPT>
```

Figure 7.8. ActiveX control: JavaScript.

Calling JavaScript Functions from HTML

Figure 7.9 shows a piece of HTML code that calls the JavaScript function `call-netmeeting()`. The functions of the code can be found from Figures 7.4 and 7.5. Basically, once the mouse clicks the Start A/V button or Stop A/V button, `call-netmeeting()` will be called and executed to handle the relevant NetMeeting tasks.

ActiveX Control (continued)

```
......
1   <tr>
2    <td width="30%" height="58" align="center" valign="middle">
3     <form method="post" name="call" action="">
4      <input type="button" name="button" value="Start A / V"
5          onClick="callnetmeeting()">
6     </form>
7    </td>
8   </tr>
......
```

Figure 7.9. ActiveX control: calling JavaScript.

7.3 Camera Control

When conducting experiments, it is helpful for users to be able to see results and apparatus from a number of angles or viewpoints. In the Web-based laboratory, this can be achieved by adjusting the camera's eyeshot. Figure 7.10 shows the situation in the coupled-tank experiment, where the camera's eyeshot can be zoomed in, zoomed out, moved left, moved right, turned up and turned down by clicking the corresponding buttons.

The capability to control the camera's eyeshot lies in the camera adjustment system, as shown in Figure 7.11. Basically, the camera is placed on a servo unit, which in turn is controlled by the control server through the AD1641S-2X control box [40]. The servo unit can be rotated as well as shifted up and down, while the camera's lens can also be adjusted. An appropriate combination of these operations will result in visual effects that are more satisfactory.

The complete eyeshot adjustment system consists of two parts: (1) a client subsystem that receives mouse inputs from the panel and transfers the commands to the control server; and (2) a server subsystem that receives the commands, interprets them, and controls the adjustment unit of the camera. The client program is embedded in the Web page and runs on the user's local computer. The server program resides on the control server, which is located in the real laboratory. The electrical connection between the control server and control box (AD1641S-2X) is via an RS-232 interface. In the following sections, we will discuss these two subsystems.

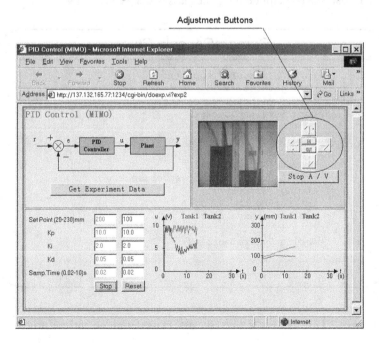

Figure 7.10. Coupled-tank experiment: adjusting the camera's eyeshot.

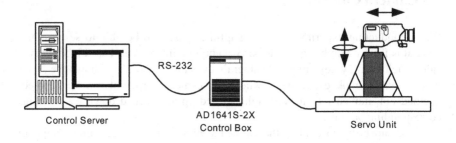

Figure 7.11. Camera adjustment system.

7.3.1 Client

We use a Java applet to handle issues related to receiving commands from the panel. The class responsible for this is CameraConsole, which is given in Figures 7.12 to 7.15.

Class Definition and Constructor

Figure 7.12 lists the code for defining the class and the constructor.

```
                CameraConsole Class

 1   import java.applet.Applet;
 2   import java.io.*;
 3   import java.net.InetAddress;
 4   import java.net.Socket;

 5   public class CameraConsole extends Applet
 6   {
 7     private Socket sock;
 8     private DataOutputStream dataout;
 9     String servHost;
10     int servPort;
11     boolean standalone;

12     public CameraConsole()
13       {
14       }
```

Figure 7.12. CameraConsole class: class definition and constructor.

1–4   Tell Java that the program uses the `Applet`, `io`, `InetAddress` and `Socket` packages.

5   Derive the `CameraConsole` class from the `Applet` class.

7–11   Define variables and objects for the class.

12–14   Define the constructor. Here the constructor contains nothing because we have left the initialization in the `init()` method.

`init()` Method

Figure 7.13 lists the code for the `init()` method. As mentioned earlier, the `init()` method is executed once the applet is loaded. In this case, `init()` will try to connect to the control server when the applet is active. An explanation of the code follows.

```
                    CameraConsole Class (continued)

15   public void init()
16   {
17     String at = getParameter("servHost");
18     servHost = (at == null) ? "137.132.165.77" : at;
19     at = getParameter("servPort");
20     servPort = (at == null)?3001:
                  Integer.valueOf(at).intValue();
21     makeConnection();
22   }

23   private void makeConnection()
24   {
25     try
26     {
27       InetAddress addr = InetAddress.getByName(servHost);
28       sock = new Socket(addr, servPort);
29       dataout = new DataOutputStream(new
30           BufferedOutputStream(sock.getOutputStream()));
31     }
32     catch(IOException E)
33     {
34       System.out.println(" IOExecption in client!!");
35       System.out.println(E.getMessage());
36     }
37   }
```

Figure 7.13. `CameraConsole` class: definition of the `init()` method.

17–20   Retrieve/assign the server name and port number for the network connection. The Java code first checks whether the HTML code has assigned parameters for it. If not, it assigns the default server name (137.132.165.77) and port number (3001) to the variables servHost and servPort, respectively. To embed the Java class in the HTML code, the parameters for the class should be provided. One can regard these parameters as arguments for the class. For example, to include the CameraConsole class in the Web page, one should include the following in the HTML file.

```
<applet codebase="http://137.132.165.77:1234/"
    code="CameraConsole.class"
    name="CameraConsole"
    width=0 height=0>
    <param name=servHostvalue=137.132.165.77>
    <param name=servPort value=3001>
</applet>
```

The contents enclosed in the <param> tags are parameters for the class. A <param> contains two parts: name and value.

21   Connection to the control server. This prepares for further communication between the client and the control server.

SendCmd() Method

Figure 7.14 lists the code for defining the SendCmd() method, which sends out the command string to the control server. In the HTML code, it is this method that is called to send the command string. The following code shows how to send moving up and moving left commands to the control server. As shown, the string "u" denotes the moving up command, while "l" denotes the moving left command. The other commands can be sent out in a similar way.

```
<a hef='javascriptdocument.
    CameraConsole.SendCmd("u");'>
<img src="http://137.132.165.77:1234/up_up.jpg"
    width="35" height="35" border="0" name="up"
    alt="up">
</a>
<a href='javascript:document.
    CameraConsole.SendCmd("l");'>
<img src="http://137.132.165.77:1234/left_up.jpg"
```

```
width="35" height="35" border="0" name="left"
alt="left">
</a>
```

```
                CameraConsole Class (continued)

38     public void SendCmd(String cmd)
39     {
40         char CHR10 = '\n';
41         cmd = cmd + CHR10;
42         try
43         {
44             dataout.writeUTF(cmd);
45             dataout.flush();
46         }
47         catch(IOException _ex)
48         {
49             System.out.println(" Oops! ");
50         }
51     }
```

Figure 7.14. CameraConsole class: SendCmd() method.

Stop() Method

Figure 7.15 lists the code for the Stop() method, which deals with the event when the applet exits. It closes the data stream and the socket if the event happens. Lastly, the overall embed CameraConsole applet is shown in Figure 7.16.

```
                CameraConsole Class (continued)

52     public void stop()
53     {
54         try
55         {
56             dataout.close();
57             sock.close();
58         }
59         catch(IOException _ex){ }
60     }
61 }
```

Figure 7.15. CameraConsole class: Stop() method.

```
1    <applet codebase="http://137.132.165.77:1234/"
2    code="CameraConsole.class"
3            name="CameraConsole"
4            width=0 height=0>
5            <param name=servHost value=137.132.165.77>
6            <param name=servPort value=3001>
7    </applet>
```

Figure 7.16. Embed the `CameraConsole` applet.

7.3.2 Server

Hardware

The AD1641S-2X Receiver [40] is a control box capable of controlling pan, tilt, zoom, focus, iris, and other auxiliary functions at a camera site. It receives command codes from a PC via RS-232 and translates the codes into actions for the pan-and-tilt unit (servo unit) or the lens system of the camera. The receiver can be set up as follows.

- Camera number

  A 10-position DIP switch with a CAMERA ID label is used to associate a specific camera number with the receiver for individual control by the matrix-switching system. Since there is no matrix-switching system in the experiment, the DIP switch is set to 1.

- Lens voltage

  The AD1641S-2X can be adjusted for a range of camera lens servo voltages. The lens output voltage can be adjusted from 7 to 12 volts using a potentiometer with the label LENS ADJ. This control is located on the side panel of the receiver near the CAMERA ID switches.

- Configuration

  An internal DIP switch located on the main PCB, labeled S7, is provided to set the configuration for the receiver.

- RS-232 receiver

  For models using RS-232, the S1 and S2 DIP switches on the RS-232 receiver module must be set up. For RS-232, switch positions 3 and S7 must be off. Switch S11 specifies the type of code, and switch S9 is for the baud rate.

The output of the AD1641S-2X control box is a 12-pin connector labeled J20 on the main PCB. The function of each pin is given in Table 7.1.

Table 7.1. Pin function of the connector.

Pin No.	Function
01	Focus
02	Zoom
03	Iris
04	Lens common
04	Pan/tilt common
06	Tilt down
07	Tilt up
08	Pan/tilt common
09	Pan right
10	Pan left

The ZoomCam Model 46 camera [40] has terminals that can be connected to a remote controller, as shown in Figure 7.17. Here, the controller is the AD1641S-2X receiver. Since the camera can be set to an auto-focus mode, only the zoom in and zoom out functions of the camera need to be controlled.

In summary, for the server subsystem, the control flow is as follows. The PC sends ASCII command codes to the receiver via the RS-232 port. The receiver then applies the necessary voltages to drive the camera lens and the pan-and-tilt unit.

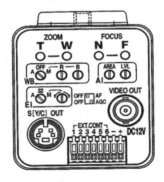

Figure 7.17. Control terminals on back panel of the camera.

Software

The system software consists essentially of a Visual Basic program that runs on the controller server. All the codes are saved in ASCII format in several files. Here, we will discuss some essential codes as examples. The most important file is Main-Form.frm, a Visual Basic Form file, as shown in Figures 7.18, 7.19 and 7.21–7.30. The procedure to create the whole system will now be discussed.

Application Form

Figure 7.18 lists the code to create the main form for the application and define its property.

1   Define the version of the program: VERSION 5.00.

2–3   As with ActiveX, one of the pleasures of programming with Visual Basic is the wealth of components already available. Many components come with the Visual Basic system, while hundreds of others are readily available from third-party developers. These components usually come in the form of VBX controls (16-bit architecture for earlier versions of VB), OCX controls (16- and 32-bit), or DLLs (dynamic linked libraries). Although all three are really DLLs, the first two usually have visual elements associated with them and are more object-oriented. Plain DLLs are usually just libraries of functions and procedures that extend the language. The code here will use components included in the two OCX files, namely, MSWINSCK.OCX and MS-COMM32.OCX [25].

5–14   Define the application window's property.

```
           MainForm.frm (continued)

 1   VERSION 5.00
 2   Object = "{248DD890-BB45-11CF-9ABC-0080C7E7B78D}#1.0#0";
                              "MSWINSCK.OCX"
 3   Object = "{648A5603-2C6E-101B-82B6-000000000014}#1.1#0";
                              "MSCOMM32.OCX"

 4   Begin VB.Form Command_Local

 5       Caption         =   "Camera Control Console"
 6       ClientHeight    =   3684
 7       ClientLeft      =   60
 8       ClientTop       =   348
 9       ClientWidth     =   4680
10       LinkTopic       =   "Camera Control Console"
11       Picture         =   "MainForm.frx":0000
12       ScaleHeight     =   3684
13       ScaleWidth      =   4680
14       StartUpPosition =   3   'Windows Default
```

Figure 7.18. Visual Basic code: application form.

CommandButton Objects

Figure 7.19 lists the code for creating buttons on the application form. The code can be conveniently written using the integrated development environment. In Figure 7.19, only the codes for creating the command buttons Left and Right are presented. Other buttons can be created in a similar manner. Figure 7.20 shows the resulting operation panel for the camera control server

```
MainForm.frm (continued)

15      Begin VB.CommandButton Command_Left
16          Caption         =   "Left"
17          Height          =   375
18          Left            =   360
19          TabIndex        =   2
20          Top             =   1440
21          Width           =   1095
22      End

23      Begin VB.CommandButton Command_Right
24          Caption         =   "Right"
25          Height          =   375
26          Left            =   3240
27          TabIndex        =   3
28          Top             =   1440
29          Width           =   1095
30      End
        . . . . . .
```

Figure 7.19. Visual Basic code: CommandButton objects.

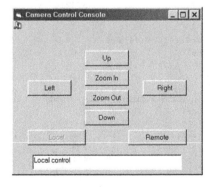

Figure 7.20. Operation panel for the camera-control server.

TextBox Object

The code in Figure 7.21 creates a `TextBox` object on the panel to display texts such as "Local control," "Listening," "Remote control" (see Figure 7.20). Since the text box only serves as a display window, no input is allowed (Line 82).

```
                    MainForm.frm (continued)

79        Begin VB.TextBox Text1
80            Height       =    375
81            Left         =    480
82            Locked       =    -1    'True
83            TabIndex     =    6
84            Top          =    3240
85            Width        =    3735
86        End
```

Figure 7.21. Visual Basic code: `TextBox` object.

Other Objects

Figure 7.22 lists the code for creating objects to handle network tasks. The classes are defined in the class libraries `MSWINSCK.OCX` and `MS-COMM32.OCX` [25].

```
                    MainForm.frm (continued)

87        Begin MSWinsockLib.Winsock Winsock1
88            Left          =    1080
89            Top           =    0
90            _ExtentX      =    593
91            _ExtentY      =    593
92            _Version      =    393216
93        End

94        Begin VB.Timer Timer1
95            Left          =    600
96            Top           =    0
97        End

98        Begin MSCommLib.MSComm MSComm1
99            Left          =    0
100           Top           =    0
101           _ExtentX      =    995
102           _ExtentY      =    995
103           _Version      =    393216
104           DTREnable     =    -1    'True
105       End

106  End
```

Figure 7.22. Visual Basic code: other objects.

Methods for Objects

The objects created so far are basically empty objects because no functions or subroutines have been defined for them. To make these objects useful, appropriate functions, subroutines, or methods must be created.

Local Variables

Figure 7.23 shows the code for declaring local variables. These variables only exist within the context of the procedure in which they are declared. In our case, these variables can be used in `MainForm.frm` because they are declared before and outside all the methods. Essentially, the various methods communicate with each other via these variables.

```
MainForm.frm (continued)

112   Dim Repno As Integer
113   Dim OutStr As String
114   Dim counter As Integer
```

Figure 7.23. Visual Basic code: local variables.

Subroutines for Sending Commands

Figure 7.24 defines the subroutines for sending commands to the receiver controller. Details follow.

115   Define subroutine `RepeatSend()` with two arguments: S, the string to be sent to the receiver controller; and N, an integer for determining the time interval for the timer event.

116   Open the communication port.

118   Set the number of times that the command string is to be sent to the receiver controller. To successfully execute the command, the command string must be sent out to the controller for at least a certain number of times. This operation is completed together with that for the timer.

119   Disable all buttons to disallow inputs from buttons when the command is being sent.

120   The time interval for the timer. Each timer control has an interval property that specifies the number of milliseconds that pass between one timer event and the next. Unless it is disabled, a timer will continue to receive an event (appropriately named the timer event) at intervals that are roughly equal.

```
                    MainForm.frm (continued)

115   Sub RepeatSend(S As String, N As Integer)
116      MSComm1.PortOpen = True
117      OutStr = S
118      counter = N
119      Call DisableAllButtons
120      Timer1.Interval = 53
121   End Sub

122   Private Sub Timer1_Timer()
123      If counter > 0 Then
124         counter = counter - 1
125         MSComm1.Output = OutStr
126      Else
127         Timer1.Interval = 0
128         MSComm1.PortOpen = False
129         If Command_Local.Enabled = False Then
130            Call EnableAllButtons
131         End If
132      End If
133   End Sub
```

Figure 7.24. Visual Basic code: `RepeatSend()` subroutine.

122   Define the routine for the timer. This is the routine that will be automatically executed when the timer event happens.

123–125   When the value of the counter is still greater than zero, send out the command string.

126   Otherwise, reset the timer and other components to the default state. That is, set the timer interval to zero, close the communication port, and enable the command buttons (provided that the panel runs in local mode).

Figure 7.25 defines subroutines to manually send the command string to the receiver controller. These subroutines called the subroutines defined in Figure 7.24, and are called when one of the command buttons Left, Right, Up, Down, Zoom In, or Zoom Out is clicked. The figure only lists the codes for defining the subroutines for the Left button and Right button. Routines for other buttons can be defined in a similar way and are thus omitted here.

Subroutines to Disable or Enable Command Buttons

Figure 7.26 defines subroutines to disable or enable the command buttons. When the system is still in the process of executing some specified operations, no inputs from the command buttons should be accepted. For example, when sending the command string to the controller receiver, no new command can be accepted and hence the command buttons must be disabled. After sending the string, the buttons can be set back to the normal state to accept new commands.

MainForm.frm (continued)

```
134  Private Sub Command_Left_Click()
135      Call RepeatSend("La", Repno)
136  End Sub

137  Private Sub Command_Right_Click()
138      Call RepeatSend("Ra", Repno)
139  End Sub
 ...
```

Figure 7.25. Visual Basic code: subroutines for command buttons.

MainForm.frm (continued)

```
152  Sub DisableAllButtons()
153      Command_Up.Enabled = False
154      Command_Down.Enabled = False
155      Command_Left.Enabled = False
156      Command_Right.Enabled = False
157      Command_Zoom_In.Enabled = False
158      Command_Zoom_Out.Enabled = False
159  End Sub

160  Sub EnableAllButtons()
161      Command_Up.Enabled = True
162      Command_Down.Enabled = True
163      Command_Left.Enabled = True
164      Command_Right.Enabled = True
165      Command_Zoom_In.Enabled = True
166      Command_Zoom_Out.Enabled = True
167  End Sub
```

Figure 7.26. Visual Basic code: disable or enable the buttons.

Subroutine for Local or Remote Control

Figure 7.27 lists the subroutine for local control. As shown in Figure 7.20, the server program can run in either a local control or a remote control mode. In the former, the camera is controlled by manually clicking the command buttons. This mode of control provides a convenient way to troubleshoot the hardware of the control system. By clicking the command buttons, we can check whether there is any response for the intended operations.

In the remote mode, the server program receives commands from the client, translates them into command strings, and sends them to the controller box. Figure 7.28 lists the code for this mode.

MainForm.frm (continued)

```
168   Private Sub Command_Local_Click()
169        ' close socket
170        Winsock1.Close
171        ' enable/disable buttons
172        Call EnableAllButtons
173        Command_Remote.Enabled = True
174        Command_Local.Enabled = False

175        Text1.Text = "Local control"
176   End Sub
```

Figure 7.27. Visual Basic code: local control.

MainForm.frm (continued)

```
177   Private Sub Command_Remote_Click()
178        ' open socket
179        Winsock1.Bind Winsock1.LocalPort, Winsock1.LocalIP
180        Winsock1.Listen
181        ' enable/disable buttons
182        Call DisableAllButtons
183        Command_Remote.Enabled = False
184        Command_Local.Enabled = True
185        Text1.Text = "Listening..."
186   End Sub
```

Figure 7.28. Visual Basic code: remote control.

Server Initialization

The subroutine shown in Figure 7.29 is called once the server program begins to run. Basically, it serves as the initialization routine, and the details follow.

189   Use TCP protocol for network communication.

191   The TCP port number for the server is set to 3001. Hence, the remote user can connect to the server using the TCP protocol with an IP address of 137.132.165.77 and a port number of 3001.

193   Use COM1 as the communication port with the controller box.

195   Give default settings to the port.

197–201   Test the control unit.

204–206   When the system is started, the server runs in the local control mode.

```
        MainForm.frm (continued)

187   Private Sub Form_Load()
188       ' Use TCP protocol
189       Winsock1.Protocol = sckTCPProtocol
190       ' TCP port number
191       Winsock1.LocalPort = 3001

192       ' Use COM1.
193       MSComm1.CommPort = 1
194       ' 9600 baud, no parity, 8 data, and 1 stop bit.
195       MSComm1.Settings = "9600,N,8,1"
196       ' Open the port.
197       MSComm1.PortOpen = True
198       ' call camera 0
199       MSComm1.Output = "1#a"
200       ' Close the port.
201       MSComm1.PortOpen = False
202       ' Number of repeat
203       Repno = 8

204       ' Local control when start
205       Command_Local.Enabled = False

206       Text1.Text = "Local control"
207   End Sub
```

Figure 7.29. Visual Basic code: application initialization.

Server Subroutine

Figure 7.30 shows the server subroutine that receives the command from the client, translates the command, and transfers the results to the control unit.

```
                    MainForm.frm (continued)

222   Private Sub Winsock1_DataArrival(ByVal bytesTotal As Long)
223   Dim strData As String
224       Winsock1.GetData strData, vbString
225       Text1.Text = ""
226       For i = 1 To Len(strData)
227           Text1.Text = Text1.Text +
                              Str$(Asc(Mid$(strData, i, 1))) + " "
228       Next i
229       If MSComm1.PortOpen = False Then
230           Select Case Mid$(strData, 3, 1)
231               Case "u": Call RepeatSend("Ua", Repno)
232               Case "r": Call RepeatSend("Ra", Repno)
233               Case "d": Call RepeatSend("Da", Repno)
234               Case "l": Call RepeatSend("La", Repno)
235               Case "i": Call RepeatSend("Wa", Repno / 5)
236               Case "o": Call RepeatSend("Ta", Repno / 5)
237           End Select
238       End If
239   End Sub
```

Figure 7.30. Visual Basic code: server subroutine.

8 Controlling Physical Systems

8.1 Introduction

Among our Web-based laboratories, the laboratories for the coupled-tank and helicopter experiments are in the area of control engineering. Both laboratories are created for learning, teaching, and research in the field. In fact, control theory plays quite an important role in the control of the instruments in Web-based laboratories. In this chapter, we will discuss how control theory can affect the performance of instruments and how it can be applied to Web-based laboratories.

8.1.1 Mathematical Model

We live in a universe that is undergoing continual change. As engineers and scientists, we always deal with situations where time-dependent effects are important [41]. For example, the time-dependent behavior of fluid-flow and heat-transfer processes significantly affects the quality of the product of a chemical process.

In order to deal with problems involving time-dependent or dynamical behavior in a systematic and efficient manner, we must have a description of the objects or processes involved. We call such a description a model. A model for enhancing our understanding of the problem can take several forms. The most common of these is a mathematical one, which is a description of the underlying process in terms of mathematical relations. The concept of a mathematical model is undoubtedly familiar in elementary physics. Common examples include the relation between voltage and current for a resistor, $v = i R$, and the relation between force and deflection for a spring, $f = k x$.

It is important to remember that the precise nature of a mathematical model depends on its purpose. For example, an electrical resistor can be subjected to mechanical deformations if its mounting board is subjected to vibration. In this case, the force–deflection spring model could be used to describe the resistor's mechanical behavior. The purpose of the model should guide the selection of the model's time scale, its length scale, and the particular facet of the object's nature to be described (thermal, mechanical, electrical, fluid flow, etc.). The time scale will in turn determine whether or not time-dependent effects should be included. Similarly, the length scale partly dictates the details that should or should not be included. It is important to realize that an engineer analyzing the dynamics of high-speed machinery may treat a component as a point mass, whereas this approximation is useless to a metallurgist studying material properties at the molecular level. In general, a good model should give a reasonably good approximation of the behavior of the system under study.

8.1.2 Control System

The coupled-tank apparatus shown in Figure 8.1 is a common system used in the teaching of process-control principles in engineering courses [42]. It consists of two transparent tower-type tanks mounted on a reservoir that stores water. The water levels in the tanks can be read from the scale in front of the tank. Each tank is fitted with an outlet, which in turn is connected to a plastic hose for returning water to the reservoir.

The inflow rate of each tank is controlled by an individual pump, which is controlled by an electric circuit with input voltage ranging from 0 to 10 V. The outflow rate of water returning to the reservoir is approximately proportional to the water levels in the tanks, which are monitored by two capacitance probes with electronic circuits to provide output signals proportional to the level of water in the corresponding tank. The output voltages are in the range of 0 to 10 V. Complex tank arrangements are possible by varying the level of the internal baffle, which controls the inter-tank resistance. The controlling PC feeds two analog input signals to the coupled-tank through a DAQ card. The two analog outputs from the two tanks are sampled at a rate specified by the user.

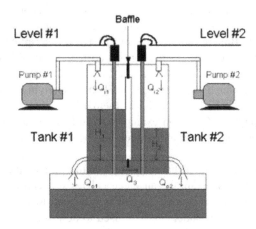

Figure 8.1. Coupled-tank apparatus.

The task of the control system is to maintain the water levels of the tanks at certain specified values or set points. However, since the dynamics of the coupled-tank system are nonlinear, it is hard, if not impossible, to accomplish this task manually by hand. To accurately control the water levels, especially under changing conditions, an automatic control system is required.

Figure 8.2 shows the block diagram of a typical control system. The signal flow of the whole system is as follows. Initially, a desired (generally nonzero) water level is fed to the system. For the moment, the actual water level is in its initial state (generally zero). Hence, the error's value is nonzero, and thus the logic element will generate an appropriate voltage to the pump via the D/A (digital to analog) channel of the DAQ card. The pump in turn controls the input flow rate of the tank to adjust the water level. The actual water level of the tank is measured by the capacitance probe and sampled by the A/D (analog to digital) channel of the DAQ card. At the input point, the actual value and the desired value are compared to generate a new control signal. After a period of time, the actual water level will reach the desired water level. There are numerous tough issues concerning the control strategy, and they form the main research focus in control theory.

In the context of this book, our focus is not on the theory of control. Instead, our aim is to build a Web-based platform for users to carry out learning and research on control theory.

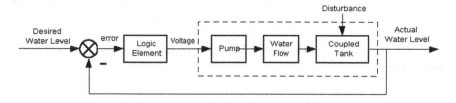

Figure 8.2. Block diagram of a control system.

8.2 Modeling of the Coupled-Tank Apparatus

For convenience, the following notations will be adopted in this chapter:

H_1 and H_2 = heights of fluid in tanks

A_1 and A_2 = cross-sectional areas of tanks

Q_{i1} and Q_{i2} = pump flow rates into tanks

Q_3 = pump flow rate of fluid between tanks

Using Bernoulli's equation for steady nonviscous incompressible flow (which states that the outlet flow in each tank is proportional to the square root of the head of water in the tank), we have

$$\begin{cases} Q_{o1} = \alpha_1 \sqrt{H_1} \\ Q_{o2} = \alpha_2 \sqrt{H_2} \end{cases} \tag{8.1}$$

Similarly, as the flow between the two tanks is proportional to the square root of the head differential,

$$Q_3 = \alpha_3 \sqrt{H_1 - H_2} \tag{8.2}$$

The constants α_1, α_2, and α_3 in the equations above depend on the coefficient of discharge, the cross-sectional area of each orifice, and the gravitational constant. From the water-flow directions in the tanks, the following relationships can be readily obtained:

$$\begin{cases} A_1 \dfrac{dH_1}{dt} = Q_{i1} - Q_{o1} - Q_3 \operatorname{sgn}(H_1 - H_2) \\ A_2 \dfrac{dH_2}{dt} = Q_{i2} - Q_{o2} - Q_3 \operatorname{sgn}(H_2 - H_1) \end{cases} \tag{8.3}$$

where $\operatorname{sgn}(\cdot)$ is the sign function

$$\operatorname{sgn}(x) = \begin{cases} 1, & x \ge 0 \\ -1, & x < 0 \end{cases} \tag{8.4}$$

Combining Equations (8.1) to (8.3), the following nonlinear dynamical equations can be obtained:

$$\begin{cases} A_1 \dfrac{dH_1}{dt} = Q_{i1} - \alpha_1 \sqrt{H_1} - \alpha_3 \operatorname{sgn}(H_1 - H_2) \sqrt{|H_1 - H_2|} \\ A_2 \dfrac{dH_2}{dt} = Q_{i2} - \alpha_2 \sqrt{H_2} - \alpha_3 \operatorname{sgn}(H_2 - H_1) \sqrt{|H_1 - H_2|} \end{cases} \tag{8.5}$$

In addition, the dynamics of the pumps connected to the tanks can be approximated by

$$\begin{cases} Q_1 = k_1 u_1 + c_1 \\ Q_2 = k_2 u_2 + c_2 \end{cases} \tag{8.6}$$

where

Q_1 and Q_2 = inflow rates of tanks 1 and 2

u_1 and u_2 = control signals for pumps 1 and 2

k_1, c_1 and k_2, c_2 = associated constants for pumps 1 and 2

Assume that $Q_{i1} = Q_1$ and $Q_{i2} = Q_2$. Substituting Equation (8.6) into Equation (8.5), we obtain the nonlinear model of the coupled-tank as follows:

$$\begin{cases} A_1 \dfrac{dH_1}{dt} = (-\alpha_1\sqrt{H_1} - \alpha_3 \operatorname{sgn}(H_1 - H_2)\sqrt{|H_1 - H_2|}) + c_1 + k_1 u_1 \\ A_2 \dfrac{dH_2}{dt} = (-\alpha_2\sqrt{H_2} - \alpha_3 \operatorname{sgn}(H_2 - H_1)\sqrt{|H_1 - H_2|}) + c_2 + k_2 u_2 \end{cases}$$ (8.7)

It is not an easy task to control the system given by Equation (8.5) or Equation (8.7). However, we can simplify the model with a simple trick by incorporating the pre-feedback control law for the control system. Assume that the coupled-tank is controlled with the pre-feedback law

$$\begin{cases} Q_{i1} = [\alpha_1\sqrt{H_1} + \alpha_3 \operatorname{sgn}(H_1 - H_2)\sqrt{|H_1 - H_2|} - c_1] + (k_1 u_1 + c_1) \\ Q_{i2} = [\alpha_2\sqrt{H_2} + \alpha_3 \operatorname{sgn}(H_2 - H_1)\sqrt{|H_1 - H_2|} - c_2] + (k_2 u_2 + c_2) \end{cases}$$ (8.8)

Substituting Equation (8.8) into Equation (8.5), we obtain a simplified linear model for the coupled-tank,

$$\begin{cases} \dfrac{dH_1}{dt} = \dfrac{k_1}{A_1} u_1 \\ \dfrac{dH_2}{dt} = \dfrac{k_2}{A_2} u_2 \end{cases}$$ (8.9)

Compared with Equation (8.7), the model above is much simpler and easier to control. Thus, in the Web-based laboratory, we prepare two control schemes: one without the pre-feedback law and another with the pre-feedback law.

8.3 Control Algorithms

There are four control schemes that have been implemented in the Web-based laboratory setup for the coupled-tank experiment. They are: (1) manual control; (2) PID control; (3) general state-space control; and (4) fuzzy logic control. In the following, we will introduce how these algorithms can be applied to the coupled-tank apparatus.

8.3.1 Manual Control

Figure 8.3 shows the block diagram of the system using manual control, which consists of directly feeding the control inputs given by the user to the pumps without the use of any automatic controller. The user is expected to adjust the values of the control inputs to achieve the desired water levels in the tanks.

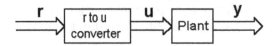

Figure 8.3. Block diagram of manual control.

The user interface for manual control is shown in Figure 8.4. Note that this can be used to determine critical frequencies of the process, which will in turn provide useful information for selecting various gains in other control algorithms such as PID control and general state-space control.

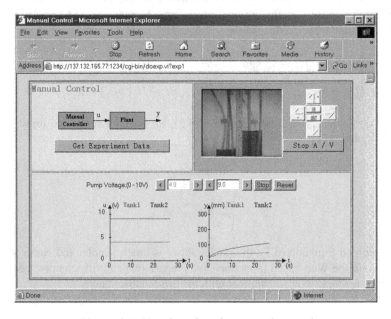

Figure 8.4. User interface for manual control.

8.3.2 PID Control

Figure 8.5 shows the block diagram of the overall control system for the coupled-tank apparatus. Here **r** is the reference input or the set points for the water levels in the tanks.

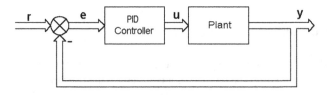

Figure 8.5. Block diagram of the system using a PID controller.

The continuous-time PID controller is given by

$$\mathbf{u} = K_{\text{p}}\,\mathbf{e} + K_{\text{i}}\int \mathbf{e}\,dt + K_{\text{d}}\,\dot{\mathbf{e}} \tag{8.10}$$

where

$\mathbf{e} = \mathbf{r} - \mathbf{y}$ = tracking error

K_{p}, K_{i}, and K_{d} = proportional, integral, and derivative gains

In the coupled-tank experiment, the PID controller is realized through LabVIEW and the appropriate discrete-time input is

$$\mathbf{u}(k) = K_{\text{p}}\,\mathbf{e}(k) + K_{\text{i}}\,T_S\sum_{j=0}^{k}\mathbf{e}(j) + K_{\text{d}}\,\frac{\mathbf{e}(k) - \mathbf{e}(k-1)}{T_S} \tag{8.11}$$

Once PID control is selected, the user is expected to input the values of the two reference inputs (set points) and the values of the proportional, integral, and differential gains. These values can be obtained by tuning the controller using various established procedures. The user interface for PID control is shown in Figure 8.6.

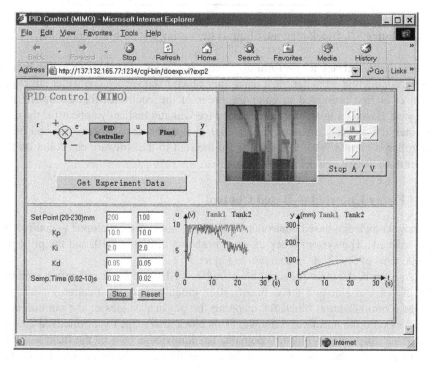

Figure 8.6. PID control for the coupled-tank.

8.3.3 General State-Space Control

Figure 8.7 shows the block diagram for the control of the coupled-tank using a generalized controller modeled in state space. Here, $\mathbf{r}$ is the reference input, $\mathbf{y}$ is the measured output of the coupled-tank, and $\mathbf{u}$ is the control input. The state model of the controller is given by

$$\begin{cases} \dot{x}_{\text{C}} = \mathbf{A}_{\text{C}} x_{\text{C}} + \mathbf{B}_{\text{C}} y + \mathbf{G}_{\text{C}} r \\ u = \mathbf{C}_{\text{C}} x_{\text{C}} + \mathbf{D}_{\text{C}} y + \mathbf{H}_{\text{C}} r \end{cases} \tag{8.12}$$

where x_{C} is the controller state and $\mathbf{A}_{\text{C}}$, $\mathbf{C}_{\text{C}}$, $\mathbf{D}_{\text{C}}$, $\mathbf{H}_{\text{C}}$, $\mathbf{B}_{\text{C}}$, and $\mathbf{G}_{\text{C}}$ are constant matrices of appropriate dimensions.

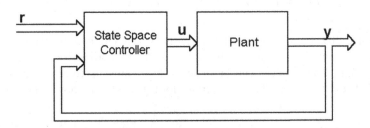

Figure 8.7. Block diagram of the system using a state-space controller.

The user interface for performing general state-space control is shown in Figure 8.8. In conducting an experiment using this general state-space controller structure, the user is first prompted to enter the order of the controller that he or she has designed. Based on this value, a user interface will automatically appear for the user to enter the various matrices. Figure 8.9 shows the case when a second-order controller is chosen. The data entered will be sent to the software controller on the server once the user clicks the OK button.

8.3.4 Fuzzy Knowledge-Based Control

A fuzzy knowledge-based controller (FKBC) has also been developed to control the coupled-tank. The system block diagram is shown in Figure 8.10, and the principal components of the FKBC are shown in Figure 8.11.

As shown, the three principal blocks of the FKBC are the fuzzification module, the inference engine and the defuzzification module. The fuzzification module includes a normalization block for mapping the physical values of the control state variables onto the normalized domain. This block also maps the normalized control output variable onto its physical domain. The knowledge base of the fuzzy controller consists of a database and a rule base. The former includes information on the membership functions and the normalization/denormalization scaling factors. The rule base represents the control policy adopted.

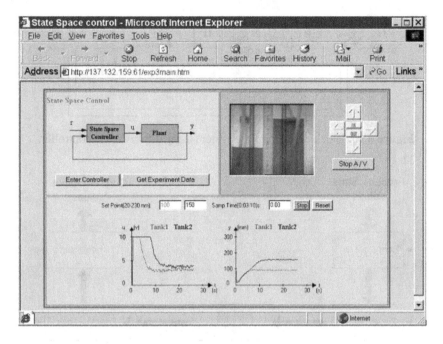

Figure 8.8. General state-space control for the coupled-tank.

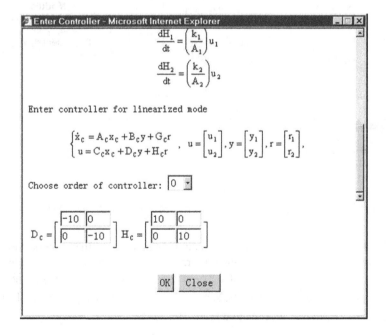

Figure 8.9. User interface for inputting matrices.

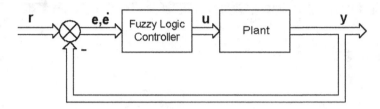

Figure 8.10. Block diagram of the system using a fuzzy logic controller.

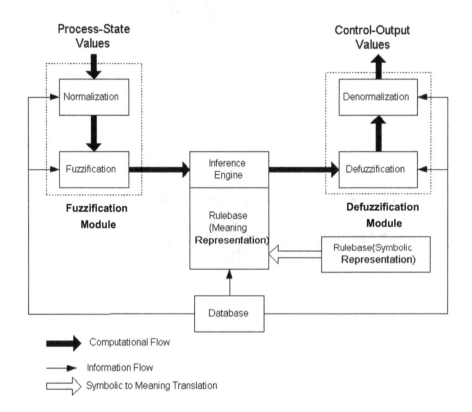

Figure 8.11. Principal components of a fuzzy knowledge-based controller.

To implement fuzzy control on the coupled-tank, we set the process state variables to be the error e and the change of error $\dot{e}$. The control output variable is the control output u. The term sets of e, $\dot{e}$, and u are denoted by $L(e)$, $L(\dot{e})$, and $L(u)$, respectively. They contain the same set of linguistic values; that is, NL (negative low), ZR (zero) and PL (positive low). Thus,

$$L(u) = L(e) = L(\dot{e}) = \{\text{NL}, \text{ZR}, \text{PL}\} \tag{8.13}$$

The user interface developed for fuzzy logic control is shown in Figure 8.12. The two tables at the bottom right corner contain rules for the two controllers. One can change the rules by clicking the corresponding entries. The membership functions for err (error), derr (derivative of error), and out (output) can be modified by clicking the corresponding buttons. On clicking these buttons, a new window pops up, as shown in Figure 8.13 to enable the user to edit the membership function.

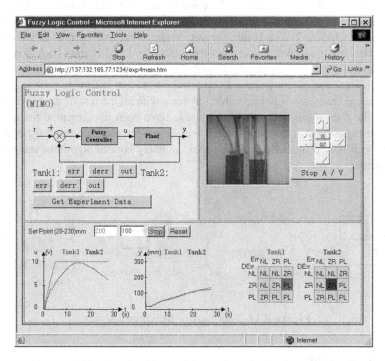

Figure 8.12. User interface of fuzzy knowledge-based control.

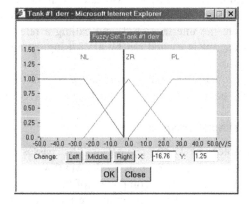

Figure 8.13. User interface for editing membership functions.

By clicking the left, middle and right buttons, the user can choose the function to edit. A vertical line then appears that can be dragged using the mouse to the desired position.

8.4 Controlling the Coupled Tank

Figure 8.14 shows the topology of the control system in the Web-based laboratory for the coupled-tank experiment. This is a typical single client/server structure, as described in Chapter 2. The control server works as the Web server as well as the local controller. It receives commands from the client and returns back control results from the control of the physical plant. The system on the server side is realized using LabVIEW and MATLAB, among which the MATLAB codes are for complicated mathematical calculations, while LabVIEW deals with all the rest of the operation.

All the four algorithms mentioned above have been implemented for the coupled-tank experiment. However, since it will be too lengthy to present these one by one, we will only discuss the realization of the fuzzy control algorithm and use this as a typical example.

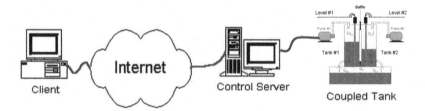

Figure 8.14. Topology of the control server.

8.4.1 VI Programs

VI programs deal with most of the issues associated with the control server, including network communication (HTTP server), sending the signal to the interface card, reading the signal from the interface card, and calling a relevant MATLAB script. Invoking of MATLAB script is carried out by a VI using dynamical data exchange (DDE).

In what follows, we will focus our interest on the control VI `localfuzzy.vi` and assume that all the commands from the client have been received by the server.

Passing Data to MATLAB Workspace

Figure 8.15 shows a piece of `localfuzzy.vi` that passes data to the MATLAB workspace. In this case, the script running in the MATLAB workspace functions as the fuzzy inference system, a critical component of the fuzzy logic control system. Functions of the key nodes of the VI program are indicated and explained as follows.

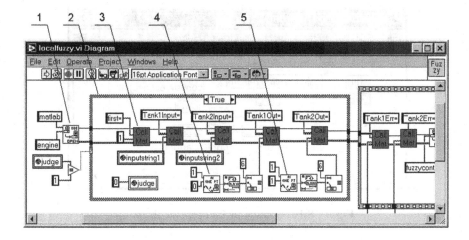

Figure 8.15. Passing data to the MATLAB workspace.

1   Establish a connection between LabVIEW and MATLAB via the dynamic data exchange (DDE) component. This is the first step in building the connection between the LabVIEW workspace and the MATLAB workspace. DDE is a protocol for exchanging data between Windows applications.

2   Execute the code inside for the case when the formula judge=1 is satisfied. For a LabVIEW program, the case structure always chooses a single subdiagram, or case, by determining an input value, which is called the selector. In this situation, the selector is judge=1.

3   Pass the string first=1 to the MATLAB workspace, where it will be interpreted as a command such as

    first=1;

That is, the variable first will be assigned a value of 1. In the same way, other variables or values can be passed. For example, the global variables that contain the control information for the fuzzy inference system, inputstring1 and inputstring2, are passed to the variables Tank1-Input and Tank2Input, respectively. As shown in Figure 8.16, the key component in the callMatlab.vi is actually the DDE VI.

4   Read data from input channel 0 of device 1. Here, device 1 is the device number of the DAQ card used by the coupled-tank, while channel 0 is the first A/D channel of the card. Channel 0 is actually connected to the capacitor probe of tank 1 and hence it can measure the water level of tank 1. The resulting data are formatted before they are passed to the variable Tank1Out in the MATLAB workspace.

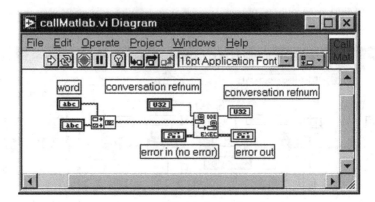

Figure 8.16. Content of `CallMatlab.vi`.

5   Same as for node 4. Data are read from channel 1, which is connected to the capacitor probe of tank 2.

The code in Figure 8.17 also passes data to the MATLAB workspace. Key components are as follows.

1   Execute the code inside the case when `judge=1` is not satisfied.

2   Pass string `first=0` to the MATLAB workspace.

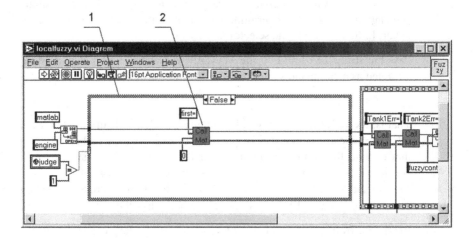

Figure 8.17. Passing data to the MATLAB workspace.

Generating Time Delay

The code inside the sequence case of Figure 8.18 generates a time delay of 182 milliseconds for the system. Key components are marked and explained as follows.

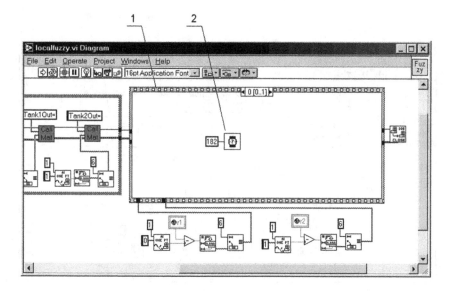

Figure 8.18. Generating a time delay.

1 Stage 1 of the sequence structure with a total of two stages. In the G language, a sequence structure assures that certain codes are executed in a specific order. The code in this sequence is executed before any other sequence when the control flow enters the sequence structure.

2 Wait 182 milliseconds. The timing function will wait for a specified number of milliseconds and then return the value.

Reading Data from the MATLAB Workspace

Figure 8.19 shows the code for the program that reads data from the MATLAB workspace and uses the result of the fuzzy inference system to control the plant.

1 Stage 2 of the sequence structure. The code in this sequence case is executed after stage 1.

2 Read data from channel 0 of device 1. Since the channel is connected to the capacitor probe of Tank 1, the water level of Tank 1 is obtained. Together with the global variable r1, the set point of Tank 1, the error between the set point and the real output is obtained and passed to the variable Tank1Err in the MATLAB workspace. In the same way, Tank2Err is generated and transferred.

3 Call the MATLAB script fuzzycontrol.m. After values for the variables are transferred to the MATLAB workspace, the MATLAB script for the control algorithm is called to generate control signals.

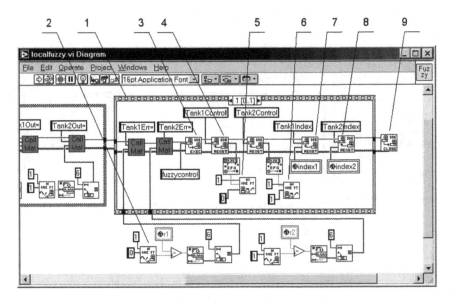

Figure 8.19. Reading data from the MATLAB workspace.

4   Read data from the MATLAB workspace. This VI reads the value of variable `Tank1Control` for the control of the pump for Tank 1.

5   Feed the control signal to the output channel 0 of device 1. Here device 1 is the DAQ card, while channel 0 is the first output channel (D/A channel) of the card. The output channel is connected to the control terminal of the pump of tank 1. Hence, the signal contained in variable `Tank1Control` is actually used to control tank 1.

6   Same as for node 5. Output channel 1 is connected to the control terminal of the pump for tank 2 and the signal contained in variable `Tank2Control` is used to control tank 2.

7–8   Read data from the MATLAB workspace and assign them to global variables.

9   Close the connection between LabVIEW and MATLAB. However, the operation does not shut down the MATLAB application, so the variables in the workspace still exist and can be used for subsequent processing or analysis.

8.4.2 MATLAB Script

Though LabVIEW is convenient for programming, it is not powerful for performing mathematical computations. Fortunately, the powerful and convenient mathematical tool MATLAB meets our computational requirements in the Web-based laboratory very well and is used in our system. The code that will be discussed shortly is for a fuzzy inference system. For convenience, only the code for tank 1 will be listed and discussed.

Translating Command Strings

Figure 8.20 lists the code for translating command strings from the client. These strings contain information for the control algorithm. To make use of this information, one must translate the command strings into MATLAB variables.

1 Determine whether the script is called for the first time. If it is, execute the code to perform initialization.

```
                     fuzzycontrol.m

1   if first==1

2        Tank1LastErr=0;
3        Tank1Derr=0;
4        Tank1Err=0;
5        Tank1Index=0;

6        Tank1RuleArray=Tank1Input(1:9);
7        Tank1ErrArray=Tank1Input(10:18);
8        Tank1DerrArray=Tank1Input(19:27);
9        Tank1OutArray=Tank1Input(28:36);

10       n=3;
11       for i=1:n
12          Tank1RuleMatrix(i,:)=Tank1RuleArray((i-1)*n+1:i*n);
13          Tank1ErrMatrix(i,:)=Tank1ErrArray((i-1)*n+1:i*n);

14          Tank1DerrMatrix(i,:)=Tank1DerrArray((i-1)*n+1:i*n);
15          Tank1OutMatrix(i,:)=Tank1OutArray((i-1)*n+1:i*n);
16       end

17       ErrScale=1;
18       DerrScale=50;
19       OutScale=10;
20       DiscreteNumber=100;

21       Tank1ErrMatrix=Tank1ErrMatrix/ErrScale;
22       Tank1DerrMatrix=Tank1DerrMatrix/DerrScale;
23       Tank1OutMatrix=Tank1OutMatrix/OutScale;

24       first=0;
25   end
```

Figure 8.20. Translating the command string.

2–5 Split the command strings into their respective variables. `Tank1Rule-Array` stores fuzzy rules, `Tank1ErrArray` carries the membership function of the error, `Tank1DerrArray` carries the membership function of the differential of the error, and `Tank1OutArray` carries the membership function for the control output.

10–16 Translate the arrays into a two-dimensional matrix for convenience in further processing.

17–23 Expand or contract the scales of the membership functions.

24 Set the variable `first` to 0, which means that MATLAB has already executed this part of the code. Henceforth, MATLAB will skip this part of the code.

25 End of `if` statement.

Mapping the Real Value into the Fuzzy Value

Figure 8.21 lists the code for mapping the real value into the fuzzy value. All real values must be mapped into fuzzy values for the fuzzy logic operations.

```
                    fuzzycontrol.m (continued)

26   Tank1Derr=Tank1Err-Tank1LastErr;
27   Tank1LastErr=Tank1Err;

28   Tank1Index=getindex(Tank1ErrMatrix,Tank1DerrMatrix,
                                      Tank1Err,Tank1Derr);

29   for i=1:n
30      if i==1
31         Tank1Err(1,i)=getleft(Tank1ErrMatrix(i,2),...
32                   Tank1ErrMatrix(i,3), Tank1Err);
33         Tank1Derr(1,i)=getleft(Tank1DerrMatrix(i,2),...
34                   Tank1DerrMatrix(i,3), Tank1Derr);
35      elseif i==n
36         Tank1Err(1,i)=getright(Tank1ErrMatrix(i,1),...
37                   Tank1ErrMatrix(i,2),Tank1Err);
38         Tank1Derr(1,i)=getright(Tank1DerrMatrix(i,1),...
39                   Tank1DerrMatrix(i,2),Tank1Derr);
40      else
41         Tank1Err(1,i)=getcenter(Tank1ErrMatrix(i,1),
                                    Tank1ErrMatrix(i,2),...
42                   Tank1ErrMatrix(i,3),Tank1Err);
43         Tank1Derr(1,i)=getcenter(Tank1DerrMatrix(i,1),...
44         Tank1DerrMatrix(i,2),Tank1DerrMatrix(i,3),
                                      Tank1Derr);
45      end
46   end
```

Figure 8.21. Mapping the real value into the fuzzy value.

26–27   Calculate the real value for `Tank1Derr` (differential error of tank 1).

  28   Determine the current fuzzy rule. To generate the control signals, all the rules are in fact are involved. However, among them, there is one rule that contributes most. This function is used to find out such a rule for display on the client GUI.

29–45   Map real values into fuzzy values.

Obtaining Fuzzy Result

Figure 8.22 lists the code for obtaining the fuzzy result.

```
                 fuzzycontrol.m (continued)

47   for i=1:n
48     for j=1:n
49       Row=(i-1)*n+j;
50       Tank1Column=Tank1RuleMatrix(i,j)+(n+1)/2;
51       Tank1Temp1(Row,Tank1Column)=min(Tank1Err(1,j),
                                            Tank1Derr(1,i));
52     end
53   end

54   for i=1:n
55     Tank1Temp2(1,i)=max(Tank1Temp1(:,i));
56   end

57   for i=1:n
58     if i==1
59       for j=1:DiscreteNumber
60         Tank1Temp3(i,j)=min(Tank1Temp2(1,i),
                  getleft(Tank1OutMatrix(i,2),...
61                Tank1OutMatrix(i,3),j*2/DiscreteNumber-1));
62       end
63     elseif i==n
64       for j=1:DiscreteNumber
65         Tank1Temp3(i,j)=min(Tank1Temp2(1,i),
                  getright(Tank1OutMatrix(i,1),...
66                Tank1OutMatrix(i,2),j*2/DiscreteNumber-1));
67       end
68     else
69       for j=1:DiscreteNumber
70         Tank1Temp3(i,j)=min(Tank1Temp2(1,i),
                  getcenter(Tank1OutMatrix(i,1),...
71                Tank1OutMatrix(i,2),Tank1OutMatrix(i,3),
                  j*2/DiscreteNumber-1));
72       end
73     end
74   end
```

Figure 8.22. Obtaining the fuzzy result.

Mapping the Fuzzy Value back into the Real Value

Figure 8.23 lists the code to map the fuzzy result back into the real value. The fuzzy result cannot be applied to the real-valued world. It must be converted back into the real value before it is applied to the plant.

fuzzycontrol.m (continued)

```
75   Tank1NumSum=0;
76   Tank1DenSum=0;
77   for i=1:DiscreteNumber
78     Tank1Temp4=max(Tank1Temp3(:,i));
79     Tank1NumSum=Tank1NumSum+i*Tank1Temp4;
80     Tank1DenSum=Tank1DenSum+Tank1Temp4;
81   end

82   Tank1Temp5=(Tank1NumSum/Tank1DenSum)*2/DiscreteNumber-1;
83   Tank1Control=Tank1Control+Tank1Temp5*1;
```

Figure 8.23. Mapping the fuzzy value back into the real value.

Limiting the Output Range

Figure 8.24 lists the code for limiting the output range. Since the control signal for the coupled-tank apparatus has a certain range, we must limit the signal before it is applied.

fuzzycontrol.m (continued)

```
84   if Tank1Control<0
85       Tank1Control=0;
86   end
87   if Tank1Control>10
88       Tank1Control=10;
89   end
```

Figure 8.24. Limiting the output range.

9 Multicast Design

9.1 Introduction

In unicast mode, network communications operate between one sender and one receiver. For example, when a user sends an e-mail to another user, a network connection is established between the sender and a mail exchanger, commands are exchanged, and the body of the e-mail message is transmitted. When a user visits a Web site, a network connection is established between the user and the Web server, commands are exchanged, and the user's computer receives the body of the Web page.

Figure 9.1 illustrates the data flow under this mode [43]. In the scenario shown, three copies of data (D) are sent point-to-point as D1, D2, and D3 to Receivers 1, 2, and 3 in a shared conferencing application. These are "unicast" transmissions sent point-to-point from a sender to a receiver. Hence, under a unicast mode of operation, if multiple users are to log onto the server at the same time, each of them must establish an exclusive connection with the server. Some information from the server may be carried over the network many times, once for each recipient, or broadcast to everyone on the network.

While unicast may be the natural choice in many applications, it may consume unnecessary bandwidth and limit the number of participants in applications that involve many parties. Imagine having to establish hundreds, or maybe thousands, of connections for audio and video download, and both the server and the network may collapse. The Web-based laboratories illustrated so far also run under a unicast environment.

Instead, consider the scenario that is shown in Figure 9.2 [43], where the server places a single packet onto the network and the network determines an optimal route to all clients, duplicating the packet only when necessary [44–47]. The packet will travel outward in a tree pattern, duplicating itself at branches in the network path from the server to all the clients. This is IP multicast, and this kind of data transmission will be able to greatly increase communication efficiency.

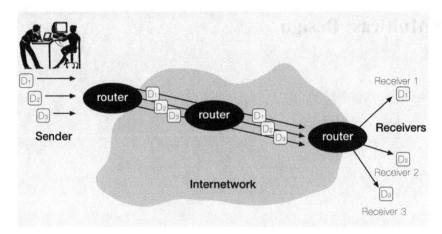

Figure 9.1. Data flow in point-to-point unicast.

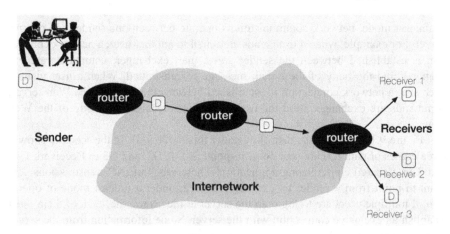

Figure 9.2. Data flow in multicast mode.

With multicast technology, it becomes possible to create Web-based laboratories that support multiple users simultaneously. The laboratory developers and users may benefit greatly from the laboratory's multicast capability. For the developers, the multicast mode helps to increase the ability to communicate, collaborate, and at least leverage more value from the network investment. For the users, they are allowed to log onto the same laboratory simultaneously and cooperate in various ways. Therefore, experienced users can demonstrate the experiment for novice users, users of common interest can collaborate to perform or finish an experiment together, and so on. Specifically, it may be beneficial to implement the Web-based laboratory under a multicast mode when there is a shortage of equipment. In this chapter, we will study the philosophy of using multicast technology to implement the Web-based laboratories.

9.2 IP Multicast

IP multicast is an extension of IP. It is an efficient and standard-based solution with broad support from industry. Under IP multicast, groups of receivers can participate in multicast sessions, with receivers in a group receiving only the traffic for the session for the group. Given a network that is inherently multicast-capable, there are two ways to design the network. One option is to employ a central server to which the clients unicast their messages and which then multicasts the messages out. The second method is to have each computer working on a peer-to-peer basis. That is, each member of the group may multicast its messages directly to other members. This design will result in a system that may have a neater architecture in some circumstances.

The two structures have their own advantages and disadvantages. In our Web-based laboratories, however, the first architecture is chosen. This is because the laboratory is a typical client/server system, where there is no underlying need for a client to multicast to other clients but the laboratory server will have to send video and results on a real-time basis to clients. Essentially, the server will multicast to all the clients, while each client unicasts to the server.

9.2.1 Multicast Protocols

As mentioned in Chapter 2, the TCP protocol is a very good choice for reliable communications. However, the protocol provides point-to-point connections only and is not designed for multicast. As a result, multicast traffic has to be handled at the transport layer with UDP instead of TCP.

The UDP provides only minimal services, such as port multiplexing and error detection. If a packet is detected to be erroneous under UDP, it is simply discarded. Also, losses and disordering may vary by recipient, or some recipients may receive the data as intended while others may experience various losses. With UDP, however, neither the sender nor the recipient will receive notification of such network errors. This adds to the complexity of datagram-based networking.

The other complication lies in the fact that multicast is currently available under controlled environments. It is not possible for a randomly selected computer on the Internet to communicate using IP multicast.

9.2.2 Multicast Groups

For the purpose of multicasting, the idea of a central gathering point for a multicast group is implemented. In the current version of IP (IPv4), there are 268 million multicast groups, identified by the IP addresses 224.0.0.0 to 239.255.255.255.

The Internet Assigned Numbers Authority (IANA) maintains lists of registered users and assigns new numbers for new users or groups. The address range from 224.0.0.0 to 224.0.0.255 is reserved for permanent assignment for a variety of applications. Some well-known addresses have been assigned to groups as follows.

- All systems on this subnet – 224.0.0.1
- All routers on this subnet – 224.0.0.2
- All DVMRP (distance vector multicast routing protocol) routers – 224.0.0.4
- All OSPF (open shortest path first) routers – 224.0.0.5
- All OSPF designated routers – 224.0.0.6
- All RIP2 (routing information protocol) routers – 224.0.0.9
- All PIM (protocol independent multicast) routers – 224.0.0.13
- All CBT (core-based trees) routers – 224.0.0.15

DVMRP, OSPF, RIP2, PIM, and CBT [44–47] are routing protocols used by routers to determine the optimal path along which to forward packets. The complete list appears in RFC 1700. The remaining multicast addresses, 224.0.1.0 to 239.255.255.255, are either assigned to various multicast applications or currently unassigned. The set from 239.0.0.0 to 239.255.255.255 is reserved for various "administratively scoped" applications that do not necessarily have an Internet-wide scope.

When a user joins a particular group, he or she will have to announce it to the underlying network infrastructure. The network will then attempt to ensure that the user will receive all messages sent to that group across the entire multicast-enabled archipelago to which the user is connected. To send a message to a group, one simply drops it onto the network and addresses it to the appropriate group. The network will then attempt to deliver the message to all members of that group.

9.2.3 Time-to-Live

For ease of administration, multicast supports a special time-to-live (TTL) feature whereby a user can limit how far a message can travel. For example, one can restrict a multicast group to a local intranet or even within a local Ethernet. TTL is based on hop count. A number is defined for the TTL of a specific application. Passage through the router decrements the TTL by one. When the number reaches zero, the packet is discarded without any error notification to the sender. In other words, the TTL number determines the scope of the network that the packet can traverse.

There are two aspects that must be considered for TTL. First of all, the user has to configure the routers and tunnels of the network appropriately. Secondly, the user must choose an appropriate time-to-live for the messages to be sent. The value of time-to-live depends on the local network configuration. A TTL of 1 will restrict a packet to a local Ethernet, while 63 typically restricts it to a single multicast island. Table 9.1 shows the values of TTL and the scope of each.

Table 9.1. TTLs and their scopes.

TTL	Scope
0	Restricted to the same host. Will not be output by any interface.
1	Restricted to the same subnet. Will not be forwarded by a router.
<32	Restricted to the same site, organization, or department.
<64	Restricted to the same region.
<128	Restricted to the same continent.
<255	Unrestricted in scope. Global.

9.2.4 Internet Group Management Protocol

Multicast packets from remote sources must be relayed by routers, which should only forward them onto the local network if there is a recipient for the multicast host group on the LAN. To learn the existence of host group members on the multicast routers' directly attached subnets, the Internet group management protocol (IGMP) is used. The system functions through the sending of IGMP queries and having IP hosts reporting their host group memberships. The basic version of IGMP dates from 1988. It is now a full Internet standard and is described in RFC 1112 (see, for example, [48]).

IGMP is loosely similar to ICMP of [49] and is implemented over IP. IGMP messages are encapsulated in IP datagrams. IGMP has only two types of packets, host membership query and host membership report, with the same simple fixed format containing some control information in the first word of the payload and a class D address in the second word. Table 9.2 shows the packet format of an IGMP datagram.

Table 9.2. IGMP packet format.

Version (bits 0–3)	Type (bits 4–7)	Code (bits 8–15)	Checksum (bits 16–31)
Multicast group address (Class D)			

To determine whether a host on a local subnet belongs to a multicast group, the multicast router on the subnet periodically sends a hardware (data link layer) multicast IGMP host membership query message to all the end nodes on its LAN asking them to report back their memberships. The query is sent to the all-hosts group (network address 224.0.0.1), and a TTL of 1 is used so that these queries are not propagated outside the LAN. Each host sends back one IGMP host membership report message to the group address so that all group members see it.

When a process requests its host to join a new multicast host group, the driver creates a hardware multicast address. At the same time, an IGMP host membership report with the group address is immediately sent. The host's network interface is expected to map the IP host group addresses to the local network addresses whenever it is necessary to update its multicast reception filter. Each host keeps track of its host group memberships, and when the last process on the host leaves a group, the group is no longer reported by the host.

Periodically, the local multicast router sends an IGMP host membership query to the "all-hosts" group to verify current memberships. If all member hosts reported memberships at the same time, frequent traffic congestion might result. This is avoided by having each host delay its report by a random interval if it has not seen a report for the same group from another host. As a result, only one membership report is sent in response for each active group address, although many hosts may have memberships.

9.2.5 Developing Multicast Groups

NUSNET-III (National University of Singapore Network III), the environment under which our Web-based laboratories are built, supports multicast. The network is a campus-wide one and interconnects 104 departments in 90 buildings over a campus area of 150 hectares. It serves a population of 24,000 students and 2,700 staff. NUSNET-III consists of multiple LANs connected together by local routers. A dedicated 3Com router is used to provide multicast service for the entire SPnP segment, which uses DVMRP instead of the PIM-DENSE mode, as the rest of the campus routers do.

With such an infrastructure, multicast implementation of Web-based laboratories can be carried out within the campus. The following two steps are required to develop a multicast group.

- Configure the network settings to be multicast-enabled. For a Web-based laboratory, the network must be enabled at least campus-wide so that it can be accessed at least within the campus.

- Choose a multicast group and a time-to-live that lets all the desired users connect to the multicast server but prevents messages from traveling too far.

9.3 System Architecture

Among the Web-based laboratories that have been created, the frequency modulation experiment has been implemented under multicast. We will now use it as an example to discuss the principle of multicast Web-based laboratories.

9.3.1 Hardware

Figure 9.3 shows a block diagram of the hardware structure of the system. The structure is quite similar to the one under unicast. The main difference is that the Internet is multicast-enabled. As illustrated Figure 9.3, the users of the Web-based laboratory are separated into two groups: a main user and observers. The main user is the same as the user under unicast, who has full access to all the instruments in the Web-based laboratory. On the other hand, the observers are only allowed to watch how the experiment is being carried out by the main user. At any time, there may be multiple observers but there can only be one main control user. This makes sure that the instruments or apparatus will not get conflicting commands from two independent users or clients, and the experiment can be conducted smoothly. Of course, it is conceivable that the users may be communicating through e-mails or a chat channel and the main user may be influenced to carry out procedures directly by other observers on other continents.

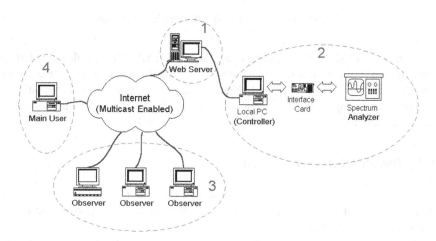

Figure 9.3. Hardware structure under multicast.

9.3.2 Software

Figure 9.4 summarizes the software structure of the system, which is similar to that under unicast. A WWW server with Red Hat Linux 7.0 and an Apache HTTP Server host the Web pages for the experiment. A Mysql database system is installed to manage user authentication. The GNU C program that transmits command strings from the client side to the controller PC and passes sampled data in the reverse direction also runs on the Linux server. In addition, a Java server application that multicasts the real-time spectrum analyzer display and other sampled data from the controller PC, as well as a simple queuing system server, also runs on the Linux server.

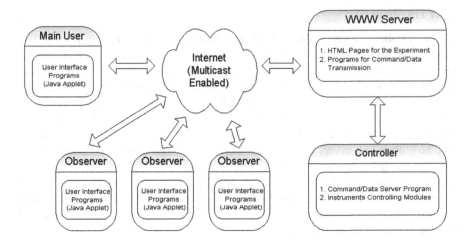

Figure 9.4. Software structure under multicast.

On the user side, Java applets embedded in HTML files are downloaded for running on the client machine to provide a user-friendly interface. Two Java applets are available for the main user and observers separately. For the implementation of multicast in an applet, the Java code needs to be signed in order to step out of the sandbox using the test certificate provided by Microsoft J++.

9.3.3 Double Client/Server Mode

As discussed in Chapter 2, Figure 9.5 shows the double client/server structure, which consists of two client/server pairs: a client and Web server pair, and a Web server and controller pair.

Under multicast, the system functions as follows. The main user initiates a request to the Web server to start the experiment, resulting in the downloading of a Java applet onto the client machine for the client GUI interface. The client then establishes a connection with the program `transit.c` running on the Web server. The program asks for a connection to the controller PC. The `Controller.vi`, which resides on the controller PC, accepts the request, which results in a link from the client to the controller being established for exchange of commands and data. The link is released by closing all the sockets when the experiment is over.

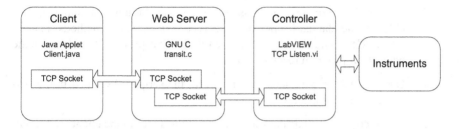

Figure 9.5. Double client/server structure.

9.4 System Implementation

9.4.1 User Authentication

In the realization of a multicast Web-based laboratory, only one main user can have the privilege of controlling all the equipment and apparatus in a session, even though there may be many observing users.

After a user has gained access to conduct the experiment and becomes the main user, all subsequent requests by other users must be blocked and directed to another Web page so that these users can observe the experiment and become observing users. To understand this process, we will now give a brief description of the Common Gateway Interface (CGI), a tool for dealing with client/server interaction.

Common Gateway Interface – CGI

A CGI program allows us to create exciting, dynamic, and interactive Web pages. It is supported by almost all Web servers and browsers. Basically, CGI is a specification defining how a program interacts with a, HTTP server [25].

CGI programs can be developed in C, C++, Visual Basic, TCL, REXX, Python, Icon, AppletScript, UNIX shell script, and even as DOS batch files. However, Perl is the most common language used for CGI programs. The reasons for this are as follows. First, Perl, with its powerful pattern-matching and file-manipulation facilities, has very good text-handling capability. Second, because CGI programs are often time-sensitive and dynamic in nature, the possibility for rapid coding and prototyping under Perl is very helpful.

CGI script is simply a program that in some way communicates with Web documents based on HTML, text, image or any other appropriate type of files on the Web. The following illustrates the interaction between the client and the server when a piece of CGI script is called by the Web browser on the client.

1. A new session is started by the Web server to execute the CGI script.

2. A set of environment variables giving both the server and client system information, such as gateway interface, server software, and IP address of the remote system are created for use in the script.

3. The user's parameters are passed to the script through environment variables or the standard input of the server system. Three methods, namely GET, POST, and HEAD, are defined in the CGI protocol to determine the way a CGI program receives data.

4. Once the user's parameters are received, the script is executed in the session established in step 1.

5. The Web server sends back any output of the script to the client, and it will be displayed in the client's Web browser in the format specified by the server.

Authentication for the Main User

The authentication of the main user is coded in Perl and runs on the Web server. The flowchart of the authentication system is illustrated in Figure 9.6, which shows that the parameter interpretation module extracts parameters from the CGI request and determines the submodule that should be called.

If the request is a logon one, the logon module will verify the user ID and password given by the user. After the information has been found legal, a session ID is generated and written onto a data file, referred to as the session database, to indicate that a user has logged on. At the same time, an access grant is returned to the user. On the other hand, if the user ID or password is not valid, the logon module returns an access denial.

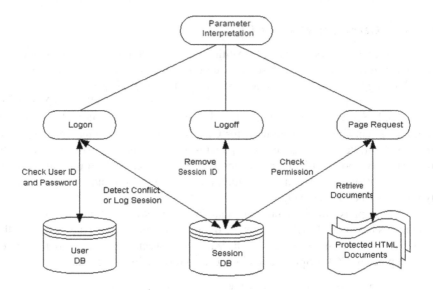

Figure 9.6. User authentication.

If the request is a page request, the page request module will be called. The module first checks the access permission of the current user by querying the session database. If the user has logged on and his session has not expired yet, the appropriate HTML document, which is protected from being accessed by other means, will be sent to the client's browser.

The logoff module is called when the user requests for a logoff. It removes the current active session ID from the session database to allow other users to access the protected Web pages.

Authentication for the Observers

The authentication for the observers actually consists of two parts: authentication and queuing. The former is similar to that for the main user. The latter tries to determine a successor for the main user from the observers.

After the user ID and password provided by the main user are verified and proved legal, a session ID is generated and is written into a data file named session.db, which is located in the cgi-bin/auth-freqmod1 directory. When the main user logs out, the session ID is removed to allow other users access. This provides a simple way to check if control has already been given on the instruments in the laboratory. If session.db is empty, it will be taken that no one is currently conducting the experiment and the requesting user will be allowed to gain control. On the other hand, if session.db is filled with a session ID, subsequent requesting users will be directed to observe the experiment instead.

Table 9.3 lists the CGI programs on the authentication functions above. The whole authentication procedure involves four programs in Perl: Preauth.pl, Auth1.pl, Auth2.pl, and Auth3.pl.

The program Preauth.pl checks whether anyone has already been given access to conduct the experiment by testing out the file size of session.db. If the instrument is unavailable, it will bring the user to the observer login interface. Otherwise, the main user interface is provided.

Table 9.3. Perl programs.

Program	Description
Preauth.pl	To check if another user is given control of the instrument.
Auth1.pl	To verify the user ID and password and keep track of the login history.
Auth2.pl	To double-check if the instrument is really available right before the first observer is taking over. Then, it registers with session.db.
Auth3.pl	To remove the corresponding session ID.

The username and password for authentication will be requested on the observer login page. If the observer does not have an account, he can still log on using the guest account with a username of `guest` and a password of `welcome`. The user ID and password given are verified by `auth1.pl` and, if proved legal, the user will be granted access. In addition, the system keeps track of all the observers' login histories using a data file entitled `clients.db`.

Once the observer is granted access, a Java signed applet will be downloaded onto the client machine to enable the user to view the remote experiment. However, if the main user decides not to continue with the experimental session and logs off, the first observer in the queue will be prompted to take over. The program `auth2.pl` double-checks whether the instrument is still available right before the first observer is taking over. The purpose of doing so is to prevent the chaotic situation where another user logs onto the system and is given control of the instrument before the first observer agrees to take over. If the instrument is available, the program will register using `session.db` on behalf of the first observer and will inform subsequent users that the instruments are in use.

In every client program downloaded to the main user and observers, there is a routine that generates a signal for sending to the server every 1 ms. If the server receives this signal, it will conclude that the client is working well and is still online. On the other hand, if the server does not receive this signal for 10 ms, it will assume that the Internet connection is broken and remove the login status of the client.

9.4.2 Real-Time Transfer of Spectrum Analyzer Display

Figure 9.7 shows the data flow for the spectrum analyzer display. As shown, the data communication between the controller PC and the main user is accomplished by `spectraserver.c`, a server program running on the Web server on port 9002. The Java applet `spectralclient.java` running on the main user side sends a request for a TCP connection to `spectraserver.c`. The program in turn sends a connection request to the controller and accepts the request from the client. The controller PC then accepts the request and hence a link from the main user to the controller PC is established. At the same time, the connection between `spectraserver.c` and `fmexpserver.java` is also set up through the same client/server interaction using TCP on port 9003.

The display of the spectrum and other parameters is based on data passing through the GPIB from the real spectrum analyzer. To reduce the data traffic on the network, the server at the controller PC will send a new spectrum only if there is a significant change. Once the link is being set up, the controller keeps sampling the instrument and pumping the sampled data to the program `spectraserver.c`. The data are then sent to the main user and `fmexpserver.java`. The applet for the main user, `spectralclient.java`, will then reconstruct the spectrum in the user interface according to the collected data. Meanwhile, `fmexpserver.java` will carry out some simple processing on the data before multicasting them to the observers in the multicast group.

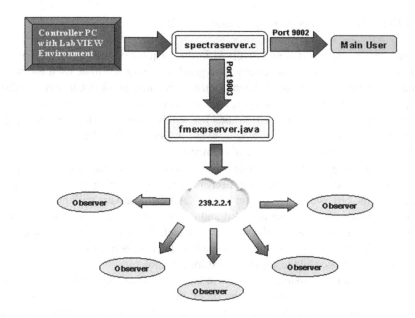

Figure 9.7. Data flow for the spectrum analyzer display.

Since IP multicast uses UDP rather than TCP, the packets received may be out of order or missing. However, neither the sender nor observers will receive notification of any such network errors. For our purposes, the occasional loss of data is quite acceptable. In order to keep things simple, the data received from `spectraserver.c` in bytes will be multicast to the observers as a sequence of UTF-8 encoded characters. The decoding would not succeed and hence cause problems if packets are corrupted. With this feature, some degree of reliability is provided.

Since the data are multicast using the UDP protocol, data packets may be received in error. This may result in the failure in the subsequent reconstruction of the spectrum. To overcome this problem, the data can be broken into smaller packets, with each packet divided into two parts, length and data, as shown in Figure 9.8. Very simply, if the length of the first part is not 4 bytes, the packet is discarded. In addition, if the length of the data packet is not as expected, it is also discarded. With this strategy, reliability is ensured to a certain extent.

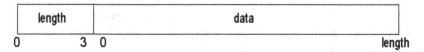

Figure 9.8. Data packet for the spectrum analyzer.

9.4.3 Real-Time Transfer of Command Strings

The procedures and instruments involved in the frequency modulation experiment are so complicated that it is necessary for a good user interface to be used for carrying out the experiment. This has been discussed in some depth in Chapter 3. Basically, events such as mouse dragging and clicking are captured and are used to change the positions of displayed buttons and knobs as well as for controlling the real instruments. To handle these events, event listeners such as `MouseListener` and `MouseMotionListener` are implemented.

To allow observers to view an existing remote experimental session while the experiment is conducted by the main user, the captured events must also be transferred to all the observers on a real-time basis. All the observers will then be able to see the controls that have been adjusted and the resulting changes on the apparatus or signals. In the frequency modulation experiment, the status of the instruments is sent to the observers every second. These include the connectivity of the connectors, the setting of buttons, and the angles turned for the knobs.

Even though it is possible for the main user to multicast this information to the selected group address to reach all the observing users, a lot of processing is involved and it will be costly to the main user in terms of system resources. Since this may affect the progress of the experimental work, a dedicated server application, `multicastServer.java`, is developed instead.

As shown in Figure 9.9, the same communication scheme as described for the double client/server structure is used for exchanging the command strings between the main user and the controller PC. The Java applet running on the main user side sends a request for TCP connection to the program, `transit.c`, running on the Web server on port 3001. The program in turn sends a connection request to the controller PC on port 2055 as well as accepting the request from the client. The controller PC then accepts the request and creates a link from the main user to the controller PC being established. The `client.java` program also establishes a connection with `multicastServer.java` to transfer the command strings to the server application.

The connection between `transit.c` and `multicastServer.java` is also set up through the same client/server interaction using TCP on ports 3003 and 3004 at the same time. Command strings from the main user to the controller PC will have one copy sent to `multicastServer.java` via port 3003, and feedback is received on port 3004.

This dedicated server `multicastServer.java` works as a middleman for the main user reaching all the observers. All the information received at this server will be multicast to the appropriate group address, as shown in Table 9.4, after making appropriate comparisons. A timer is implemented locally rather than asking for the remaining time from the main user periodically.

The server creates six multicast sockets bound to the specified local ports. It then sets the time-to-live of packets to 63 to restrict the packets to travel around the same region and creates the datagram streams (`DatagramOutputStream`). To make textual communications easier, we attach an `OutputStreamWriter` using UTF-8 [50] encoding on top of these byte streams. By this time, the output streams associated with the multicast sockets are retrieved and ready for data to be sent.

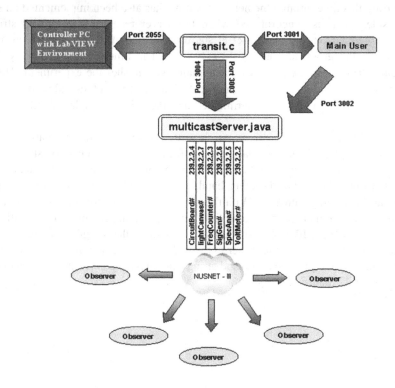

Figure 9.9. Data flow for command strings.

Table 9.4. IP multicast addresses for instrument modules.

Instrument Module	Command String Starting with	IP Multicast Address
Circuit board	`CircuitBoard#`	`239.2.2.4`
Client	`lightCanvas#`	`239.2.2.7`
Frequency counter	`FreqCounter#`	`239.2.2.3`
Signal generator	`SigGen#`	`239.2.2.6`
Spectrum analyzer	`SpecAna#`	`239.2.2.5`
Volt meter	`VoltMeter#`	`239.2.2.2`

A timer is implemented on the main user machine to give the time that remains in the existing experimental session. In order to reduce data traffic and the delay for transferring this time through the network, a timer has also been implemented on the server side. This is synchronized when the server receives a command string `Timer#start` from the main user at startup. The output of this timer is in turn multicast to the group at address `239.2.2.7`. The timer is terminated by the command string `Timer#stop` when the main user finishes the experiment. Then, `No Experiment Session` is multicast to all instrument modules to inform them that the current session is terminated and the original display should be restored.

Note that the command strings are formatted to indicate the originating modules. For example, all the command strings from the signal generator starts with `SigGen#`. `SigGen#groundConn#conn` is sent to the server if the ground connector is to be joined. On the other hand, `SigGen#groundConn#disc` is for disjoining the ground connector. With this design, it is easier for the server to identify where the command strings come from and for this information to be multicast to their corresponding IP multicast addresses. Basically, the design is that the server acts as a middleman for the main user to reach the observers, and it is the observer's responsibility to interpret the command strings and make the corresponding changes on the client GUI interface.

10 An Implementation Example

10.1 Introduction

In previous chapters, we have addressed the key topics and components in the design of Web-based laboratories. In this chapter, we will take the coupled-tank experiment as an example to show how the various subsystems fit and work together in the creation of a Web-based laboratory.

Figure 10.1 gives the overall structure for the coupled-tank experiment. On the server computer, a series of LabVIEW-based programs control the coupled-tank through a DAQ card by calling MATLAB based programs that implement some control algorithms. At the same time, a Visual Basic program controls the pan, tilt, and zoom of a camera through the serial port, while Microsoft NetMeeting processes the video stream received from the camera through a video capture card.

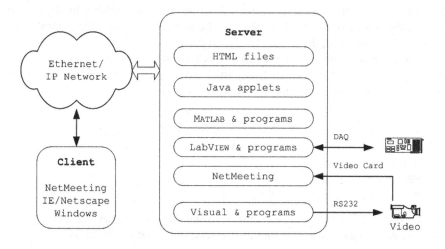

Figure 10.1. Overall structure for the coupled-tank experiment.

The system is started by running the LabVIEW Internet kit on the server. This specifies a home directory for holding the entire related HTML applet, picture, and other files and provides HTTP service for the client.

On the client computer, NetMeeting and Internet Explorer or Netscape are needed, in addition to an Internet connection, for conducting the remote experiment.

In the following sections, details on all the important subsystems will be provided.

10.2 Camera Control Sub-System

To enable the user to view the coupled-tank from various angles, the system uses a pan-, till-, and zoom-enabled camera that can be remotely controlled. This camera is connected to the server through an RS-232 serial port. A Visual Basic application has been developed to run on the server to receive commands from the remote user through a TCP/IP channel, convert them to an appropriate format, and then send the converted commands to the camera.

The source code for camera control is contained in two separate files that together form a project. The first file, camera_control_console.vbp, is a standard management file and is given in Section A.1. This file is almost the same as that created by the Visual Basic development system in standard projects, except for some minor changes in the project name and user information. In particular, the line

```
Form = MainForm.frm
```

specifies to the system that a user-defined form file, MainForm.frm, is to be used in the project.

This MainForm.frm file forms the second file of the project and is shown in Section A.2. Its main purpose is to create functions that can be called by the remote user for the control of the camera. Also, for the purpose of testing, it provides a user interface for controlling the camera locally on the server side.

For the remote control of the camera, a TCP/IP object, Winsock1, and a serial port object, MSComm1, are created and initialized for the purpose of forwarding the user's commands. These are done in the following lines.

```
Winsock1.Protocol = sckTCPProtocol
Winsock1.Bind Winsock1.LocalPort, Winsock1.LocalIP
Winsock1.LocalPort = 3001
Winsock1.Listen
MSComm1.CommPort = 1
MSComm1.Settings = "9600,N,8,1"
```

Basically, the program receives commands from the remote user via Winsock1, converts them to an appropriate format, and sends them out via MSComm1.

The following lines give some details on the command reception, conversion, and delivery processes.

```
Winsock1.GetData strData, vbString
Select Case Mid$(strData, 3, 1)
    Case "u": Call RepeatSend("Ua", Repno)
    Case "r": Call RepeatSend("Ra", Repno)
    Case "d": Call RepeatSend("Da", Repno)
    Case "l": Call RepeatSend("La", Repno)
    Case "i": Call RepeatSend("Wa", Repno / 5)
    Case "o": Call RepeatSend("Ta", Repno / 5)
End Select
MSComm1.Output = OutStr
```

The first line fetches the command string, the Select Case statement carries out the conversion, and the last line delivers the command string to the serial port MSComm1.

To facilitate testing the pan, tilt, and zoom functionality of the camera locally, six control buttons, Command_Right, Command_Left, Command_Up, Command_Down, Command_Zoomin, and Command_Zoomout, are defined in the MainForm.frm file in Section A.2.

10.3 Video Transmission Subsystem

The experiment uses Microsoft NetMeeting for transmitting video to the user for the remote monitoring of the experimental process. The video signal from the camera is first input to the video card in the server. The server NetMeeting application delivers the video stream to the NetMeeting object on the remote client side. As long as the video card and its driver work properly, a basic configuration of the NetMeeting application is the only thing that is needed.

Specifically, for Windows 2000 and above, NetMeeting is installed automatically together with the operating system. To set it up properly, one can look for the NetMeeting icon on the server and run the application, click Call under the main menu, and then select the Automatically Accept Calls option as shown in Figure 10.2. This overrides the default and ensures that video feedback is delivered to the remote client automatically.

10.4 Client Interface

On the client side, a series of HTML files embedded with key objects such as Java applets and NetMeeting have to be provided for the client PC to create the remote user interface. As shown in working flow and relationship style in Figure 10.3, these files provide a series of interfaces for the user to log on, log off, input data, view the control process, and obtain experimental results. A detailed explanation of these files will be provided in the following subsections.

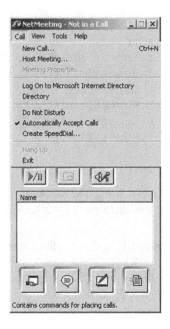

Figure 10.2. NetMeeting configuration.

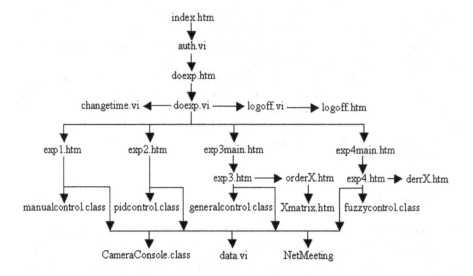

Figure 10.3. File relationship in the client GUI.

10.4.1 index.htm

Since the experiment utilizes real apparatus, only one user should be given control at any one time. An authorization and login subsystem is thus needed, and this is provided by the first index.htm file in the stack of Figure 10.3.

Section B.1 gives the complete listing for index.htm, which includes creation of the user interface for logging on and also for authentication. As an example, the following lines check for the validity of the user inputs before submission to the server for authentication.

```
function check(input) {
  var testarray=new Ar-
  ray("a","b","c","d","e","f","g","h","i","j","k",
  "l","m","n","o","p","q","r","s","t","u","v","w",
  "x","y","z","A","B","C","D","E","F","G","H","I",
  "J","K","L","M","N","O","P","Q","R","S","T","U",
  "V","W","X","Y","Z"," ",".");
  var ok = true;
  if (input=="") ok=false;
  else {
    for (var i=0; i<input.length; i++) {
      var chr = input.charAt(i);
      var found = false;
      for (var j=0; j<testarray.length; j++) {
        if (chr==testarray[j]) found = true;
      }
      if (!found) ok = false;
    }
  }
  return ok;
}
```

Once the user input is validated, the following lines send the user information to a file auth.vi on the server for authentication through a CGI request:

```
<form action="http://137.132.165.77/cgi-bin/auth.vi"
  method=POST name=userInput>
```

10.4.2 doexp.htm

After successful authentication, the server will send back a Web page that allows the user to choose one of the controllers (manual, PID, state space, and fuzzy) that can be used for the experiment. This Web page is given in the file doexp.htm, which is listed in Section B.2.

The file also includes a display showing the time that remains for the user to finish the experiment (limited to 30 minutes) and also a manual logout link. The important lines follow:

```
currenttime=30;
function timecalculate(){
  if(currenttime==0){
    ...
    alert("        Time is up!          ");
    document.location.href="http://137.132.165.77/
      cgi-bin/doexp.vi?timeout";
  }
  document.forms["settime"].elements[0].value
    =currenttime;
  currenttime--;
  setTimeout("timecalculate()",60000);
}
```

10.4.3 exp1.htm

Clicking "Manual Control" on the page provided by doexp.htm will allow the user to control the coupled-tank through manual means. The GUI for this is provided by the file exp1.htm. Given in Section B.3, exp1.htm is a large file and hosts a few Java applet and NetMeeting objects for the manual control experiment.

Specifically, the following codes insert an applet file for the adjustment of the camera positions and zoom

```
<applet codebase="http://137.132.165.77/java"
    code="CameraConsole.class" name="CameraConsole"
    width=0 height=0>
    <param name=servHost value=137.132.165.77>
    <param name=servPort value=3001></applet>
```

The codes below insert an applet file for all the other aspects in the manual control GUI:

```
<applet name=myapplet code-
    base="http://137.132.165.77/java/"
    code="manualcontrol.class" width=500
    height=200></applet>
```

To adjust the remote camera, a standard interface on the client is created for turning the camera up, down, left, and right, as well as zooming it in and out. The following codes show that when an adjustment button is pressed, the appropriate hyper link is activated. The hyperlink in turn calls the corresponding javascript function, which then calls the Java applet CameraConsole.class to send out the control command.

```
<a href=
    'javascript:document.CameraConsole.SendCmd("l");'>
    <img src ="http://137.132.165.77/left_up.jpg"
```

```
   width="35" height="35" border="0" name="left"
   alt="left"></a>
<a href=
   'javascript:document.CameraConsole.SendCmd("i");'>
   <img src="http://137.132.165.77/zoomin.jpg" bor-
   der="0" name="zoomin" alt="zoom in" width="35"
   height="18"></a>
<a href=
   'javascript:document.CameraConsole.SendCmd("u");'>
   <img src="http://137.132.165.77/up_up.jpg"
   width="35" height="35" border="0" name="up"
   alt="up"></a>
<a href  =
   'javascript:document.CameraConsole.SendCmd("o");'>
   <img src="http://137.132.165.77/zoomout.jpg" bor-
   der="0" name="zoomout" alt="zoom out" width="35"
   height="18"></a>
<a href=
   'javascript:document.CameraConsole.SendCmd("r");'>
   <img src="http://137.132.165.77/right_up.jpg"
   width="35" height="35" border="0" name="right"
   alt="right"></a>
<a href=
   'javascript:document.CameraConsole.SendCmd("d");'>
   <img src="http://137.132.165.77/down_up.jpg"
   width="35" height="35" border="0" name="down"
   alt="down"></a>
```

Also, on the client interface that shows the video capture, a NetMeeting object has to be inserted for receiving the video stream from the server. This object is connected to NetMeeting on the server on the basis of point-to-point communication. The following codes show how this connection is made when the user clicks the "Start A/V" button on the GUI.

```
<object width="180" name="Netmeeting"
   classid="CLSID:3E9BAF2D-7A79-11d2-9334-
   0000F875AE17" height="156">
   <param name="MODE" value="RemoteNoPause">
   <embed name="NetMeeting" classid=
   "CLSID:3E9BAF2D-7A79-11d2-9334-0000F875AE17"
   type="application/oleobject"
   param_mode="RemoteNoPause" width="220"
   height="156">
   </embed></object>
```

Apart from video feedback, the remote user can also retrieve experimental data from the coupled-tank apparatus for further analysis. This is provided by the following function:

```
function getdata(){
    var running;
    running=document.myapplet.returnrunning();
    if (running=="yes"){
        alert(" To get the experiment data, click Stop
        to stop the controller first, click Reset to
        clean the previous data.");
    } else {
        mywin=open(
        "http://137.132.165.77/cgi-bin/data.vi",
        "datawindow","width=520,height=300,status=no,
        scrollllbars=yes,toolbar=no,menubar=no");
    }
}
```

The applet for the other aspects for the manual control of the apparatus will be described in the next few subsections.

10.4.4 exp2.htm, exp3.htm, and exp4.htm

Clicking "PID Control," "General State Space Control," and "Fuzzy Control" on the controller option provided by doexp.htm will activate exp2.htm, exp3.htm, and exp4.htm instead of exp1.htm. Complete listings of the HTML programs, exp2.htm, exp3.htm, and exp4.htm, are given in Sections B.4, B.5, and B.6, respectively.

The interfaces for camera adjustment and video feedback are the same as for manual control. However, the applets for the controller GUI are now given by pid-control.class, generalcontrol.class, and fuzzycontrol.class.

10.4.5 manualcontrol.java

As described in Subsections 10.4.3 and 10.4.4, the implementation of the controller GUI is carried out by using Java applet objects, which are created by compiling the corresponding Java source-code files. Each of the four controllers will require an individual Java file, and this is illustrated in the compilation relationship in Figure 10.4. The compilation process and method that can be used depends on the tools available. For example, if JDK is used to compile manualcontrol.java in the path directory, the following command should be executed under DOS:

```
C:\path\Javac manualcontrol.java
```

If javac.exe is not in the current path or not set in the PATH option in the system batch file, the entire path will need to be added. Figure 10.5 shows the results of an example compilation and illustrates that the Java file contains a deprecated API in an earlier version.

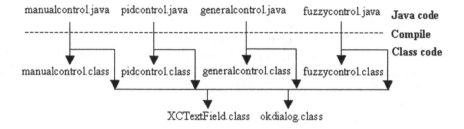

Figure 10.4. Java files and relationships.

```
C:\WINNT\System32\cmd.exe                                    _ |□| x|

C:\Books\Coupletank\Java>\jdk1.3.1_01\bin\javac manualcontrol.java
Note: manualcontrol.java uses or overrides a deprecated API.
Note: Recompile with -deprecation for details.

C:\Books\Coupletank\Java>_
```

Figure 10.5. Compiling `manualcontrol.java`.

The applet `manualcontrol.class` provides the manual control interface for the remote user to give inputs to control the pump voltages and to monitor the water levels. The entire source code is given in Section B.7. Specifically, the file `XCTextField.class` is invoked for obtaining user inputs, and the class `okdialog.class` is used to give a warning message if the input is improper or out of range:

```
XCTextField v1=new XCTextField(4);
XCTextField v2=new XCTextField(4);
okdialog.createokdialog("Pump voltage is 0-10 V!");
```

In addition, a client socket object is created to establish a TCP/IP connection with the server socket on the server. This is for the purpose of setting up a reliable network communication for sending experimental data on the water levels:

```
Socket con;
Socket con1;
PrintStream output;
PrintStream outStream;
DataInputStream inStream;
try {
```

```
      InetAddress add = InetAddress.
        getByName("137.132.165.77");
      Con = new Socket(add,6666);
      Output = new PrintStream(con.getOutputStream());
      System.out.println(con);
    } catch(Exception e) {System.out.println(e);}
    try {
      InetAddress add1 = InetAddress.
        getByName("137.132.165.77");
      con1 = new Socket(add1,5555);
      outStream = new PrintStream
        (con1.getOutputStream());
      inStream = new DataInputStream
        (con1.getInputStream());
      System.out.println(con1);
    } catch(Exception e) {System.out.println(e);}
```

A thread interface `Runnable` is then implemented to receive experimental data on the water levels continuously:

```
public class manualcontrol extends java.applet.Applet
    implements Runnable, ActionListener {
Thread runner;
  ...
}
```

At the same time, the functions `update()` and `paint()` are used to draw and update two curves on these levels in real time:

```
public void update (Graphics g){
  paint(g);
}
public void paint(Graphics g){
}
```

10.4.6 pidcontrol.java, generalcontrol.java, and fuzzycontrol.java

Similarly, controller GUIs for PID, general state-space, and fuzzy logic controllers are implemented by compiling the files pidcontrol.java, generalcontrol.java, and fuzzycontrol.java. These are listed in Sections B.7, B.8, and B.9, respectively.

Apart from some differences due to the nature of the controllers, the same XCTextField.class and okdialog.class classes are involved in obtaining user inputs, while thread interfaces and client socket objects are created for receiving and plotting experimental curves.

10.4.7 NetMeeting

Receiving and displaying the video transmitted from the server through the use of Microsoft NetMeeting is straightforward as long as Windows-based computers are used. The code for setting this up (invoked when the user presses the "Start A/V" button on the GUI) is included in Section B.3 and is given below:

```
Function connection()
  Netmeeting.CallTo("137.132.165.178")
end Function
Function disconnection()
  Netmeeting.LeaveConference()
end Function
...
function callnetmeeting() {
  if (!onshow) {
    connection();
    document.forms["call"].button.value="Stop A/V";
    onshow=true;
    //document.images["power"].src="stop_up.jpg";
  }
  else {
    onshow=false;
    disconnection();
    document.forms["call"].button.value="Start A/V";
    //document.images["power"].src="start_up.jpg";
  }
} ...
<form method="post" name="call" action="">
  <input type="button" name="button" value=
  "Start A/V" onClick="callnetmeeting()"></form>
```

10.5 Coupled-Tank Control and Algorithm

The previous subsections have outlined how the user GUI is created and how user inputs and experimental results are transferred. In this section, we will present details on how the coupled-tank apparatus is actually controlled through the use of LabVIEW and MATLAB.

As mentioned in Chapter 6, LabVIEW is based on the use of a graphical programming methodology. Compilation is not needed, and the developed vi programs will run on the LabVIEW system platform. Similarly, all of the MATLAB m files will run under the MATLAB platform without any need for compilation.

In the remote laboratory system, LabVIEW programs respond to a CGI request, and control the coupled-tank according to the selected control algorithm implemented under MATLAB. Figure 10.6 illustrates the relationship between the various files used in this process. The first four programs are for CGI processing, and the others are used for coupled-tank control.

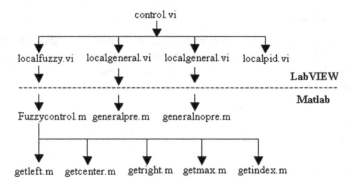

Figure 10.6. vi and m file relationship.

In addition to being used for the control of the experimental apparatus, a few LabVIEW programs have also been written for system-control purposes such as in user authentication. The various LabVIEW and MATLAB programs that have been written for the coupled-tank experiment will now be outlined.

10.5.1 auth.vi

As shown in Figure 10.3, the LabVIEW auth.vi CGI file is for the verification of the user ID and password after receiving an appropriate HTTP request. This logon process has to be successfully completed first before an authorized user is sent the doexp.htm file to select the controller to be used in the experiment. Figure 10.7 shows the important aspects of this graphics program.

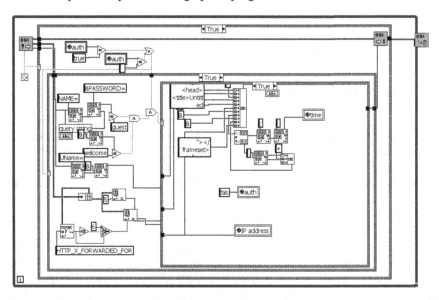

Figure 10.7. Graphics program auth.vi.

10.5.2 doexp.vi and control.vi

As indicated in Figure 10.3, after the user has selected the controller, the do-exp.vi CGI file will be invoked to send back a specific experiment page to the user according to the controller chosen. Figure 10.8 shows the important page in the vi graphics program for manual control. Figure 10.9 shows the graphics program page for the PID controller.

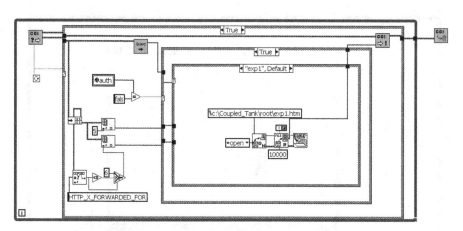

Figure 10.8. Graphic program page for manual control.

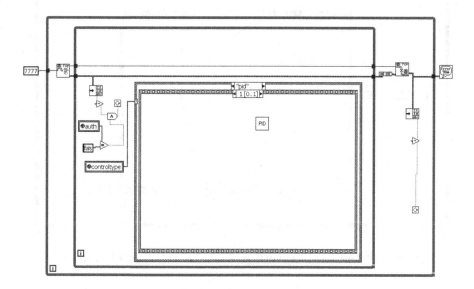

Figure 10.9. Graphic program page for selecting PID controller.

For the PID, state-space, and fuzzy controllers, the `control.vi` program is invoked to receive commands from the client via TCP/IP instead of through a CGI request. `control.vi` in turns calls other `vi` programs, `localpid.vi`, `local-general.vi`, and `localfuzzy.vi`, to control the coupled-tank according to the controller selected. Figures 10.10, 10.11, and 10.12 show the implementation for PID, state-space, and fuzzy controllers, respectively.

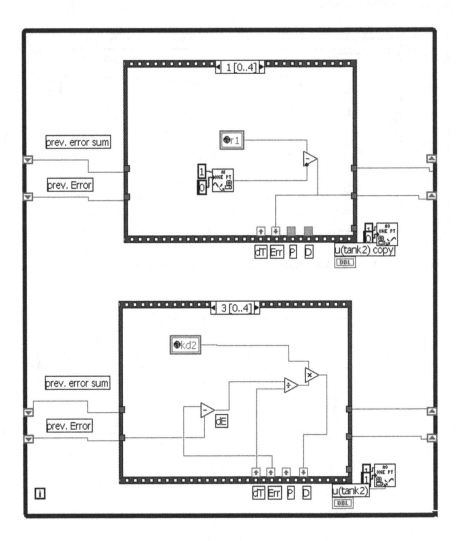

Figure 10.10. Graphics program page for implementing the PID controller.

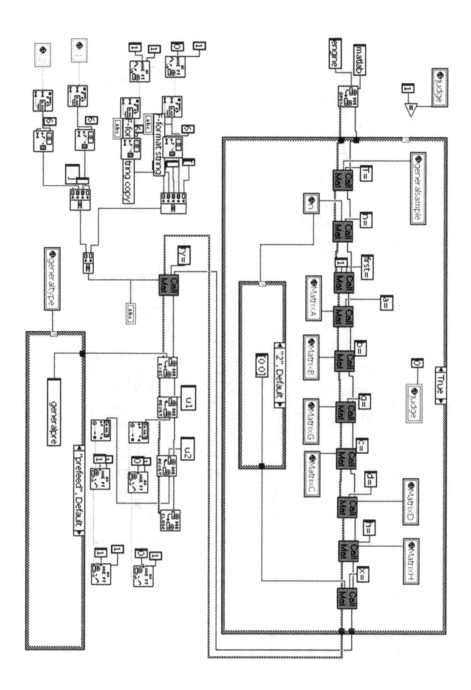

Figure 10.11. Graphics program page for implementing the state-space controller.

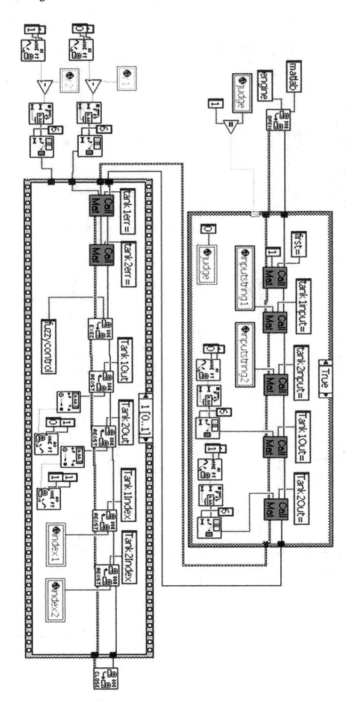

Figure 10.12. Graphics program page for implementing the fuzzy controller.

10.5.3 `fuzzycontrol.m`

The MATLAB `fuzzycontrol.m` file is invoked by the LabVIEW `local-fuzzy.vi` program to implement the control algorithm for the fuzzy logic control of the coupled-tank apparatus. This solution separates the tasks of instrument control and network communication from that of algorithm implementation, which can be done more effectively under MATLAB.

The complete listing for `fuzzycontrol.m` is given in Section C.1. Specifically, the `getleft.m` file is invoked by `fuzzycontrol.m` for obtaining the left fuzzy point:

```
function y =
   getleft(LeftPoint,RightPoint,currentpoint)
   if currentpoint<LeftPoint
     y = 1;
   elseif currentpoint>=LeftPoint &
     currentpoint<RightPoint
     y = (RightPoint-currentpoint)/
       RightPoint-LeftPoint);
   else
     y = 0;
   end
```

the `getcenter.m` file is invoked for obtaining the center fuzzy point:

```
Function y = getcenter
   (LeftPoint,CenterPoint,RightPoint,currentpoint)
   if currentpoint<LeftPoint
     y = 0;
   elseif currentpoint>=LeftPoint &
     currentpoint<CenterPoint
     y = (currentpoint-LeftPoint)/
       (CenterPoint-LeftPoint);
   elseif currentpoint>=CenterPoint &
     currentpoint<RightPoint
     y = (RightPoint-currentpoint)/
       (RightPoint-CenterPoint);
   else
     y = 0;
   end
```

while the `getright.m` file is invoked for obtaining the right fuzzy point:

```
function y = getright
   (LeftPoint,RightPoint,currentpoint)
   if currentpoint<LeftPoint
     y = 0;
   elseif currentpoint>=LeftPoint
     & currentpoint<RightPoint
```

```
     y = (currentpoint-LeftPoint)/
         (RightPoint-LeftPoint);
  else
     y = 1;
end
```

Similarly, the getmax.m file is invoked by fuzzycontrol.m for obtaining the maximum fuzzy point:

```
function y = getmax(matrix,InputValue)
  n = 3;
  MaxValue = 0;
  MaxIndex = 1;
  for i=1:n
    if i==1
      TempValue =
        getleft(matrix(i,2),matrix(i,3),InputValue);
    elseif i==n
      TempValue =
        getright(matrix(i,1),matrix(i,2),InputValue);
    else
      TempValue = getcenter(matrix(i,1),matrix(i,2),
        matrix(i,3),InputValue);
    end
    if TempValue>MaxValue
      MaxValue = TempValue;
      MaxIndex = i;
    end
  end
  y = MaxIndex;
```

whereas the getindex.m file is invoked for obtaining the index of the main fuzzy rule used:

```
function y = getindex
  (matrix1,matrix2,InputValue1,InputValue2)
  n = 3;
  i = getmax(matrix1,InputValue1);
  j = getmax(matrix2,InputValue2);
  y = (j-1)*n+i;
```

10.5.4 generalpre.m and generalnopre.m

In the same manner, the implementation of the general state-space control algorithm with and without pre-feedback is given in generalpre.m and generalnopre.m, and these are listed in Section C.2 and Section C.3, respectively.

Appendix A. Source Codes for Camera Control

A.1 `camera_control_console.vbp`

```
Type=Exe
Form=MainForm.frm
Reference=*\G{00020430-0000-0000-C000-00000000046}
    #2.0#0#C:\WINNT\system32\stdole2.tlb#OLE Automation
Object={248DD890-BB45-11CF-9ABC-0080C7E7B78D}#1.0#0; MSWINSCK.OCX
Object={648A5603-2C6E-101B-82B6-000000000014}#1.1#0; MSCOMM32.OCX
IconForm="Command_Local"
Startup="Command_Local"
Command32=""
Name="Camera_Control_Console"
HelpContextID="0"
CompatibleMode="0"
MajorVer=1
MinorVer=0
RevisionVer=0
AutoIncrementVer=0
ServerSupportFiles=0
VersionCompanyName="NUS"
CompilationType=0
OptimizationType=0
FavorPentiumPro(tm)=0
CodeViewDebugInfo=0
NoAliasing=0
BoundsCheck=0
OverflowCheck=0
FlPointCheck=0
FDIVCheck=0
UnroundedFP=0
StartMode=0
Unattended=0
Retained=0
ThreadPerObject=0
MaxNumberOfThreads=1
[MS Transaction Server]
AutoRefresh=1
```

A.2 MainForm.frm

```
VERSION 5.00
Object = "{248DD890-BB45-11CF-9ABC-0080C7E7B78D}#1.0#0";
    "MSWINSCK.OCX"
Object = "{648A5603-2C6E-101B-82B6-000000000014}#1.1#0";
    "MSCOMM32.OCX"
Begin VB.Form Command_Local
   Caption         =   "Camera Control Console"
   ClientHeight    =   3684
   ClientLeft      =   60
   ClientTop       =   348
   ClientWidth     =   4680
   LinkTopic       =   "Camera Control Console"
   Picture         =   "MainForm.frx":0000
   ScaleHeight     =   3684
   ScaleWidth      =   4680
   StartUpPosition =   3   'Windows Default
   Begin VB.CommandButton Command_Zoom_Out
      Caption      =   "Zoom Out"
      Height       =   375
      Left         =   1800
      TabIndex     =   8
      Top          =   1680
      Width        =   1095
   End
   Begin VB.CommandButton Command_Zoom_In
      Caption      =   "Zoom In"
      Height       =   375
      Left         =   1800
      TabIndex     =   7
      Top          =   1200
      Width        =   1095
   End
   Begin VB.TextBox Text1
      Height       =   375
      Left         =   480
      Locked       =   -1   'True
      TabIndex     =   6
      Top          =   3240
      Width        =   3735
   End
   Begin VB.CommandButton Command_Remote
      Caption      =   "Remote"
      Height       =   375
      Left         =   2880
      TabIndex     =   5
      Top          =   2640
      Width        =   1455
   End
   Begin VB.CommandButton Command_Local
      Caption      =   "Local"
      Height       =   375
```

```
      Left              =    360
      TabIndex          =    4
      Top               =    2640
      Width             =    1455
End
Begin MSWinsockLib.Winsock Winsock1
      Left              =    1080
      Top               =    0
      _ExtentX          =    593
      _ExtentY          =    593
      _Version          =    393216
End
Begin VB.CommandButton Command_Right
      Caption           =    "Right"
      Height            =    375
      Left              =    3240
      TabIndex          =    3
      Top               =    1440
      Width             =    1095
End
Begin VB.CommandButton Command_Left
      Caption           =    "Left"
      Height            =    375
      Left              =    360
      TabIndex          =    2
      Top               =    1440
      Width             =    1095
End
Begin VB.Timer Timer1
      Left              =    600
      Top               =    0
End
Begin VB.CommandButton Command_Down
      Caption           =    "Down"
      Height            =    375
      Left              =    1800
      TabIndex          =    1
      Top               =    2160
      Width             =    1095
End
Begin VB.CommandButton Command_Up
      Caption           =    "Up"
      Height            =    375
      Left              =    1800
      TabIndex          =    0
      Top               =    720
      Width             =    1095
End
Begin MSCommLib.MSComm MSComm1
      Left              =    0
      Top               =    0
      _ExtentX          =    995
      _ExtentY          =    995
      _Version          =    393216
```

```
          DTREnable        =    -1  'True
      End
End
Attribute VB_Name = "Command_Local"
Attribute VB_GlobalNameSpace = False
Attribute VB_Creatable = False
Attribute VB_PredeclaredId = True
Attribute VB_Exposed = False
Dim Repno As Integer
Dim OutStr As String
Dim counter As Integer
Sub DisableAllButtons()
    Command_Up.Enabled = False
    Command_Down.Enabled = False
    Command_Left.Enabled = False
    Command_Right.Enabled = False
    Command_Zoom_In.Enabled = False
    Command_Zoom_Out.Enabled = False
End Sub
Sub EnableAllButtons()
    Command_Up.Enabled = True
    Command_Down.Enabled = True
    Command_Left.Enabled = True
    Command_Right.Enabled = True
    Command_Zoom_In.Enabled = True
    Command_Zoom_Out.Enabled = True
End Sub
Sub RepeatSend(S As String, N As Integer)
    ' Open the port.
    MSComm1.PortOpen = True
    ' Set the command string
    OutStr = S
    ' Set how many times the command string is going to be sent
    counter = N
    ' Disable all buttons
    Call DisableAllButtons
    ' Set timer interval to output the command string 15 times per
     second
    Timer1.Interval = 53
End Sub
Private Sub Command_Down_Click()
    Call RepeatSend("Da", Repno)
End Sub
Private Sub Command_Left_Click()
    Call RepeatSend("La", Repno)
End Sub
Private Sub Command_Local_Click()
    ' close socket
    Winsock1.Close
    ' enable/disable buttons
    Call EnableAllButtons
    Command_Remote.Enabled = True
    Command_Local.Enabled = False
    Text1.Text = "Local control"
```

```vb
End Sub
Private Sub Command_Remote_Click()
    ' open socket
    Winsock1.Bind Winsock1.LocalPort, Winsock1.LocalIP
    Winsock1.Listen
    ' enable/disable buttons
    Call DisableAllButtons
    Command_Remote.Enabled = False
    Command_Local.Enabled = True
    Text1.Text = "Listening..."
End Sub
Private Sub Command_Right_Click()
    Call RepeatSend("Ra", Repno)
End Sub
Private Sub Command_Up_Click()
    Call RepeatSend("Ua", Repno)
End Sub
Private Sub Command_Zoom_In_Click()
    Call RepeatSend("Wa", Repno / 5)
End Sub
Private Sub Command_Zoom_Out_Click()
    Call RepeatSend("Ta", Repno / 5)
End Sub
Private Sub Form_Load()
    ' Use TCP protocol
    Winsock1.Protocol = sckTCPProtocol
    ' TCP port number
    Winsock1.LocalPort = 3001
    ' Use COM1.
    MSComm1.CommPort = 1
    ' 9600 baud, no parity, 8 data, and 1 stop bit.
    MSComm1.Settings = "9600,N,8,1"
    ' Open the port.
    MSComm1.PortOpen = True
    ' call camera 0
    MSComm1.Output = "1#a"
    ' Close the port.
    MSComm1.PortOpen = False
    ' Number of repeat
    Repno = 8
    ' Local control when start
    Command_Local.Enabled = False
    Text1.Text = "Local control"
End Sub
Private Sub Timer1_Timer()
    If counter > 0 Then
        counter = counter - 1
        ' Write the command
        MSComm1.Output = OutStr
    Else
        ' Disable the timer
        Timer1.Interval = 0
        ' Close the port.
        MSComm1.PortOpen = False
```

```
                ' Enable all buttons if in local control mode
                If Command_Local.Enabled = False Then
                    Call EnableAllButtons
                End If
        End If
    End Sub
    Private Sub Winsock1_Close()
        ' Listen again
        Winsock1.Close
        Winsock1.Listen
        Text1.Text = "Listening..."
    End Sub
    Private Sub Winsock1_ConnectionRequest(ByVal requestID As Long)
        If Winsock1.State <> sckClosed Then
            Winsock1.Close
            Text1.Text = "Closed!"
        End If
        Winsock1.Accept requestID
        Text1.Text = "Accepted..."
    End Sub
    Private Sub Winsock1_DataArrival(ByVal bytesTotal As Long)
    Dim strData As String
        Winsock1.GetData strData, vbString
        Text1.Text = ""
        For i = 1 To Len(strData)
            Text1.Text = Text1.Text + Str$(Asc(Mid$(strData, i,    1)))
    + " "
        Next i
        If MSComm1.PortOpen = False Then
            Select Case Mid$(strData, 3, 1)
                Case "u": Call RepeatSend("Ua", Repno)
                Case "r": Call RepeatSend("Ra", Repno)
                Case "d": Call RepeatSend("Da", Repno)
                Case "l": Call RepeatSend("La", Repno)
                Case "i": Call RepeatSend("Wa", Repno / 5)
                Case "o": Call RepeatSend("Ta", Repno / 5)
            End Select
        End If
    End Sub
    Private Sub Winsock1_Error(ByVal Number As Integer, Description As
        String, ByVal Scode As Long, ByVal Source As String, ByVal
        HelpFile As String, ByVal HelpContext As Long, CancelDisplay As
        Boolean)
        Text1.Text = "Error: No." + Str$(Winsock1.State)
        If Winsock1.State <> sckClosed Then
            Winsock1.Close
        End If
    End Sub
```

Appendix B. Source Codes for Interface Design

B.1 index.htm

```
<html>
<head>
<title>Web based virtual laboratory</title>
<meta http-equiv="Content-Type" content="text/html; charset=iso-
   8859-1">
<SCRIPT LANGUAGE="JavaScript">
function check(input) {
   var testarray=new
   Array("a","b","c","d","e","f","g","h","i","j","k","l","m","n",
   "o","p","q","r","s","t","u","v","w","x","y","z","A","B","C",
   "D","E","F","G","H","I","J","K","L","M","N","O","P","Q","R",
   "S","T","U","V","W","X","Y","Z"," ",".");
   var ok = true;
   if (input=="") ok=false;
   else {
     for (var i = 0; i < input.length; i++) {
       var chr = input.charAt(i);
       var found = false;
       for (var j = 0; j <  testarray.length; j++) {
         if (chr == testarray[j]) found = true;
       }
       if (!found) ok = false;
     }
   }
   return ok;
}
function doit() {
   var just=true;
   var name=document.forms[0].UName.value;
   if (!check(name)) {
     alert("please enter your real name!");
     just=false;
   }
   if (just==true)
```

```
                document.userInput.submit();
        }
        </SCRIPT>
        </head>
        <body bgcolor="#000000" text="#000000" valign="MIDDLE"
            link="#0000FF" vlink="#FF0000" alink="#00FF00"
            background="http://vlab.ee.nus.edu.sg/vlab/background_body.gif"
            >
        <br>
        <center>
          <p><font size="+3"><font color="#FF0000">Logon
            Information</font> </font></p>
          <p><font size="3"><b><font
            color="#FF3333"><blink>Important:</blink></font></b></font>
            You must use I.E. 4.0 or above and install netmeeting
            3.0 first!</p>
          <p>To carry out the experiments in the Virtual Laboratory, you
            must now logon.
          <p>Please write down your name and your institute.</p>
          <p>If you don't have a registered UserID, use '<font
            color=red><b><u>guest</u></b></font>'as UserID and'<font
            color=red><b><u>welcome</u></b></font>'as Password.</p>
          <center>
           <p>
           <form action="http://137.132.165.77/cgi-bin/auth.vi"
           method=POST name=userInput>
             <input type=HIDDEN name=MODE value=LOGIN>
             <table border=0 width="156">
               <tr>
                 <td>Name:</td>
                 <td><input type=TEXT size=15 name="UName"></td>
               </tr>
               <tr>
                 <td>Institute:</td>
                 <td><input type=TEXT size=15 name="Institute"></td>
               </tr>
               <tr>
                 <td>UserID:</td>
                 <td><input type=TEXT size=15 name=NAME></td>
               </tr>
               <tr>
                 <td>Password:</td>
                 <td><input name=PASSWORD type=PASSWORD size=15></td>
               </tr>
               <tr>
                 <td> </td>
                 <td> </td>
               </tr>
               <tr>
                 <td> </td>
                 <td> </td>
               </tr>
               <tr>
                 <td> </td>
```

```
        <td>
            <input type="button" name=Button value="Submit"
    onClick="doit()">
            <input type=RESET name="RESET">
        </td>
      </tr>
    </table>
  </form>
  </center>
</center>
</body>
</html>
```

B.2 doexp.htm

```
<html>
<head>
<title>conduct experiment</title>
<meta http-equiv="Content-Type" content="text/html; charset=iso-
    8859-1">
<script language=javascript>
var exp1win=null;
var exp2win=null;
var exp3win=null;
var exp4win=null;
var exp5win=null;
var exp6win=null;
currenttime=30;
function quit(){
if(exp1win!==null){exp1win.close();}
if(exp2win!==null){exp2win.close();}
if(exp3win!==null){exp3win.close();}
if(exp4win!==null){exp4win.close();}
if(exp5win!==null){exp5win.close();}
if(exp6win!==null){exp6win.close();}
}
function changetime(t){
currenttime=t;
document.forms["settime"].elements[0].value=currenttime;
}
function timecalculate(){
if(currenttime==0) {
if(exp1win!==null){exp1win.close();}
if(exp2win!==null){exp2win.close();}
if(exp3win!==null){exp3win.close();}
if(exp4win!==null){exp4win.close();}
if(exp5win!==null){exp5win.close();}
if(exp6win!==null){exp6win.close();}
alert("    Time is up!        ");
document.location.href="http://137.132.165.77/cgi-
    bin/doexp.vi?timeout";
}
```

```
document.forms["settime"].elements[0].value=currenttime;
currenttime--;
setTimeout("timecalculate()",60000);
}
function closewindow(){
if(exp1win!==null){exp1win.close();}
if(exp2win!==null){exp2win.close();}
if(exp3win!==null){exp3win.close();}
if(exp4win!==null){exp4win.close();}
if(exp5win!==null){exp5win.close();}
if(exp6win!==null){exp6win.close();}
}
function doexp1(){
exp1win=window.open("http://137.132.165.77/cgi-
    bin/doexp.vi?exp1","expwindow");
}
function doexp2(){
exp2win=window.open("http://137.132.165.77/cgi-
    bin/doexp.vi?exp2","expwindow");
}
function doexp3(){
exp3win=window.open("http://137.132.165.77/exp3main.htm",
    "expwindow");
}
function doexp4(){
exp4win=window.open("http://137.132.165.77/exp4main.htm",
    "expwindow");
}
function doexp5()
{
    exp5win=window.open("http://137.132.165.77/cgi-
    bin/doexp.vi?exp5","expwindow");
}
function doexp6()
{
    exp6win=window.open("http://137.132.165.77/cgi-
    bin/doexp.vi?exp6","expwindow");
}
</script>
</head>
<body bgcolor="#FFFFFF" onLoad="timecalculate()"
    background="http://vlab.ee.nus.edu.sg/vlab/background_body.gif"
    onunload="quit()">
<center>
  <p><font color="#FF3333" size="5">Coupled-Tank System
    Experiments</font></p>
  <p>Congratulations! You have successfully logged on to the
    Virtual Laboratory.</p>
  <p>Please proceed with any one of the six experiments here. </p>
  <p>You have a total of <b><font color="#FF3333">30</font></b>
    minutes to use
    the Virtual Laboratory.</p>
  After <font color="#FF3333"><b>30</b></font> minutes, you will
    be logged off automatically.
```

```
      <form name="settime">
      <input type="text" name="timeleft" size="3"
      onfocus="this.blur()">
      minutes left!
      </form>
      <table align="center" border="0" width="50%" cellspacing="0"
      cellpadding="0">
      <tr>
         <td width="32%" height="30" align="center"><font size="4"
      color="#006600"><a href="javascript:doexp1()">
         Exp 1: </a></font> <font color="#000099"> </font></td>
         <td width="88%" height="30"><font color="#FFCC00"><b><font
      color="#CC9900">Manual Control</font></b></font></td>
      </tr>
      <tr>
         <td width="32%" height="31" align="center"><font size="4"
      color="#006600"><a href="javascript:doexp2()">
         Exp 2: </a></font> <font color="#000099"></font></td>
         <td width="88%" height="31"><font color="#FFCC00"><b><font
      color="#CC9900">PID Control (MIMO)</font></b></font></td>
      </tr>
      <tr>
         <td width="32%" height="35" align="center"><font size="4"
      color="#006600"><a href="javascript:doexp3()">
         Exp 3: </a></font> <font color="#000099"></font></td>
         <td width="88%" height="35"><font color="#FFCC00"><b><font
      color="#CC9900">General State-Space Control
      (MIMO)</font></b></font></td>
      </tr>
      <tr>
         <td width="32%" height="32" align="center"><font size="4"
      color="#006600"><a href="javascript:doexp4()">
         Exp 4: </a></font><font color="#000099"></font></td>
         <td width="88%" height="32"><font color="#FFCC00"><b><font
      color="#CC9900">Fuzzy Logic Control
      (MIMO)</font></b></font></td>
      </tr>
      <tr>
         <td width="32%" height="50" align="center"><font size="4"><a
      href="http://137.132.165.77/cgi-bin/logoff.vi?"
      onClick="closewindow()">Logoff</a></font></td>
         <td width="68%" height="50"> </td>
      </tr>
   </table>
</center></body></html>
```

B.3 `exp1.htm`

```
<html>
<head>
  <title>Manual Control</title>
<SCRIPT LANGUAGE="JavaScript">
```

```
onshow=false
zoomin1 = new Image
zoomin1.src = 'http://137.132.165.77/zoomin_up.jpg'
zoomin2 = new Image
zoomin2.src = 'http://137.132.165.77/zoomin_down.jpg'
zoomout1 = new Image
zoomout1.src = 'http://137.132.165.77/zoomout_up.jpg'
zoomout2 = new Image
zoomout2.src = 'http://137.132.165.77/zoomout_down.jpg'
start1 = new Image
start1.src = 'http://137.132.165.77/start_up.jpg'
start2 = new Image
start2.src = 'http://137.132.165.77/start_down.jpg'

up1 = new Image
up1.src = 'http://137.132.165.77/up_up.jpg'
up2 = new Image
up2.src = 'http://137.132.165.77/up_down.jpg'
right1 = new Image
right1.src = 'http://137.132.165.77/right_up.jpg'
right2 = new Image
right2.src = 'http://137.132.165.77/right_down.jpg'
down1 = new Image
down1.src = 'http://137.132.165.77/down_up.jpg'
down2 = new Image
down2.src = 'http://137.132.165.77/down_down.jpg'
left1 = new Image
left1.src = 'http://137.132.165.77/left_up.jpg'
left2 = new Image
left2.src = 'http://137.132.165.77/left_down.jpg'
function img_act(imgName) {
    imgOn = eval(imgName + "2.src");
    document[imgName].src = imgOn;
    window.status=imgName;
}
function img_inact(imgName) {
    imgOff = eval(imgName + "1.src");
    document[imgName].src = imgOff;
    window.status="";
}
function callnetmeeting() {
    if (!onshow) {
        connection();
        document.forms["call"].button.value="Stop A / V";
        onshow=true;
        //document.images["power"].src="stop_up.jpg";
    }
    else {
        onshow=false;
        disconnection();
        document.forms["call"].button.value="Start A / V";
        //document.images["power"].src="start_up.jpg";
    }
}
```

```
function getdata(){
    var running;
    running=document.myapplet.returnrunning();
    if (running=="yes"){
        alert(" To get the experiment data, click Stop to stop the
    controller first,click Reset to clean the previous data.");
        }
        else {
            mywin=open("http://137.132.165.77/cgi-
    bin/data.vi","datawindow","width=520,height=300,status=no,
    scrollllbars=yes,toolbar=no,menubar=no");
        }
}
</SCRIPT>
<script language="VBScript" TYPE="text/vbscript">
Function connection()
    Netmeeting.CallTo("137.132.165.178")
end Function
Function disconnection()
    Netmeeting.LeaveConference()
end Function
</script>
<SCRIPT LANGUAGE="JavaScript">
<!--
// NCompass ScriptActive(TM) -- do not remove this comment
ua = navigator.appName;
ua = ua.toLowerCase();
if ((ua.indexOf('netscape',0)) != -1) {document.writeln('<EMBED
    SRC=\"experiment1.AXS\" WIDTH=1 HEIGHT=1
    LANGUAGE=\"VBScript\">');
}
//-->
</SCRIPT>
<script language="JavaScript">
<!--
// NCompass ScriptActive(TM) -- do not remove this comment
ua = navigator.appName;
ua = ua.toLowerCase();
if ((ua.indexOf('netscape',0)) != -1) {document.writeln('<EMBED
    TYPE=\"application/oleobject\" CLASSID=\"CLSID:3472D900-5A27-
    11CF-8B11-00AA00C00903\" NAME=\"CallToBtn\" WIDTH=99
    HEIGHT=23>');
}
//-->
</script>
</head>
<body bgcolor="#CCCCCC" >
<table width="720" border="3" height="430" align="center"
    bordercolor="#666666">
  <tr>
    <td bgcolor="#CCFFFF" height="165" valign="top" width="346">
      <table width="56%" border="0" height="22" cellpadding="0"
    cellspacing="0">
        <tr>
```

```
        <td height="24" width="280"><b><font
color="#FF3333">Manual Control</font></b></td>
        <td height="24" width="50" align="center"><applet
codebase="http://137.132.165.77/java"
code="CameraConsole.class" name="CameraConsole" width=0
height=0>
            <param name=servHost value=137.132.165.77>
            <param name=servPort value=3001>
          </applet></td>
    </tr>
  </table>
  <blockquote>
    <form>
      <p><img src="http://137.132.165.77/Manual.gif"
align="middle"  >
        <input type="button" name="button" value="Get
Experiment Data" onClick="getdata()">
      </p>
    </form>
  </blockquote>
</td>
<td bgcolor="#99CCFF" align="center" width="354" height="165"
valign="middle">
  <table width="92%" border="0" cellpadding="0"
cellspacing="0">
    <tr>
      <td rowspan="2" width="70%" valign="top"
align="left"><object width="180"  name="Netmeeting"
classid="CLSID:3E9BAF2D-7A79-11d2-9334-0000F875AE17"
height="156">
          <param name = "MODE" value = "RemoteNoPause">
          <embed name="NetMeeting"  classid="CLSID:3E9BAF2D-
7A79-11d2-9334-0000F875AE17" type="application/oleobject"
param_mode="RemoteNoPause" width="220" height="156">
          </embed></object></td>
        <td width="30%" height="98" align="center">
        <table width="67%" border="0" cellpadding="0"
cellspacing="0">
          <tr>
            <td width="33%">¡¡</td>
            <td width="19%" align="center"><a
href='javascript:document.CameraConsole.SendCmd("u");'><img
src="http://137.132.165.77/up_up.jpg" width="35" height="35"
border="0" name="up" alt="up"></a></td>
            <td width="48%">¡¡</td>
          </tr>
          <tr>
            <td align="right" width="33%"><a
href='javascript:document.CameraConsole.SendCmd("l");'><img
src="http://137.132.165.77/left_up.jpg" width="35" height="35"
border="0" name="left" alt="left"></a></td>
            <td width="19%" align="center">
              <table width="75%" border="0" cellpadding="0"
cellspacing="0">
```

```
        <tr>
          <td><a
href='javascript:document.CameraConsole.SendCmd("i");'><img
src="http://137.132.165.77/zoomin.jpg" border="0" name="zoomin"
alt="zoom in" width="35" height="18"></a></td>
          </tr>
          <tr>
          <td><a
href='javascript:document.CameraConsole.SendCmd("o");'><img
src="http://137.132.165.77/zoomout.jpg" border="0"
name="zoomout" alt="zoom out" width="35" height="18"></a></td>
          </tr>
          </table>
        </td>
        <td width="48%" align="left"><a
href='javascript:document.CameraConsole.SendCmd("r");'><img
src="http://137.132.165.77/right_up.jpg" width="35" height="35"
border="0" name="right" alt="right"></a></td>
      </tr>
      <tr>
        <td height="2" width="33%"> </td>
        <td height="2" width="19%" align="center"><a
href='javascript:document.CameraConsole.SendCmd("d");'><img
src="http://137.132.165.77/down_up.jpg" width="35" height="35"
border="0" name="down" alt="down"></a></td>
        <td height="2" width="48%"> </td>
      </tr>
    </table>
  </td>
</tr>
<tr>
  <td width="30%" height="58" align="center"
valign="middle">
    <form method="post" name="call" action="">
    <input type="button" name="button" value="Start A /
V" onClick="callnetmeeting()">
    </form>
  </td>
</tr>
    </table>
  </td>
</tr>
<tr bgcolor="#CCFFCC" align="center">
  <td colspan="2" height="195"><applet name=myapplet
  codebase="http://137.132.165.77/java/"
  code="manualcontrol.class" width=500 height=200>
  </applet> </td>
</tr>
</table>
</body>
</html>
```

B.4 exp2.htm

```
<html>
<head>
<title>PID Control (MIMO)</title>
<SCRIPT LANGUAGE="JavaScript">
onshow=false
zoomin1 = new Image
zoomin1.src = 'http://137.132.165.77/zoomin_up.jpg'
zoomin2 = new Image
zoomin2.src = 'http://137.132.165.77/zoomin_down.jpg'
zoomout1 = new Image
zoomout1.src = 'http://137.132.165.77/zoomout_up.jpg'
zoomout2 = new Image
zoomout2.src = 'http://137.132.165.77/zoomout_down.jpg'
start1 = new Image
start1.src = 'http://137.132.165.77/start_up.jpg'
start2 = new Image
start2.src = 'http://137.132.165.77/start_down.jpg'
up1 = new Image
up1.src = 'http://137.132.165.77/up_up.jpg'
up2 = new Image
up2.src = 'http://137.132.165.77/up_down.jpg'
right1 = new Image
right1.src = 'http://137.132.165.77/right_up.jpg'
right2 = new Image
right2.src = 'http://137.132.165.77/right_down.jpg'
down1 = new Image
down1.src = 'http://137.132.165.77/down_up.jpg'
down2 = new Image
down2.src = 'http://137.132.165.77/down_down.jpg'
left1 = new Image
left1.src = 'http://137.132.165.77/left_up.jpg'
left2 = new Image
left2.src = 'http://137.132.165.77/left_down.jpg'
function img_act(imgName) {
    imgOn = eval(imgName + "2.src");
    document[imgName].src = imgOn;
    window.status=imgName;
}
function img_inact(imgName) {
    imgOff = eval(imgName + "1.src");
    document[imgName].src = imgOff;
    window.status="";
}
function callnetmeeting() {
    if (!onshow) {
        connection();
        document.forms["call"].button.value="Stop A / V";
        onshow=true;
    }
    else {
        onshow=false;
```

```
            disconnection();
            document.forms["call"].button.value="Start A / V";
        }
}
function getdata() {
    var running;
    running=document.myapplet.returnrunning();
    if (running=="yes") {
        alert(" To get the experiment data, click Stop to stop the
    controller first,click Reset to clean the previous data.");
        }
        else {
            mywin=open("http://137.132.165.77/cgi-
        bin/data.vi","datawindow","width=520,height=300,status=no,
        scrollbars=yes,toolbar=no,menubar=no");
        }
}
</SCRIPT>
<script language="VBScript" TYPE="text/vbscript">
Function connection()
    Netmeeting.CallTo("137.132.165.178")
end Function
Function disconnection()
    Netmeeting.LeaveConference()
end Function
</script>
<SCRIPT LANGUAGE="JavaScript">
<!--
// NCompass ScriptActive(TM) -- do not remove this comment
ua = navigator.appName;
ua = ua.toLowerCase();
if ((ua.indexOf('netscape',0)) != -1) {
    document.writeln('<EMBED SRC=\"experiment1.AXS\" WIDTH=1
    HEIGHT=1 LANGUAGE=\"VBScript\">');
}
//-->
</SCRIPT>
<script language="JavaScript">
<!--
// NCompass ScriptActive(TM) -- do not remove this comment
ua = navigator.appName;
ua = ua.toLowerCase();
if ((ua.indexOf('netscape',0)) != -1) {
    document.writeln('<EMBED TYPE=\"application/oleobject\"
    CLASSID=\"CLSID:3472D900-5A27-11CF-8B11-00AA00C00903\"
    NAME=\"CallToBtn\" WIDTH=99 HEIGHT=23>');
}
//-->
</script>
</head>
<body bgcolor="#CCCCCC" >
<table width="728" border="3" height="430" align="center"
    bordercolor="#666666">
  <tr>
```

```
<td bgcolor="#CCFFFF" height="197" valign="top" width="369"
align="center">
  <table width="100%" border="0" height="22" cellpadding="0"
cellspacing="0">
    <tr>
     <td height="24" width="280"><b><font color="#FF3333">PID
Control (MIMO)</font></b></td>
     <td height="24" width="203" align="center"><applet
codebase="http://137.132.165.77/java"
code="CameraConsole.class" name="CameraConsole" width=0
height=0>
          <param name=servHost value=137.132.165.77>
          <param name=servPort value=3001>
        </applet></td>
    </tr>
  </table>
    <form>
     <p><img src="http://137.132.165.77/pid.gif" align="middle"
width="340" height="91" > </p>
     <p><input type="button" name="Submit" value="Get
Experiment Data" onClick="getdata()"> </p>
    </form>
</td>
<td bgcolor="#99CCFF" align="center" width="340" height="197"
valign="middle">
  <table width="90%" border="0" cellpadding="0"
cellspacing="0">
    <tr>
      <td rowspan="2" width="70%" valign="top"
align="left"><object width="180"  name="Netmeeting"
classid="CLSID:3E9BAF2D-7A79-11d2-9334-0000F875AE17"
height="156">
          <param name = "MODE" value = "RemoteNoPause">
          <embed name="NetMeeting"  classid="CLSID:3E9BAF2D-
7A79-11d2-9334-0000F875AE17" type="application/oleobject"
param_mode="RemoteNoPause" width="220" height="156">
          </embed></object></td>
        <td width="30%" height="98" align="center">
         <table width="63%" border="0" cellpadding="0"
cellspacing="0">
           <tr>
             <td width="33%">¡¡</td>
             <td width="31%" align="center"><a
href='javascript:document.CameraConsole.SendCmd("u");'><img
src="http://137.132.165.77/up_up.jpg" width="35" height="35"
border="0" name="up" alt="up"></a></td>
             <td width="36%">¡¡</td>
           </tr>
           <tr>
             <td align="right" width="33%"><a
href='javascript:document.CameraConsole.SendCmd("l");'><img
src="http://137.132.165.77/left_up.jpg" width="35" height="35"
border="0" name="left" alt="left"></a></td>
             <td width="31%" align="center">
```

```html
                    <table width="75%" border="0" cellpadding="0"
    cellspacing="0">
                        <tr>
                          <td><a
    href='javascript:document.CameraConsole.SendCmd("i");'><img
    src="http://137.132.165.77/zoomin.jpg" border="0" name="zoomin"
    alt="zoom in" width="35" height="18"></a></td>
                        </tr>
                        <tr>
                          <td><a
    href='javascript:document.CameraConsole.SendCmd("o");'><img
    src="http://137.132.165.77/zoomout.jpg" border="0"
    name="zoomout" alt="zoom out" width="35" height="18"></a></td>
                        </tr>
                      </table>
                    </td>
                    <td align="left" width="36%"><a
    href='javascript:document.CameraConsole.SendCmd("r");'><img
    src="http://137.132.165.77/right_up.jpg" width="35" height="35"
    border="0" name="right" alt="right"></a></td>
                  </tr>
                  <tr>
                    <td height="2" width="33%"> </td>
                    <td height="2" width="31%" align="center"><a
    href='javascript:document.CameraConsole.SendCmd("d");'><img
    src="http://137.132.165.77/down_up.jpg" width="35" height="35"
    border="0" name="down" alt="down"></a></td>
                    <td height="2" width="36%"> </td>
                  </tr>
                </table>
              </td>
            </tr>
            <tr>
              <td width="30%" height="58" align="center"
    valign="middle">
                <form method="post" name="call" action="">
                  <input type="button" name="button" value="Start A /
    V" onClick="callnetmeeting()">
                </form>
              </td>
            </tr>
          </table>
        </td>
    </tr>
    <tr bgcolor="#CCFFCC" align="center">
      <td colspan="2" height="218"><applet name=myapplet
      codebase="http://137.132.165.77/new1/" code="pidcontrol.class"
      width=715 height=200>
        </applet> </td>
    </tr>
  </table>
</body>
</html>
```

B.5 `exp3.htm`

```
<html>
<head>
<title>General Control (MIMO)</title>
<SCRIPT LANGUAGE="JavaScript">
function selectmatrix(){
  var myindex=document.forms["dimension"].select.selectedIndex;
  if (myindex>0) {
    var
    myvalue=document.forms["dimension"].select.options[myindex].
    value;
    // alert("the index is"+myindex+"the value is"+myvalue);
    myWin= open(myvalue, "displayWindow","
    width=500,height=300,status=no,scrollbars=yes,toolbar=no,
    menubar=no");
    document.forms["dimension"].select.value="order";
  }
}
function entercontroller(){
myWin=open("http://137.132.165.77/controller.htm","displaywindow",
    "width=550,height=450,status=no,scrollbars=yes,toolbar=no,
    menubar=no");
}
function helpwin(){
myWin=open("http://137.132.165.77/help.htm","helpwindow","
    width=550,height=450,status=no,scrollbars=yes,toolbar=no,
    menubar=no");
}
function getdata(){
var running;
running=document.myapplet.returnrunning();
if (running=="yes"){
alert(" To get the experiment data, click Stop to stop the
    controller first,click Reset to clean the previous data.");
}
else{ mywin=open("http://137.132.165.77/cgi-
    bin/data.vi","datawindow","width=500,height=300,status=no,scrol
    lbars=yes,toolbar=no,menubar=no"); }
}
var controltype="prefeed@";
function yesfeed(){
controltype="prefeed@";
document.myapplet.gettype(controltype); }
function nofeed(){
controltype="nonprefeed@";
document.myapplet.gettype(controltype); }
onshow=false
zoomin1 = new Image
zoomin1.src = 'http://137.132.165.77/zoomin_up.jpg'
zoomin2 = new Image
zoomin2.src = 'http://137.132.165.77/zoomin_down.jpg'
zoomout1 = new Image
```

```
zoomout1.src = 'http://137.132.165.77/zoomout_up.jpg'
zoomout2 = new Image
zoomout2.src = 'http://137.132.165.77/zoomout_down.jpg'
start1 = new Image
start1.src = 'http://137.132.165.77/start_up.jpg'
start2 = new Image
start2.src = 'http://137.132.165.77/start_down.jpg'
up1 = new Image
up1.src = 'http://137.132.165.77/up_up.jpg'
up2 = new Image
up2.src = 'http://137.132.165.77/up_down.jpg'
right1 = new Image
right1.src = 'http://137.132.165.77/right_up.jpg'
right2 = new Image
right2.src = 'http://137.132.165.77/right_down.jpg'
down1 = new Image
down1.src = 'http://137.132.165.77/down_up.jpg'
down2 = new Image
down2.src = 'http://137.132.165.77/down_down.jpg'
left1 = new Image
left1.src = 'http://137.132.165.77/left_up.jpg'
left2 = new Image
left2.src = 'http://137.132.165.77/left_down.jpg'
function img_act(imgName) {
    imgOn = eval(imgName + "2.src");
    document[imgName].src = imgOn;
    window.status=imgName;
}
function img_inact(imgName) {
    imgOff = eval(imgName + "1.src");
    document[imgName].src = imgOff;
    window.status="";
}
function callnetmeeting() {
    if (!onshow) {
        connection();
        onshow=true;
        document.forms["call"].button.value="Stop A / V";
        //document.images["power"].src="stop_up.gif";
    }
    else {
        onshow=false;
        disconnection();
        document.forms["call"].button.value="Start A / V";
        //document.images["power"].src="start_up.gif";
    }
}
function sendtest(){
    var testvalue="12345";
    document.myapplet.getvalue(testvalue);
}
</SCRIPT>
<script language="VBScript" TYPE="text/vbscript">
Function connection()
```

```
Netmeeting.CallTo("137.132.165.178")
end Function

Function disconnection()
Netmeeting.LeaveConference()
end Function
</script>
<SCRIPT LANGUAGE="JavaScript">
<!--
// NCompass ScriptActive(TM) -- do not remove this comment
ua = navigator.appName;
ua = ua.toLowerCase();
if ((ua.indexOf('netscape',0)) != -1) {document.writeln('<EMBED
    SRC=\"experiment1.AXS\" WIDTH=1 HEIGHT=1
    LANGUAGE=\"VBScript\">');
}
//-->
</SCRIPT>
<script language="JavaScript">
<!--
// NCompass ScriptActive(TM) -- do not remove this comment
ua = navigator.appName;
ua = ua.toLowerCase();
if ((ua.indexOf('netscape',0)) != -1) {document.writeln('<EMBED
    TYPE=\"application/oleobject\" CLASSID=\"CLSID:3472D900-5A27-
    11CF-8B11-00AA00C00903\" NAME=\"CallToBtn\" WIDTH=99
    HEIGHT=23>');
}
//-->
</script>
</head>
<body bgcolor="#CCCCCC" >
<table width="730" border="3" bordercolor="#666666"
    align="center">
  <tr>
    <td width="51%" height="158" valign="top" bgcolor="#CCFFFF"
    align="center">
      <table width="100%" border="0" cellpadding="0"
    cellspacing="0">
        <tr>
          <td><b><font color="#FF3333">State Space Control
    (MIMO)</font></b></td>
          <td><applet codebase="http://137.132.165.77/java"
    code="CameraConsole.class" name="CameraConsole" width=0
    height=0>
              <param name=servHost value=137.132.165.77>
              <param name=servPort value=3001>
            </applet></td>
        </tr>
      </table>
      <form name="dimension">
        <table width="100%" border="0" cellpadding="0"
    cellspacing="0">
          <tr align="center">
```

```
        <td width="100%" height="33" colspan="2"><img
src="http://137.132.165.77/general.gif" align="middle"  ></td>
      </tr>
      <tr align="center" valign="top">
        <td width="100%" height="12" colspan="2">With Pre-
feedback? Yes
          <input type="radio" name="feed"  checked
onClick="yesfeed()">
          No
          <input type="radio" name="feed"  onClick="nofeed()">
          <input type="button" name="help" value="help"
onClick="helpwin()">
        </td>
      </tr>
      <tr align="center" valign="bottom">
        <td width="100%" height="4" colspan="2"></td>
      </tr>
      <tr align="center" valign="bottom">
        <td width="100%" height="19" colspan="2">
          <input type=button value="Enter Controller"
onClick="entercontroller()" name="button2">
          <input type="button" name="Submit" value="Get
Experiment Data" onClick="getdata()">
        </td>
      </tr>
    </table>
  </form>
</td>
<td width="49%" height="158" align="center" bgcolor="#99CCFF">
  <table width="90%" border="0" cellpadding="0"
cellspacing="0">
    <tr>
      <td rowspan="2" width="70%" valign="top" align="left">
        <object width="180"  name="Netmeeting"
classid="CLSID:3E9BAF2D-7A79-11d2-9334-0000F875AE17"
height="156">
          <param name = "MODE" value = "RemoteNoPause">
          <embed name="NetMeeting"  classid="CLSID:3E9BAF2D-
7A79-11d2-9334-0000F875AE17" type="application/oleobject"
param_mode="RemoteNoPause" width="220" height="156">
          </embed></object>
                </td>
      <td width="30%" height="98" align="center">
        <table width="63%" border="0" cellpadding="0"
cellspacing="0">
          <tr>
            <td>¡¡</td>
            <td align="center"><a
href='javascript:document.CameraConsole.SendCmd("u");'><img
src="http://137.132.165.77/up_up.jpg" width="35" height="35"
border="0" name="up" alt="up"></a></td>
            <td>¡¡</td>
          </tr>
          <tr>
```

```
                <td align="right"><a
href='javascript:document.CameraConsole.SendCmd("l");'><img
src="http://137.132.165.77/left_up.jpg" width="35" height="35"
border="0" name="left" alt="left"></a></td>
                <td align="center">
                    <table width="75%" border="0" cellpadding="0"
cellspacing="0">
                        <tr>
                            <td><a
href='javascript:document.CameraConsole.SendCmd("i");'><img
src="http://137.132.165.77/zoomin.jpg" border="0" name="zoomin"
alt="zoom in" width="35" height="18"></a></td>
                        </tr>
                        <tr>
                            <td><a
href='javascript:document.CameraConsole.SendCmd("o");'><img
src="http://137.132.165.77/zoomout.jpg" border="0"
name="zoomout" alt="zoom out" width="35" height="18"></a></td>
                        </tr>
                    </table>
                </td>
                <td align="left"><a
href='javascript:document.CameraConsole.SendCmd("r");'><img
src="http://137.132.165.77/right_up.jpg" width="35" height="35"
border="0" name="right" alt="right"></a></td>
            </tr>
            <tr>
                <td height="2"> </td>
                <td height="2" align="center"><a
href='javascript:document.CameraConsole.SendCmd("d");'><img
src="http://137.132.165.77/down_up.jpg" width="35" height="35"
border="0" name="down" alt="down"></a></td>
                <td height="2"> </td>
            </tr>
        </table>
    </td>
  </tr>
  <tr>
    <td width="30%" height="58" align="center"
valign="middle">
        <form method="post" name="call" action="">
        <input type="button" name="button" value="Start A /
V" onClick="callnetmeeting()">
        </form>
    </td>
  </tr>
</table>
</td>
</tr>
<tr align="center" bgcolor="#CCFFCC">
 <td colspan="2" height="197"><applet
 codebase="http://137.132.165.77/java"
 code="generalcontrol.class" name=myapplet width=500 height=220>
    </applet></td>
```

```
   </tr>
 </table>
 </body>
 </html>
```

B.6 exp4.htm

```
<html>
<head>
<title>Fuzzy Control (MIMO)</title>
<SCRIPT LANGUAGE="JavaScript">
function showerr1(){
mywin=open("http://137.132.165.77/err1.htm","err1Window",
    "width=460,height=350,status=no,scrollbars=no,toolbar=no,
    menubar=no");
}
function showderr1(){
mywin=open("http://137.132.165.77/derr1.htm","derr1Window",
    "width=460,height=350,status=no,scrollbars=no,toolbar=no,
    menubar=no");
}
function showout1(){
mywin=open("http://137.132.165.77/out1.htm","out1Window",
    "width=460,height=350,status=no,scrollbars=no,toolbar=no,
    menubar=no");
}
function showerr2(){
mywin=open("http://137.132.165.77/err2.htm","err2Window",
    "width=460,height=350,status=no,scrollbars=no,toolbar=no,
    menubar=no");
}
function showderr2(){
mywin=open("http://137.132.165.77/derr2.htm","derr2Window",
    "width=460,height=350,status=no,scrollbars=no,toolbar=no,
    menubar=no");
}
function showout2(){
mywin=open("http://137.132.165.77/out2.htm","out2Window",
"width=460,height=350,status=no,scrollbars=no,toolbar=no,menubar=n
    o");
}
onshow=false
zoomin1 = new Image
zoomin1.src = 'http://137.132.165.77/zoomin_up.jpg'
zoomin2 = new Image
zoomin2.src = 'http://137.132.165.77/zoomin_down.jpg'
zoomout1 = new Image
zoomout1.src = 'http://137.132.165.77/zoomout_up.jpg'
zoomout2 = new Image
zoomout2.src = 'http://137.132.165.77/zoomout_down.jpg'
start1 = new Image
start1.src = 'http://137.132.165.77/start_up.jpg'
```

```
start2 = new Image
start2.src = 'http://137.132.165.77/start_down.jpg'
up1 = new Image
up1.src = 'http://137.132.165.77/up_up.jpg'
up2 = new Image
up2.src = 'http://137.132.165.77/up_down.jpg'
right1 = new Image
right1.src = 'http://137.132.165.77/right_up.jpg'
right2 = new Image
right2.src = 'http://137.132.165.77/right_down.jpg'
down1 = new Image
down1.src = 'http://137.132.165.77/down_up.jpg'
down2 = new Image
down2.src = 'http://137.132.165.77/down_down.jpg'
left1 = new Image
left1.src = 'http://137.132.165.77/left_up.jpg'
left2 = new Image
left2.src = 'http://137.132.165.77/left_down.jpg'
    function img_act(imgName) {
        imgOn = eval(imgName + "2.src");
        document[imgName].src = imgOn;
    window.status=imgName;
    }
    function img_inact(imgName) {
        imgOff = eval(imgName + "1.src");
        document[imgName].src = imgOff;
    window.status="";
    }
function callnetmeeting() {
if (!onshow) {
connection();
document.forms["call"].button.value="Stop A / V";
onshow=true;
//document.images["power"].src="stop_up.jpg";
}
else {
onshow=false;
disconnection();
document.forms["call"].button.value="Start A / V";
//document.images["power"].src="start_up.jpg";
}
}
function getdata(){
var running;
running=document.myapplet.returnrunning();
if (running=="yes"){
alert(" To get the experiment data, click Stop to stop the
    controller first,click Reset to clean the previous data.");
}
else{ mywin=open("http://137.132.165.77/cgi-
    bin/data.vi","datawindow","width=520,height=300,status=no,
    scrollbars=yes,toolbar=no,menubar=no");}
}
</SCRIPT>
```

```
<script language="VBScript" TYPE="text/vbscript">
Function connection()
Netmeeting.CallTo("137.132.165.178")
end Function
Function disconnection()
Netmeeting.LeaveConference()
end Function
</script>
<SCRIPT LANGUAGE="JavaScript">
<!--
// NCompass ScriptActive(TM) -- do not remove this comment
ua = navigator.appName;
ua = ua.toLowerCase();
if ((ua.indexOf('netscape',0)) != -1) {document.writeln('<EMBED
    SRC=\"experiment1.AXS\" WIDTH=1 HEIGHT=1
    LANGUAGE=\"VBScript\">');
}
//-->
</SCRIPT>
<script language="JavaScript">
<!--
// NCompass ScriptActive(TM) -- do not remove this comment
ua = navigator.appName;
ua = ua.toLowerCase();
if ((ua.indexOf('netscape',0)) != -1) {document.writeln('<EMBED
    TYPE=\"application/oleobject\" CLASSID=\"CLSID:3472D900-5A27-
    11CF-8B11-00AA00C00903\" NAME=\"CallToBtn\" WIDTH=99
    HEIGHT=23>');
}
//-->
</script>
</head>
<body bgcolor="#CCCCCC" >
<table width="734" border="3" height="402" align="center"
    bordercolor="#666666">
  <tr>
    <td bgcolor="#CCFFFF" height="213" valign="top" width="371"
    align="center">
      <table width="100%" border="0" height="22" cellpadding="0"
    cellspacing="0">
        <tr>
          <td height="24" width="280"><b><font
    color="#FF3333">Fuzzy Logic Control (MIMO)</font></b></td>
          <td height="24" width="202" align="center"><applet
    codebase="http://137.132.165.77/java"
    code="CameraConsole.class" name="CameraConsole" width=0
    height=0>
              <param name=servHost value=137.132.165.77>
              <param name=servPort value=3001>
            </applet></td>
        </tr>
      </table>
      <form>
```

```
      <table width="75%" border="0" cellpadding="0"
cellspacing="0">
        <tr>
          <td><img src="http://137.132.165.77/fuzzy.gif"
align="middle" width="337" height="91"  ></td>
        </tr>
        <tr>
          <td>Tank1:
            <input type="button" name="err" value="err"
onClick="showerr1()">
            <input type="button" name="Derr" value="derr"
onClick="showderr1()">
            <input type="button" name="out" value="out"
onClick="showout1()">
            Tank2:
            <input type="button" name="err2" value="err"
onClick="showerr2()">
            <input type="button" name="Derr2" value="derr"
onClick="showderr2()">
            <input type="button" name="out2" value="out"
onClick="showout2()">
          </td>
        </tr>
        <tr>
          <td height="4"></td>
        </tr>
        <tr>
          <td>
            <input type="button" name="Button" value="Get
Experiment Data" onClick="getdata()">
          </td>
        </tr>
      </table>
    </form>
</td>
<td bgcolor="#99CCFF" align="center" width="343" height="213"
valign="middle">
  <table width="92%" border="0" cellpadding="0"
cellspacing="0">
    <tr>
      <td rowspan="2" width="70%" valign="top"
align="left"><object width="180"  name="Netmeeting"
classid="CLSID:3E9BAF2D-7A79-11d2-9334-0000F875AE17"
height="156">
          <param name = "MODE" value = "RemoteNoPause">
          <embed name="NetMeeting"  classid="CLSID:3E9BAF2D-
7A79-11d2-9334-0000F875AE17" type="application/oleobject"
param_mode="RemoteNoPause" width="220" height="156">
          </embed></object></td>
      <td width="30%" height="98" align="center">
        <table width="60%" border="0" cellpadding="0"
cellspacing="0">
          <tr>
            <td>¡¡</td>
```

```html
          <td align="center"><a
href='javascript:document.CameraConsole.SendCmd("u");'><img
src="http://137.132.165.77/up_up.jpg" width="35" height="35"
border="0" name="up" alt="up"></a></td>
          <td>¡¡</td>
        </tr>
        <tr>
          <td align="right"><a
href='javascript:document.CameraConsole.SendCmd("l");'><img
src="http://137.132.165.77/left_up.jpg" width="35" height="35"
border="0" name="left" alt="left"></a></td>
          <td align="center">
            <table width="75%" border="0" cellpadding="0"
cellspacing="0">
              <tr>
                <td><a
href='javascript:document.CameraConsole.SendCmd("i");'><img
src="http://137.132.165.77/zoomin.jpg" border="0" name="zoomin"
alt="zoom in" width="35" height="18"></a></td>
              </tr>
              <tr>
                <td><a
href='javascript:document.CameraConsole.SendCmd("o");'><img
src="http://137.132.165.77/zoomout.jpg" border="0"
name="zoomout" alt="zoom out" width="35" height="18"></a></td>
              </tr>
            </table>
          </td>
          <td align="left"><a
href='javascript:document.CameraConsole.SendCmd("r");'><img
src="http://137.132.165.77/right_up.jpg" width="35" height="35"
border="0" name="right" alt="right"></a></td>
        </tr>
        <tr>
          <td height="2"> </td>
          <td height="2" align="center"><a
href='javascript:document.CameraConsole.SendCmd("d");'><img
src="http://137.132.165.77/down_up.jpg" width="35" height="35"
border="0" name="down" alt="down"></a></td>
          <td height="2"> </td>
        </tr>
      </table>
    </td>
  </tr>
  <tr>
    <td width="30%" height="58" align="center"
valign="middle">
      <form method="post" name="call" action="">
        <input type="button" name="button" value="Start A /
V" onClick="callnetmeeting()">
      </form>
    </td>
  </tr>
</table>
```

```
   </td>
  </tr>
  <tr bgcolor="#CCFFCC">
   <td colspan="2" height="199"><applet
   codebase="http://137.132.165.77/java/"
   code="fuzzycontrol.class" width=710 height=200 name="myapplet">
     </applet> </td>
  </tr>
 </table>
 </body>
 </html>
```

B.7 manualcontrol.java

```java
import java.net.*;
import java.io.*;
import java.awt.*;
import java.awt.event.*;
public class manualcontrol extends java.applet.Applet implements
    Runnable, ActionListener {
int[] x1=new int[200];
int[] y1=new int[200];
int[] x2=new int[200];
int[] y2=new int[200];
int[] ux1=new int[200];
int[] uy1=new int[200];
int[] ux2=new int[200];
int[] uy2=new int[200];
int m=0;
int n=0;
int j1=290;//use to record the points on the x axis
int j2=290;
int i=0;//use to read three bytes from the server side
int k=0;//use to change time
int height1=0;
int height2=0;
int um=0;
int un=0;
int uj1=70;//use to record the points on the x axis
int uj2=70;
int ui=0;//use to read three bytes from the server side
int uk=0;//use to change time
int uheight1=0;
int uheight2=0;
int value1int;
int value2int;
long timevalue1=0;
long timevalue2=0;
long timeaverage=0;
int loopvalue=0;
long timeoffset=0;
long alltime=0;
```

```
boolean changetime=false;
int timeperiod=10;
Button run=new Button("Run");
Button reset=new Button("Reset");
Button t1down=new Button("<");
Button t1up=new Button(">");
Button t2down=new Button("<");
Button t2up=new Button(">");
XCTextField v1=new XCTextField(4);
XCTextField v2=new XCTextField(4);
String voltage1;
String voltage2;
String voltage;
Socket con;
Socket con1;
PrintStream output;
PrintStream outStream;
DataInputStream inStream;
boolean temp=false;
boolean temp1=false;
boolean utemp=false;
boolean utemp1=false;
//Panel panel1=new Panel();
Thread runner;
String flowvalue1;
String flowvalue2;
String uvalue1;
String uvalue2;
Font f=new Font("TimesRoman", Font.BOLD,14);
char[] currchar1=new char[3];
char[] currchar2=new char[3];
char[] currchar3=new char[3];
char[] currchar4=new char[3];
char[] currchar5=new char[5];
byte[] currLine=new byte[23];
Color greencolor=new Color(204,255,204);
String timevaluestring;
int timevalue;
int timeindex=0;
int timeleft=0;
int pointnumber1=0;
int pointnumber2=0;
int pointnumber3=0;
boolean resetalready=false;
int shift=0;
public void init(){
this.setBackground(greencolor);
v1.setForeground(Color.red);
v2.setForeground(Color.blue);
v1.setText("0.0");
v2.setText("0.0");
v1.button1=run;
v2.button1=run;
t1down.addActionListener(this);
```

```
t1up.addActionListener(this);
t2down.addActionListener(this);
t2up.addActionListener(this);
add(new Label("Pump Voltage:(0 - 10V)"));
add(t1down);
add(v1);
add(t1up);
add(t2down);
add(v2);
add(t2up);
add(run);
add(reset);
}
public void start() {
try {
InetAddress add= InetAddress.getByName("137.132.165.77");
con=new Socket(add, 6666);
output=new PrintStream(con.getOutputStream());
System.out.println(con);
} catch(Exception e) {System.out.println(e);}
Try {
InetAddress add1=InetAddress.getByName("137.132.165.77");
con1=new Socket(add1,5555);
outStream=new PrintStream(con1.getOutputStream());
inStream=new DataInputStream(con1.getInputStream());
System.out.println(con1);
} catch(Exception e) {System.out.println(e);}
runner=new Thread(this);
}
public void stop() {
runner.stop();
try {
con.close();
con1.close();}catch (Exception e){};
}
public void run() {
while (true){    //write and read
try {
outStream.println("waiting");
inStream.readFully(currLine);
} catch (Exception e) {System.out.println(e);}
//convert bytes to char
for(i=0;i<3;i++) {
currchar1[i]=(char)currLine[i];
currchar2[i]=(char)currLine[i+3];
currchar3[i]=(char)currLine[i+6];
currchar4[i]=(char)currLine[i+9];
}
for(i=0;i<5;i++) {
currchar5[i]=(char)currLine[18+i];}
//build a string by the chars
timevaluestring=new String(currchar5);
timevalue=Integer.parseInt(timevaluestring.trim());
if(resetalready) {
```

```
timevalue=0;
resetalready=false;}
System.out.println("timevalue is "+timevalue);
timeindex=timevalue/200;
timeleft=timevalue%200;
if (timeleft>100) timeindex++;
flowvalue1=new String(currchar1);
flowvalue2=new String(currchar2);
height1=180-Integer.parseInt(flowvalue1.trim());
height2=180-Integer.parseInt(flowvalue2.trim());
uvalue1=new String(currchar3);
uvalue2=new String(currchar4);
//draw the voltage
uheight1=180-Integer.parseInt(uvalue1.trim());
uheight2=180-Integer.parseInt(uvalue2.trim());
j1=j1+timeindex;
j2=j2+timeindex;
uj1=uj1+timeindex;
uj2=uj2+timeindex;
x1[m]=j1;
y1[m]=height1;
x2[m]=j2;
y2[m]=height2;
ux1[m]=uj1;
uy1[m]=uheight1;
ux2[m]=uj2;
uy2[m]=uheight2;
if (x1[m]<=340) {
pointnumber1++;
}
else if (x1[m]<=390) {
pointnumber2++;
}
else {
pointnumber3++;
}
if (x1[m]>=440) {
shift=m-pointnumber1;
for (n=0;n<m-pointnumber1;n++) {
x1[n]=x1[n+pointnumber1]-50;
y1[n]=y1[n+pointnumber1];
x2[n]=x2[n+pointnumber1]-50;
y2[n]=y2[n+pointnumber1];
ux1[n]=ux1[n+pointnumber1]-50;
uy1[n]=uy1[n+pointnumber1];
ux2[n]=ux2[n+pointnumber1]-50;
uy2[n]=uy2[n+pointnumber1];
}
j1=x1[m-pointnumber1];
j2=j1;
uj1=ux1[m-pointnumber1];
uj2=uj1;
m=m-pointnumber1;
pointnumber1=pointnumber2;
```

```
pointnumber2=pointnumber3;
pointnumber3=0;
k++;
temp=true;
uk++;
utemp=true;
}
m++;
repaint();
}
}
public void actionPerformed(ActionEvent e) {
String Text1;
String Text2;
If (e.getSource()==t1down) {
String firstvalue1=v1.getText();
Float firstvalue1f=new
    Float(Float.valueOf(firstvalue1).floatValue()*10f);
int firstvalueint1=firstvalue1f.intValue();
firstvalueint1=firstvalueint1-1;
run.setLabel("Stop");
if (firstvalueint1<0) {
v1.setText("0.0");
firstvalueint1=0;
okdialog.createokdialog("Pump voltage is 0-10 V!");
}
float textf1=(new Integer(firstvalueint1)).floatValue()/10f;
Text1=String.valueOf(textf1);
v1.setText(Text1);
Text2=v2.getText();
voltage="manual@"+Text1+" "+Text2;
output.println(voltage);
if(runner.isAlive()) {
runner.resume();
System.out.println("runner start!");
}
else {
runner.start();
System.out.println("runner resume!");
}
}
if (e.getSource()==t1up) {
String firstvalue1=v1.getText();
Float firstvalue1f=new
    Float(Float.valueOf(firstvalue1).floatValue()*10f);
int firstvalueint1=firstvalue1f.intValue();
firstvalueint1=firstvalueint1+1;
run.setLabel("Stop");
if (firstvalueint1>100) {
v1.setText("10.0");
firstvalueint1=100;
okdialog.createokdialog("Pump voltage is 0-10 V!");
}
float textf1=(new Integer(firstvalueint1)).floatValue()/10f;
```

```
Text1=String.valueOf(textf1);
v1.setText(Text1);
Text2=v2.getText();
voltage="manual@"+Text1+" "+Text2;
output.println(voltage);
if(runner.isAlive()) {
runner.resume();
System.out.println("runner start!");
}
else {
runner.start();
System.out.println("runner resume!");
}
}
if (e.getSource()==t2down) {
String firstvalue2=v2.getText();
Float firstvalue2f=new
    Float(Float.valueOf(firstvalue2).floatValue()*10f);
int firstvalueint2=firstvalue2f.intValue();
firstvalueint2=firstvalueint2-1;
run.setLabel("Stop");
if (firstvalueint2<0 ) {
v2.setText("0.0");
firstvalueint2=0;
okdialog.createokdialog("Pump voltage is 0-10 V!");
}
float textf2=(new Integer(firstvalueint2)).floatValue()/10f;
Text2=String.valueOf(textf2);
v2.setText(Text2);
Text1=v1.getText();
voltage="manual@"+Text1+" "+Text2;
output.println(voltage);
if(runner.isAlive()) {
runner.resume();
System.out.println("runner start!");
}
else {
runner.start();
System.out.println("runner resume!");
}
}
if(e.getSource()==t2up ) {
String firstvalue2=v2.getText();
Float firstvalue2f=new
    Float(Float.valueOf(firstvalue2).floatValue()*10f);
int firstvalueint2=firstvalue2f.intValue();
firstvalueint2=firstvalueint2+1;
run.setLabel("Stop");
if (firstvalueint2>100 ) {
v2.setText("10.0");
firstvalueint2=100;
okdialog.createokdialog("Pump voltage is 0-10 V!");
}
float textf2=(new Integer(firstvalueint2)).floatValue()/10f;
```

```
Text2=String.valueOf(textf2);
v2.setText(Text2);
Text1=v1.getText();
voltage="manual@"+Text1+" "+Text2;
output.println(voltage);
if(runner.isAlive()) {
runner.resume();
System.out.println("runner start!");
}
else {
runner.start();System.out.println("runner resume!");
}
}
}
public boolean action(Event evt,Object arg) {
String label=(String)arg;
/**if(label.equals("<") || label.equals(">"))
{
String param=evt.toString();
String xindex=param.substring(25,28);
int index=Integer.parseInt(xindex);
System.out.println(index);
String firstvalue1=v1.getText();
String firstvalue2=v2.getText();
//float value1f=Float.valueOf(firstvalue1).floatValue()*20f;
//float value2f=Float.valueOf(firstvalue2).floatValue()*20f;
Float firstvalue1f=new
    Float(Float.valueOf(firstvalue1).floatValue()*10f);
Float firstvalue2f=new
    Float(Float.valueOf(firstvalue2).floatValue()*10f);
int firstvalueint1=firstvalue1f.intValue();
int firstvalueint2=firstvalue2f.intValue();
System.out.println(firstvalueint1);
System.out.println(firstvalueint2);
if (index==167) {
firstvalueint1=firstvalueint1-1;
System.out.println("firstvalueint1-1");
run.setLabel("Stop");}
if (index==245) {
firstvalueint1=firstvalueint1+1;
System.out.println("firstvalueint1+1");
run.setLabel("Stop");
}
if (index==270) {
firstvalueint2=firstvalueint2-1;
System.out.println("firstvalueint2-1");
run.setLabel("Stop");
}
if (index==348) {
firstvalueint2=firstvalueint2+1;
System.out.println("firstvalueint2+1");
run.setLabel("Stop");
}
if (firstvalueint1<0 ) {
```

```
v1.setText("0.0");
firstvalueint1=0;
okdialog.createokdialog("Pump voltage is 0-10 V!");
}
else if (firstvalueint1>100) {
v1.setText("10.0");
firstvalueint1=100;
okdialog.createokdialog("Pump voltage is 0-10 V!");
}
else if (firstvalueint2<0) {
v2.setText("0.0");
okdialog.createokdialog("Pump voltage is 0-10 V!");
firstvalueint2=0;
}
else if (firstvalueint2>100) {
v2.setText("10.0");
okdialog.createokdialog("Pump voltage is 0-10 V!");
firstvalueint2=100;
}
System.out.println(firstvalueint1);
System.out.println(firstvalueint2);
value1int=firstvalueint1;
value2int=firstvalueint2;
float textf1=(new Integer(firstvalueint1)).floatValue()/10f;
float textf2=(new Integer(firstvalueint2)).floatValue()/10f;
String Text1=String.valueOf(textf1);
String Text2=String.valueOf(textf2);
//String Text11=Text1.substring(0,3);
//String Text22=Text2.substring(0,3);
System.out.println(Text1);
System.out.println(Text2);
v1.setText(Text1);
v2.setText(Text2);
voltage="manual@"+Text1+" "+Text2;
output.println(voltage);
if(runner.isAlive()) {
runner.resume();
System.out.println("runner start!");
}
else {
runner.start();System.out.println("runner resume!");
}
//System.out.println("change successful!");
} */
if (evt.target instanceof Button) {
if(label.equals("Run")) {
voltage1=v1.getText();
voltage2=v2.getText();
String value1=v1.getText();
String value2=v2.getText();
float value1f=Float.valueOf(value1).floatValue()*10f;
float value2f=Float.valueOf(value2).floatValue()*10f;
Float value1F=new Float(value1f);
Float value2F=new Float(value2f);
```

```
value1int=value1F.intValue();
value2int=value2F.intValue();
if(value1int>100) {
v1.setText("10.0");
value1int=100;
voltage1="10.0";
okdialog.createokdialog("        Pump voltage is 0-10 V!");
}
else if (value1int<0) {
v1.setText("0.0");
value1int=0;
voltage1="0.0";
okdialog.createokdialog("        Pump voltage is 0-10 V!");
}
else if (value2int>100) {
v2.setText("10.0");
value2int=100;
voltage2="10.0";
okdialog.createokdialog("        Pump voltage is 0-10 V!");
}
else if (value2int<0) {
v2.setText("0.0");
value2int=0;
voltage2="0.0";
okdialog.createokdialog("        Pump voltage is 0-10 V!");
}
run.setLabel("Stop");
voltage="manual@"+voltage1+" "+voltage2;
output.println(voltage);
if(runner.isAlive()) {
runner.resume();
System.out.println("runner start!");}
else {runner.start();System.out.println("runner resume!");
}
}
if(label.equals("Stop")) {
run.setLabel("Run");
output.println("0 0");
runner.suspend();
System.out.println("runner stop!");
//try {con1.close();}catch(Exception e){}
System.out.println("con1 closed!");
}
if(label.equals("Reset")) {
run.setLabel("Run");
v1.setText("0");
v2.setText("0");
output.println("0 0");
m=0;
um=0;
temp=false;
temp1=true;
utemp=false;
utemp1=true;
```

```
k=0;
j1=290;
j2=290;
uk=0;
uj1=70;
uj2=70;
loopvalue=0;
alltime=0;
timeperiod=10;
timeindex=0;
timeleft=0;
pointnumber1=0;
pointnumber2=0;
pointnumber3=0;
runner.suspend();
resetalready=true;
repaint();
}
}
return true;
}
public void update (Graphics g) {
paint(g);
}
public void paint(Graphics g) {
if(changetime){g.setColor(greencolor);
g.fillRect(65,185,500,30);
changetime=false;
}
if(temp) {
g.setColor(greencolor);
g.fillRect(260,50,220,200);
for (n=0;n<shift-1;n++) {
g.setColor(Color.red);
g.drawLine (x1[n+1],y1[n+1],x1[n],y1[n]);
g.setColor(Color.blue);
g.drawLine (x2[n+1],y2[n+1],x2[n],y2[n]);
}
temp=false;
}
if(temp1) {
g.setColor(greencolor);
g.fillRect(260,50,220,200);
temp1=false;
}
g.setColor(Color.black);
g.drawString(String.valueOf(k*10),285,195);
//g.drawString(String.valueOf(k+5),50,145);
g.drawString(String.valueOf((k+1)*10),335,195);
//g.drawString(String.valueOf(k+15),100,145);
g.drawString(String.valueOf((k+2)*10),385,195);
//g.drawString(String.valueOf(k+25),150,145);
g.drawString(String.valueOf((k+3)*10),435,195);
//height, time axis
```

```
g.drawLine(290,180,460,180);
g.drawLine(290,60,290,180);
// on time axis
//g.drawLine(55,128,55,132);
g.drawLine(340,178,340,182);
//g.drawLine(105,128,105,132);
g.drawLine(390,178,390,182);
//g.drawLine(155,128,155,132);
g.drawLine(440,178,440,182);
g.drawString("(s)",460,195);
g.drawString("t",465,185);
g.drawString("(mm)",295,65);
g.drawString("y",280,65);
//on height axis
g.drawLine(288,80,292,80);
g.drawString("300",265,85);
g.drawLine(288,113,292,113);
g.drawString("200",265,118);
g.drawLine(288,146,292,146);
g.drawString("100",265,151);
g.drawString("0",270,180);
int xcoords1[]={290,285,295,290};
int ycoords1[]={60,68,68,60};
int xcoords2[]={460,452,452,460};
int ycoords2[]={180,175,185,180};
g.fillPolygon(xcoords1,ycoords1,4);
g.fillPolygon(xcoords2,ycoords2,4);
if(m==0)m=0;
else if (m==1) {
g.setColor(Color.red);
g.drawLine(x1[m-1],y1[m-1],x1[m-1],y1[m-1]);
g.setColor(Color.blue);
g.drawLine(x2[m-1],y2[m-1],x2[m-1],y2[m-1]);
}
else {
g.setColor(Color.red);
g.drawLine(x1[m-2],y1[m-2],x1[m-1],y1[m-1]);
g.setColor(Color.blue);
g.drawLine(x2[m-2],y2[m-2],x2[m-1],y2[m-1]);
}
if(utemp) {
g.setColor(greencolor);
g.fillRect(40,50,220,200);
for (n=0;n<shift-1;n++) {
g.setColor(Color.red);
g.drawLine (ux1[n+1],uy1[n+1],ux1[n],uy1[n]);
g.setColor(Color.blue);
g.drawLine (ux2[n+1],uy2[n+1],ux2[n],uy2[n]);
}
utemp=false;
}
if(utemp1) {
g.setColor(greencolor);
g.fillRect(40,50,220,200);
```

```
utemp1=false;
}
g.setColor(Color.black);
g.drawString(String.valueOf(k*timeperiod),65,195);
//g.drawString(String.valueOf(k+5),50,145);
g.drawString(String.valueOf((k+1)*timeperiod),110,195);
//g.drawString(String.valueOf(k+15),100,145);
g.drawString(String.valueOf((k+2)*timeperiod),160,195);
//g.drawString(String.valueOf(k+25),150,145);
g.drawString(String.valueOf((k+3)*timeperiod),215,195);
//height, time axis
g.drawLine(70,180,240,180);
g.drawLine(70,60,70,180);
// on time axis
//g.drawLine(55,128,55,132);
g.drawLine(120,178,120,182);
//g.drawLine(105,128,105,132);
g.drawLine(170,178,170,182);
//g.drawLine(155,128,155,132);
g.drawLine(220,178,220,182);
g.drawString("(s)",240,195);
g.drawString("t",245,185);
g.drawString("(v)",75,65);
g.drawString("u",55,65);
//on height axis
g.drawLine(68,80,72,80);
g.drawString("10",45,80);
//g.drawLine(248,113,252,113);
//g.drawString("200",225,118);
g.drawLine(68,130,72,130);
g.drawString("5",50,134);
g.drawString("0",50,180);
int uxcoords1[]={70,65,75,70};
int uycoords1[]={60,68,68,60};
int uxcoords2[]={240,232,232,240};
int uycoords2[]={180,175,185,180};
g.fillPolygon(uxcoords1,uycoords1,4);
g.fillPolygon(uxcoords2,uycoords2,4);
g.setFont(f);
g.setColor(Color.red);
g.drawString("Tank1",330,65);
g.setColor(Color.blue);
g.drawString("Tank2",390,65);
g.setColor(Color.red);
g.drawString("Tank1",100,65);
g.setColor(Color.blue);
g.drawString("Tank2",160,65);
if(m==0)m=0;
else if (m==1) {
g.setColor(Color.red);
g.drawLine(ux1[m-1],uy1[m-1],ux1[m-1],uy1[m-1]);
g.setColor(Color.blue);
g.drawLine(ux2[m-1],uy2[m-1],ux2[m-1],uy2[m-1]);
}
```

```
else {
g.setColor(Color.red);
g.drawLine(ux1[m-2],uy1[m-2],ux1[m-1],uy1[m-1]);
g.setColor(Color.blue);
g.drawLine(ux2[m-2],uy2[m-2],ux2[m-1],uy2[m-1]);
}
}
}
```

B.8 pidcontrol.java

```
import java.awt.*;
import java.io.*;
import java.net.*;
import java.lang.*;
import java.util.Date;
class drawpid extends Thread {
int i=0;
int m=0;
int n=0;
int height1=0;
int height2=0;
int j1=310;
int j2=310;
int fj1=530;
int fj2=530;
int fm=0;
int fn=0;
int fheight1=0;
int fheight2=0;
int fi=0;
String timevaluestring;
int timevalue;
int timeindex=0;
int timeleft=0;
String fvalue1;
String fvalue2;
byte[] currLine =new byte[23];
char[] currchar1=new char[3];
char[] currchar2=new char[3];
char[] currchar3=new char[3];
char[] currchar4=new char[3];
char[] currchar5=new char[5];
String value1;
String value2;
int pointnumber1=0;
int pointnumber2=0;
int pointnumber3=0;
pidcontrol applet;
drawpid(pidcontrol applet) {
this.applet=applet;
}
```

```java
public void reset() {
pointnumber1=0;
pointnumber2=0;
pointnumber3=0;
i=0;
m=0;
n=0;
height1=0;
height2=0;
j1=310;
j2=310;
fj1=530;
fj2=530;
fm=0;
fn=0;
fheight1=0;
fheight2=0;
fi=0;
//loopvalue=0;
//alltime=0;
applet.timeperiod=10;
}
public void run() {
System.out.println("thread started!!!");
while(true) {
applet.output1.println("waiting");
//System.out.println("waiting");
try {
applet.instream1.readFully(currLine);
//System.out.println(currLine);
} catch (Exception e){System.out.println(e);}
if(!applet.stopalready && !applet.resetalready) {
for (i=0;i<3;i++) {
currchar1[i]=(char)currLine[i];
currchar2[i]=(char)currLine[i+3];
currchar3[i]=(char)currLine[i+6];
currchar4[i]=(char)currLine[i+9];
}
//build a string by the chars
for (i=0;i<5;i++) {
currchar5[i]=(char)currLine[18+i];
}
fvalue1=new String(currchar1);
fvalue2=new String(currchar2);
value1=new String(currchar3);
value2=new String(currchar4);
timevaluestring=new String(currchar5);
//convert string to int, i.e., the Y value.
timevalue=Integer.parseInt(timevaluestring.trim());
if (applet.settime20) {
timevalue=0;
applet.settime20=false;}
System.out.println("timevalue is "+timevalue);
timeindex=timevalue/200;
```

```
timeleft=timevalue%200;
if (timeleft>100)timeindex++;
fheight1=130-Integer.parseInt(fvalue1.trim());
fheight2=130-Integer.parseInt(fvalue2.trim());
height1=130-Integer.parseInt(value1.trim());
height2=130-Integer.parseInt(value2.trim());
System.out.println("fm is "+fm);
fj1=fj1+timeindex;
fj2=fj2+timeindex;
applet.flx1[fm]=fj1;
applet.fly1[fm]=fheight1;
applet.flx2[fm]=fj2;
applet.fly2[fm]=fheight2;
j1=j1+timeindex;
j2=j2+timeindex;
applet.x1[fm]=j1;
applet.y1[fm]=height1;
applet.x2[fm]=j2;
applet.y2[fm]=height2;
if (applet.flx1[fm]<=580) {
pointnumber1++;}
else if (applet.flx1[fm]<=630) {
pointnumber2++;
}
else {
pointnumber3++;
}
System.out.println("pointnumber1 is "+pointnumber1);
System.out.println("pointnumber2 is "+pointnumber2);
System.out.println("pointnumber3 is "+pointnumber3);
//System.out.println(fm);
if(applet.flx1[fm]>=680) {
applet.shift=fm-pointnumber1;
for (fn=0;fn<=fm-pointnumber1;fn++) {
applet.x1[fn]=applet.x1[fn+pointnumber1]-50;
applet.y1[fn]=applet.y1[fn+pointnumber1];
applet.x2[fn]=applet.x2[fn+pointnumber1]-50;
applet.y2[fn]=applet.y2[fn+pointnumber1];
applet.flx1[fn]=applet.flx1[fn+pointnumber1]-50;
applet.fly1[fn]=applet.fly1[fn+pointnumber1];
applet.flx2[fn]=applet.flx2[fn+pointnumber1]-50;
applet.fly2[fn]=applet.fly2[fn+pointnumber1];}
fj1=applet.flx1[fm-pointnumber1];
fj2=fj1;
j1=applet.x1[fm-pointnumber1];
j2=j1;
fm=fm-pointnumber1;
pointnumber1=pointnumber2;
pointnumber2=pointnumber3;
pointnumber3=0;
applet.flk++;
applet.k++;
while (applet.flx1[applet.shift]>=680){
applet.shift=fm-pointnumber1;
```

```
for (fn=0;fn<=fm-pointnumber1;fn++)    {
applet.x1[fn]=applet.x1[fn+pointnumber1]-50;
applet.y1[fn]=applet.y1[fn+pointnumber1];
applet.x2[fn]=applet.x2[fn+pointnumber1]-50;
applet.y2[fn]=applet.y2[fn+pointnumber1];
applet.flx1[fn]=applet.flx1[fn+pointnumber1]-50;
applet.fly1[fn]=applet.fly1[fn+pointnumber1];
applet.flx2[fn]=applet.flx2[fn+pointnumber1]-50;
applet.fly2[fn]=applet.fly2[fn+pointnumber1];}
fj1=applet.flx1[fm-pointnumber1];
fj2=fj1;
j1=applet.x1[fm-pointnumber1];
j2=j1;
fm=fm-pointnumber1-1;
pointnumber1=pointnumber2;
pointnumber2=pointnumber3;
pointnumber3=0;
applet.flk++;
applet.k++;}
applet.fltemp=true;
applet.temp=true;
}
fm++;
applet.flm=fm;
applet.m=fm;
applet.repaint();
}
else {applet.stopalready=false;
applet.resetalready=false;}
}
}
}
public class pidcontrol extends java.applet.Applet   {
int m=0;
int flm=0;
int n=0;
int fln=0;
boolean changetime=false;
int[] x1=new int[200];
int[] y1=new int[200];
int[] x2=new int[200];
int[] y2=new int[200];
int k=0;//use to change time
int timeperiod=10;
int shift=0;
boolean temp=false;
boolean retemp=false;
boolean stopalready=false;
boolean resetalready=false;
boolean settime20=false;
int[] flx1=new int[200];
int[] fly1=new int[200];
int[] flx2=new int[200];
int[] fly2=new int[200];
```

```
int flk=0;//use to change time
boolean fltemp=false;
boolean refltemp=false;
Font f=new Font("TimesRoman", Font.BOLD,14);
int samplerate;
String setvalue1;
String pvalue1;
String ivalue1;
String dvalue1;
String svalue1;
String value;
String setvalue2;
String pvalue2;
String ivalue2;
String dvalue2;
String svalue2;
//String value2;
XCTextField setpoint1=new XCTextField(4);
XCTextField p1=new XCTextField(4);
XCTextField i1=new XCTextField(4);
XCTextField d1=new XCTextField(4);
XCTextField s1=new XCTextField(4);
XCTextField setpoint2=new XCTextField(4);
XCTextField p2=new XCTextField(4);
XCTextField i2=new XCTextField(4);
XCTextField d2=new XCTextField(4);
XCTextField s2=new XCTextField(4);
Panel panel1=new Panel();
Panel panel2=new Panel();
PrintStream output;
DataInputStream instream;
PrintStream output1;
DataInputStream instream1;
Button run=new Button("Run");
Button reset=new Button("Reset");
boolean suspendalready=false;
Socket con;
Socket con1;
Socket con2;
Socket con3;
/** String url="http://vlab.ee.nus.edu.sg";
URL host;*/
drawpid run1=new drawpid(this);
//sendpid run2=new sendpid(this);
Color greencolor=new Color(204,255,204);
String running="no";
public void init(){
this.setBackground(greencolor);
setpoint1.setForeground(Color.red);
p1.setForeground(Color.red);
i1.setForeground(Color.red);
d1.setForeground(Color.red);
s1.setForeground(Color.red);
setpoint2.setForeground(Color.blue);
```

```
p2.setForeground(Color.blue);
i2.setForeground(Color.blue);
d2.setForeground(Color.blue);
s2.setForeground(Color.blue);
setpoint1.button1=run;
p1.button1=run;
i1.button1=run;
d1.button1=run;
s1.button1=run;
setpoint2.button1=run;
p2.button1=run;
i2.button1=run;
d2.button1=run;
s2.button1=run;
setpoint1.setText("20");
p1.setText("10.0");
i1.setText("2.0");
d1.setText("0.05");
s1.setText("0.02");
setpoint2.setText("20");
p2.setText("10.0");
i2.setText("2.0");
d2.setText("0.05");
s2.setText("0.02");
setLayout(new FlowLayout(FlowLayout.LEFT));
add(panel1);
add(panel2);
panel1.setLayout(new GridLayout(6,1,10,5));
panel1.add(new Label("Set Point (20-230)mm"));
panel1.add(new Label("          Kp      "));
panel1.add(new Label("          Ki      "));
panel1.add(new Label("          Kd      "));
panel1.add(new Label("Samp.Time (0.02-10)s"));
panel2.setLayout(new GridLayout(6,2,10,5));
panel2.add(setpoint1);
panel2.add(setpoint2);
panel2.add(p1);
panel2.add(p2);
panel2.add(i1);
panel2.add(i2);
panel2.add(d1);
panel2.add(d2);
panel2.add(s1);
panel2.add(s2);
panel2.add(run);
panel2.add(reset);
}
public void start() {
try { /**host=new URL(url);*/
InetAddress add=InetAddress.getByName("137.132.165.77");
con= new Socket(add,6666);
instream=new DataInputStream(con.getInputStream());
output=new PrintStream(con.getOutputStream());
```

```
System.out.println(con);  }catch(Exception ex)
   {System.out.println(ex);}
try { /**host=new URL(url);*/
InetAddress add=InetAddress.getByName("137.132.165.77");
con1= new Socket(add,5555);
instream1=new DataInputStream(con1.getInputStream());
output1=new PrintStream(con1.getOutputStream());
//output1.println("start");
System.out.println(con1);  }catch(Exception ex)
   {System.out.println(ex);}
try { /**host=new URL(url);*/
InetAddress add=InetAddress.getByName("137.132.165.77");
con2= new Socket(add,7777);
System.out.println(con2);  }catch(Exception ex)
   {System.out.println(ex);}
try { /**host=new URL(url);*/
InetAddress add=InetAddress.getByName("137.132.165.77");
con3= new Socket(add,8888);
System.out.println(con3);  }catch(Exception ex)
   {System.out.println(ex);}
}
public String returnrunning(){
return running;
}
public boolean action(Event evt,Object arg){
String label=(String)arg;
if (evt.target instanceof Button) {
if(label.equals("Run")) {
//judge=true;
run.setLabel("Stop");
setvalue1=setpoint1.getText();
pvalue1=p1.getText();
ivalue1=i1.getText();
dvalue1=d1.getText();
svalue1=s1.getText();
setvalue2=setpoint2.getText();
pvalue2=p2.getText();
ivalue2=i2.getText();
dvalue2=d2.getText();
svalue2=s2.getText();
Float samplef1=new
    Float(Float.valueOf(svalue1).floatValue()*1000f);
int sampleint1=samplef1.intValue();
if(sampleint1<20) {
svalue1="0.02";
s1.setText("0.02");
}
else if (sampleint1>10000) {
svalue1="10";
s1.setText("10");}
s2.setText(svalue1);
int sp1=Integer.parseInt(setvalue1);
int sp2=Integer.parseInt(setvalue2);
if (sp1>230) {
```

```
sp1=230;
setvalue1="230";
setpoint1.setText("230");
okdialog.createokdialog("        Setpoint is 20-230mm!");
}
else if (sp1<20) {
sp1=20;
setvalue1="20";
setpoint1.setText("20");
okdialog.createokdialog("        Setpoint is 20-230mm!");
}
else if (sp2>230) {
sp2=230;
setvalue2="230";
setpoint2.setText("230");
okdialog.createokdialog("        Setpoint is 20-230mm!");
}
else if (sp2<20) {
sp2=20;
setvalue2="20";
setpoint2.setText("20");
okdialog.createokdialog("        Setpoint is 20-230mm!");}
//samplerate=Integer.parseInt(svalue1);
//samplerate=1000/samplerate;
value="pid@"+setvalue1+" "+pvalue1+" "+ivalue1+" "+dvalue1+"
    "+svalue1+" "+setvalue2+" "+pvalue2+" "+ivalue2+" "+dvalue2;
output.println(value);
if(run1.isAlive()){
run1.resume();System.out.println("run1 resume!");
}
else {run1.start();System.out.println("run1 start!");}
// if(run2.isAlive()){run2.resume();System.out.println("run1
    resume!");}
// else {run2.start();System.out.println("run1 start!");}
suspendalready=false;
running="yes";
}
if(label.equals("Stop")) {
//output.println(label);
//judge=false;
run.setLabel("Run");
run1.suspend();
//run2.suspend();
stopalready=true;
System.out.println("run1 thread suspend now!");
output.println("stop@");
running="no";
suspendalready=true;
//run1.reset();
}
if(label.equals("Reset")) {
if(!suspendalready) {
run1.suspend();
//run2.suspend();
```

```
}
run.setLabel("Run");
setpoint1.setText("20");
p1.setText("10.0");
i1.setText("2.0");
d1.setText("0.05");
s1.setText("0.02");
setpoint2.setText("20");
p2.setText("10.0");
i2.setText("2.0");
d2.setText("0.05");
s2.setText("0.02");
suspendalready=true;
resetalready=true;
settime20=true;
run1.reset();
output.println("reset@");
//output1.println("start");
temp=false;
retemp=true;
fltemp=false;
refltemp=true;
running="no";
/*if(run1.isAlive()) run1.resume();
else run1.start();
*/
m=0;
flm=0;
k=0;
flk=0;
repaint();}
}
return true;
}
public void stop() {
run1.stop();
//run2.stop();
output.println("reset@");
try{con.close();con1.close();con2.close();
con3.close();
}catch(Exception e){}
}
public void destroy() {
run1.stop();
//run2.stop();
output.println("reset@");
try{con.close();con1.close();con2.close();
con3.close();
}catch(Exception e){}
}
synchronized public void update (Graphics g){
paint(g);
}
synchronized public void paint(Graphics g){
```

```
if(changetime){g.setColor(greencolor);
g.fillRect(305,135,500,30);
changetime=false;}
if(temp){
g.setColor(greencolor);
g.fillRect(300,0,200,180);
for (n=0;n<shift;n++) {
g.setColor(Color.red);
g.drawLine (x1[n+1],y1[n+1],x1[n],y1[n]);
g.setColor(Color.blue);
g.drawLine (x2[n+1],y2[n+1],x2[n],y2[n]);
}
temp=false;
}
if(retemp){g.setColor(greencolor);
g.fillRect(300,0,200,180);
retemp=false;}
/**   if(j==180){k=k+30;
g.setColor(Color.lightGray);
g.fillRect(30,30,190,125);
} */
//g.setColor(Color.black);
g.setColor(Color.black);
g.drawString(String.valueOf(k*10),305,145);
//g.drawString(String.valueOf(k+5),50,145);
g.drawString(String.valueOf((k+1)*10),355,145);
//g.drawString(String.valueOf(k+15),100,145);
g.drawString(String.valueOf((k+2)*10),405,145);
//g.drawString(String.valueOf(k+25),150,145);
g.drawString(String.valueOf((k+3)*10),455,145);
//height, time axis
g.drawLine(310,130,480,130);
g.drawLine(310,10,310,130);
// on time axis
//g.drawLine(55,128,55,132);
g.drawLine(360,128,360,132);
//g.drawLine(105,128,105,132);
g.drawLine(410,128,410,132);
//g.drawLine(155,128,155,132);
g.drawLine(460,128,460,132);
g.drawString("(s)",480,145);
g.drawString("t",485,135);
g.drawString("u",290,15);
g.drawString("(v)",314,15);
//on height axis
g.drawLine(308,30,312,30);
g.drawString("10",285,35);
g.drawLine(308,80,312,80);
g.drawString("5",290,84);
//g.drawLine(108,96,112,96);
//g.drawString("100",85,101);
g.drawString("0",290,130);
int xcoords1[]={310,305,315,310};
int ycoords1[]={10,18,18,10};
```

```
int xcoords2[]={480,472,472,480};
int ycoords2[]={130,125,135,130};
g.fillPolygon(xcoords1,ycoords1,4);
g.fillPolygon(xcoords2,ycoords2,4);
if(m==0)m=0;
else if (m==1) {
g.setColor(Color.red);
g.drawLine(x1[m-1],y1[m-1],x1[m-1],y1[m-1]);
g.setColor(Color.blue);
g.drawLine(x2[m-1],y2[m-1],x2[m-1],y2[m-1]);
}
else {
g.setColor(Color.red);
g.drawLine(x1[m-2],y1[m-2],x1[m-1],y1[m-1]);
g.setColor(Color.blue);
g.drawLine(x2[m-2],y2[m-2],x2[m-1],y2[m-1]);
}
if(fltemp) {
g.setColor(greencolor);
g.fillRect(510,0,200,180);
for (fln=0;fln<shift;fln++) {
g.setColor(Color.red);
g.drawLine (flx1[fln+1],fly1[fln+1],flx1[fln],fly1[fln]);
g.setColor(Color.blue);
g.drawLine (flx2[fln+1],fly2[fln+1],flx2[fln],fly2[fln]);
}
fltemp=false;
}
if(refltemp) {
g.setColor(greencolor);
g.fillRect(510,0,200,180);
refltemp=false;
}
g.setColor(Color.black);
g.drawString(String.valueOf(flk*10),525,145);
//g.drawString(String.valueOf(k+5),50,145);
g.drawString(String.valueOf((flk+1)*10),575,145);
//g.drawString(String.valueOf(k+15),100,145);
g.drawString(String.valueOf((flk+2)*10),625,145);
//g.drawString(String.valueOf(k+25),150,145);
g.drawString(String.valueOf((flk+3)*10),675,145);
//height, time axis
g.drawLine(530,130,700,130);
g.drawLine(530,10,530,130);
// on time axis
//g.drawLine(55,128,55,132);
g.drawLine(580,128,580,132);
//g.drawLine(105,128,105,132);
g.drawLine(630,128,630,132);
//g.drawLine(155,128,155,132);
g.drawLine(680,128,680,132);
g.drawString("(s)",700,145);
g.drawString("t",705,135);
g.drawString("(mm)",534,15);
```

```
g.drawString("y",515,15);
//on height axis
g.drawLine(528,30,532,30);
g.drawString("300",505,35);
g.drawLine(528,63,532,63);
g.drawString("200",505,68);
g.drawLine(528,96,532,96);
g.drawString("100",505,101);
g.drawString("0",510,130);
int flxcoords1[]={530,525,535,530};
int flycoords1[]={10,18,18,10};
int flxcoords2[]={700,692,692,700};
int flycoords2[]={130,125,135,130};
g.fillPolygon(flxcoords1,flycoords1,4);
g.fillPolygon(flxcoords2,flycoords2,4);
if(flm==0) flm=0;
else if (flm==1) {
g.setColor(Color.red);
g.drawLine(flx1[flm-1],fly1[flm-1],flx1[flm-1],fly1[flm-1]);
g.setColor(Color.blue);
g.drawLine(flx2[flm-1],fly2[flm-1],flx2[flm-1],fly2[flm-1]);}
else {
g.setColor(Color.red);
g.drawLine(flx1[flm-2],fly1[flm-2],flx1[flm-1],fly1[flm-1]);
g.setColor(Color.blue);
g.drawLine(flx2[flm-2],fly2[flm-2],flx2[flm-1],fly2[flm-1]);
}
g.setFont(f);
g.setColor(Color.red);
g.drawString("Tank1",350,15);
g.drawString("Tank1",570,15);
g.setColor(Color.blue);
g.drawString("Tank2",400,15);
g.drawString("Tank2",620,15);
}
}
```

B.9 generalcontrol.java

```
import java.awt.*;
import java.io.*;
import java.net.*;
import java.lang.*;
class drawgeneral extends Thread {
int fm=0;
int fn=0;
int fheight1=0;
int fheight2=0;
int fi=0;
int fj1=290;
int fj2=290;
String fvalue1;
```

```
String fvalue2;
long timevalue1=0;
long timevalue2=0;
long timeaverage=0;
int loopvalue=0;
long timeoffset=0;
long alltime=0;
int i=0;
int m=0;
int n=0;
int height1=0;
int height2=0;
int j1=70;
int j2=70;
String value1;
String value2;
byte[] currLine =new byte[23];
char[] currchar1=new char[3];
char[] currchar2=new char[3];
char[] currchar3=new char[3];
char[] currchar4=new char[3];
char[] currchar5=new char[5];
String timevaluestring;
int timevalue;
int timeindex=0;
int timeleft=0;
int pointnumber1=0;
int pointnumber2=0;
int pointnumber3=0;
generalcontrol applet;
drawgeneral(generalcontrol applet) {
this.applet=applet;
}
public void reset() {
pointnumber1=0;
pointnumber2=0;
pointnumber3=0;
fm=0;
fn=0;
fheight1=0;
fheight2=0;
fi=0;
fj1=290;
fj2=290;
i=0;
m=0;
n=0;
height1=0;
height2=0;
j1=70;
j2=70;
loopvalue=0;
alltime=0;
applet.timeperiod=10;
```

```
}
public void run() {
while(true) {
applet.output.println("waiting");
try{applet.instream.readFully(currLine);}catch (Exception e){}
for(i=0;i<3;i++) {
currchar1[i]=(char)currLine[i];
currchar2[i]=(char)currLine[i+3];
currchar3[i]=(char)currLine[i+6];
currchar4[i]=(char)currLine[i+9];}
for (i=0;i<5;i++) {
currchar5[i]=(char)currLine[18+i];}
//build a string by the chars
fvalue1=new String(currchar1);
fvalue2=new String(currchar2);
value1=new String(currchar3);
value2=new String(currchar4);
timevaluestring=new String(currchar5);
timevalue=Integer.parseInt(timevaluestring.trim());
if(applet.resetalready) {
timevalue=0;
applet.resetalready=false;}
System.out.println("timevalue is "+timevalue);
timeindex=timevalue/200;
timeleft=timevalue%200;
if (timeleft>100) timeindex++;
//convert string to int, i.e., the Y value.
fheight1=180-Integer.parseInt(fvalue1.trim());
fheight2=180-Integer.parseInt(fvalue2.trim());
height1=180-Integer.parseInt(value1.trim());
height2=180-Integer.parseInt(value2.trim());
fj1=fj1+timeindex;
fj2=fj2+timeindex;
applet.flx1[fm]=fj1;
applet.fly1[fm]=fheight1;
applet.flx2[fm]=fj2;
applet.fly2[fm]=fheight2;
j1=j1+timeindex;
j2=j2+timeindex;
applet.x1[fm]=j1;
applet.y1[fm]=height1;
applet.x2[fm]=j2;
applet.y2[fm]=height2;
if (applet.flx1[fm]<=340) {
pointnumber1++;}
else if (applet.flx1[fm]<=390) {
pointnumber2++;}
else {pointnumber3++;}
if (applet.flx1[fm]>=440) {
applet.shift=fm-pointnumber1;
for (fn=0;fn<fm-pointnumber1;fn++) {
applet.x1[fn]=applet.x1[fn+pointnumber1]-50;
applet.y1[fn]=applet.y1[fn+pointnumber1];
applet.x2[fn]=applet.x2[fn+pointnumber1]-50;
```

```
applet.y2[fn]=applet.y2[fn+pointnumber1];
applet.flx1[fn]=applet.flx1[fn+pointnumber1]-50;
applet.fly1[fn]=applet.fly1[fn+pointnumber1];
applet.flx2[fn]=applet.flx2[fn+pointnumber1]-50;
applet.fly2[fn]=applet.fly2[fn+pointnumber1];}
fj1=applet.flx1[fm-pointnumber1];
fj2=fj1;
j1=applet.x1[fm-pointnumber1];
j2=j1;
fm=fm-pointnumber1;
pointnumber1=pointnumber2;
pointnumber2=pointnumber3;
pointnumber3=0;
applet.flk++;
applet.k++;
applet.fltemp=true;
applet.temp=true;
}
fm++;
applet.flm=fm;
applet.m=fm;
//convert string to int, i.e., the Y value.
applet.repaint();
}
}
}
public class generalcontrol extends java.applet.Applet  {
boolean suspendalready=false;
int m=0;
int flm=0;
int n=0;
int fln=0;
int shift=0;
boolean resetalready=false;
boolean changetime=false;
int timeperiod=10;
int[] x1=new int[200];
int[] y1=new int[200];
int[] x2=new int[200];
int[] y2=new int[200];
int k=0;//use to change time
boolean temp=false;
boolean retemp=false;
int[] flx1=new int[200];
int[] fly1=new int[200];
int[] flx2=new int[200];
int[] fly2=new int[200];
int flk=0;//use to change time
boolean fltemp=false;
boolean refltemp=false;
Font f=new Font("TimesRoman", Font.BOLD,14);
int samplerate;
String value;
String valueget;
```

```
XCTextField setpoint1=new XCTextField(4);
XCTextField setpoint2=new XCTextField(4);
XCTextField samptime=new XCTextField(4);
String setvalue1;
String setvalue2;
String sampvalue;
String judge;
PrintStream output;
DataInputStream instream;
PrintStream output1;
DataInputStream instream1;
Button run=new Button("Run");
Button reset=new Button("Reset");
Socket con;
Socket con1;
String running="no";
/** String url="http://vlab.ee.nus.edu.sg";
URL host;*/
drawgeneral run1=new drawgeneral(this);
//sendgeneral run2=new sendgeneral(this);
Color greencolor=new Color(204,255,204);
int firstornot=0;
public void init(){
this.setBackground(greencolor);
setpoint1.setForeground(Color.red);
setpoint2.setForeground(Color.blue);
setLayout(new FlowLayout(FlowLayout.CENTER));
add(new Label("Set Point(20-230 mm):"));
add(setpoint1);
setpoint1.setText("20");
add(setpoint2);
setpoint2.setText("20");
add(new Label(" Samp.Time(0.03-10)s:"));
add(samptime);
samptime.setText("0.03");
add(run);
add(reset);
setpoint1.button1=run;
setpoint2.button1=run;
samptime.button1=run;
}
public void start() {
try{ /**host=new URL(url);*/
InetAddress add=InetAddress.getByName("137.132.165.77");
con= new Socket(add,5555);
instream=new DataInputStream(con.getInputStream());
output=new PrintStream(con.getOutputStream());
System.out.println(con);   }catch(Exception ex)
    {System.out.println(ex);}
try{ /**host=new URL(url);*/
InetAddress add=InetAddress.getByName("137.132.165.77");
con1= new Socket(add,6666);
instream1=new DataInputStream(con1.getInputStream());
output1=new PrintStream(con1.getOutputStream());
```

```
System.out.println(con1);   }catch(Exception ex)
    {System.out.println(ex);}
}
public void getvalue(String valueofmatrix){
valueget=valueofmatrix;
//firstornot=1;
}
public String returnrunning(){
return running;
}
public boolean action(Event evt,Object arg){
String label=(String)arg;
if (evt.target instanceof Button){
if(label.equals("Run")) {
    //if(valueget!=null){okdialog.createokdialog(valueget);}
if (valueget==null){okdialog.createokdialog("Please enter
    controller!");}
else {//judge=true;
judge="1";
setvalue1=setpoint1.getText();
setvalue2=setpoint2.getText();
int sp1=Integer.parseInt(setvalue1);
int sp2=Integer.parseInt(setvalue2);
sampvalue=samptime.getText();
Float samplef1=new
    Float(Float.valueOf(sampvalue).floatValue()*1000f);
int sampleint1=samplef1.intValue();
if(sampleint1<30) {
sampvalue="0.03";
samptime.setText("0.03");
}
else if (sampleint1>10000) {
sampvalue="10";
samptime.setText("10");}
if(sp1>230) {
sp1=230;
setvalue1="230";
setpoint1.setText("230");
okdialog.createokdialog("       Setpoint is 20-230mm!");}
else if (sp1<20) {
sp1=20;
setvalue1="20";
setpoint1.setText("20");
okdialog.createokdialog("       Setpoint is 20-230mm!");}
else if (sp2>230) {
sp2=230;
setvalue2="230";
setpoint2.setText("230");
okdialog.createokdialog("       Setpoint is 20-230mm!");}
else if (sp2<20) {
sp2=20;
setvalue2="20";
setpoint2.setText("20");
okdialog.createokdialog("       Setpoint is 20-230mm!");}
```

```
//valueget=judge+" "+valueget;
value="general@"+valueget+setvalue1+" "+setvalue2+" "+sampvalue+"
    "+judge;
output1.println(value);
run.setLabel("Stop");
//firstornot=0;
judge="0";
//System.out.println("run1 start!");
if(run1.isAlive()) run1.resume();
else run1.start();
running="yes";
//    if(run2.isAlive()) run2.resume();
// else run2.start();
suspendalready=false;
}
}
if(label.equals("Stop")) {
//output.println(label);
//judge=false;
run.setLabel("Run");
output1.println("stop@");
run1.suspend();
//run2.suspend();
running="no";
suspendalready=true;
//System.out.println("run2 thread suspend now!");
}
if(label.equals("Reset")) {
output1.println("reset@");
run.setLabel("Run");
setpoint1.setText("20");
setpoint2.setText("20");
temp=false;
retemp=true;
fltemp=false;
refltemp=true;
setpoint1.setText("20");
setpoint2.setText("20");
samptime.setText("0.03");
m=0;
flm=0;
k=0;
flk=0;
if(!suspendalready) {
run1.suspend();
//run2.suspend();
}
running="no";
resetalready=true;
run1.reset();
repaint();}
}
return true;
}
```

```
public void stop() {
run1.stop();
//run2.stop();
output1.println("reset@");
try{con.close();con1.close();
}catch(Exception e){}
}
synchronized public void update (Graphics g){
paint(g);
}
synchronized public void paint(Graphics g){
if(changetime){g.setColor(greencolor);
g.fillRect(65,185,500,30);
changetime=false;}
if(temp){
g.setColor(greencolor);
g.fillRect(60,50,200,180);
for (n=0;n<shift-1;n++) {
g.setColor(Color.red);
g.drawLine (x1[n+1],y1[n+1],x1[n],y1[n]);
g.setColor(Color.blue);
g.drawLine (x2[n+1],y2[n+1],x2[n],y2[n]);
}
temp=false;
}
if(retemp){g.setColor(greencolor);
g.fillRect(60,50,200,180);
retemp=false;}
/**  if(j==180){k=k+30;
g.setColor(Color.lightGray);
g.fillRect(30,30,190,125);
} */
//g.setColor(Color.black);
g.setColor(Color.black);
g.drawString(String.valueOf(k*10),65,195);
//g.drawString(String.valueOf(k+5),50,145);
g.drawString(String.valueOf((k+1)*10),115,195);
//g.drawString(String.valueOf(k+15),100,145);
g.drawString(String.valueOf((k+2)*10),165,195);
//g.drawString(String.valueOf(k+25),150,145);
g.drawString(String.valueOf((k+3)*10),215,195);
//height, time axis
g.drawLine(70,180,240,180);
g.drawLine(70,60,70,180);
// on time axis
//g.drawLine(55,128,55,132);
g.drawLine(120,178,120,182);
//g.drawLine(105,128,105,132);
g.drawLine(170,178,170,182);
//g.drawLine(155,128,155,132);
g.drawLine(220,178,220,182);
g.drawString("(s)",240,195);
g.drawString("t",245,185);
g.drawString("u",50,65);
```

```
g.drawString("(v)",74,65);
//on height axis
g.drawLine(68,80,72,80);
g.drawString("10",45,85);
g.drawLine(68,130,72,130);
g.drawString("5",50,134);
//g.drawLine(108,96,112,96);
//g.drawString("100",85,101);
g.drawString("0",50,180);
int xcoords1[]={70,65,75,70};
int ycoords1[]={60,68,68,60};
int xcoords2[]={240,232,232,240};
int ycoords2[]={180,175,185,180};
g.fillPolygon(xcoords1,ycoords1,4);
g.fillPolygon(xcoords2,ycoords2,4);
if(m==0)m=0;
else if (m==1) {
g.setColor(Color.red);
g.drawLine(x1[m-1],y1[m-1],x1[m-1],y1[m-1]);
g.setColor(Color.blue);
g.drawLine(x2[m-1],y2[m-1],x2[m-1],y2[m-1]);}
else {
g.setColor(Color.red);
g.drawLine(x1[m-2],y1[m-2],x1[m-1],y1[m-1]);
g.setColor(Color.blue);
g.drawLine(x2[m-2],y2[m-2],x2[m-1],y2[m-1]);
}
if(fltemp) {
g.setColor(greencolor);
g.fillRect(270,50,200,180);
for (fln=0;fln<shift-1;fln++) {
g.setColor(Color.red);
g.drawLine (flx1[fln+1],fly1[fln+1],flx1[fln],fly1[fln]);
g.setColor(Color.blue);
g.drawLine (flx2[fln+1],fly2[fln+1],flx2[fln],fly2[fln]);
}
fltemp=false;
}
if(refltemp){g.setColor(greencolor);
g.fillRect(270,50,200,180);
refltemp=false;
}
g.setColor(Color.black);
g.drawString(String.valueOf(flk*10),285,195);
//g.drawString(String.valueOf(k+5),50,145);
g.drawString(String.valueOf((flk+1)*10),335,195);
//g.drawString(String.valueOf(k+15),100,145);
g.drawString(String.valueOf((flk+2)*10),385,195);
//g.drawString(String.valueOf(k+25),150,145);
g.drawString(String.valueOf((flk+3)*10),435,195);
//height, time axis
g.drawLine(290,180,460,180);
g.drawLine(290,60,290,180);
// on time axis
```

```
//g.drawLine(55,128,55,132);
g.drawLine(340,178,340,182);
//g.drawLine(105,128,105,132);
g.drawLine(390,178,390,182);
//g.drawLine(155,128,155,132);
g.drawLine(440,178,440,182);
g.drawString("(s)",460,195);
g.drawString("t",465,185);
g.drawString("(mm)",294,65);
g.drawString("y",275,65);
//on height axis
g.drawLine(288,80,292,80);
g.drawString("300",265,85);
g.drawLine(288,113,292,113);
g.drawString("200",265,118);
g.drawLine(288,146,292,146);
g.drawString("100",265,151);
g.drawString("0",270,180);
int flxcoords1[]={290,285,295,290};
int flycoords1[]={60,68,68,60};
int flxcoords2[]={460,452,452,460};
int flycoords2[]={180,175,185,180};
g.fillPolygon(flxcoords1,flycoords1,4);
g.fillPolygon(flxcoords2,flycoords2,4);
if(flm==0)flm=0;
else if (flm==1) {
g.setColor(Color.red);
g.drawLine(flx1[flm-1],fly1[flm-1],flx1[flm-1],fly1[flm-1]);
g.setColor(Color.blue);
g.drawLine(flx2[flm-1],fly2[flm-1],flx2[flm-1],fly2[flm-1]);}
else {
g.setColor(Color.red);
g.drawLine(flx1[flm-2],fly1[flm-2],flx1[flm-1],fly1[flm-1]);
g.setColor(Color.blue);
g.drawLine(flx2[flm-2],fly2[flm-2],flx2[flm-1],fly2[flm-1]);
}
g.setFont(f);
g.setColor(Color.red);
g.drawString("Tank1",110,65);
g.drawString("Tank1",330,65);
g.setColor(Color.blue);
g.drawString("Tank2",160,65);
g.drawString("Tank2",380,65);
}
}
```

B.10 fuzzycontrol.java

```
import java.awt.*;
import java.io.*;
import java.net.*;
import java.lang.*;
```

```java
import java.awt.event.*;
class drawfuzzy extends Thread {
int fm=0;
int fn=0;
int fheight1=0;
int fheight2=0;
int fi=0;
int fj1=260;
int fj2=260;
String fvalue1;
String fvalue2;
int i=0;
int m=0;
int n=0;
int height1=0;
int height2=0;
int j1=40;
int j2=40;
String value1;
String value2;
byte[] currLine =new byte[23];
char[] currchar1=new char[3];
char[] currchar2=new char[3];
char[] currchar3=new char[3];
char[] currchar4=new char[3];
char[] currchar5=new char[3];
char[] currchar6=new char[3];
char[] currchar7=new char[5];
String timevaluestring;
int timevalue=0;
int timeindex=0;
int timeleft=0;
int pointnumber1=0;
int pointnumber2=0;
int pointnumber3=0;
String index1;
String index2;
fuzzycontrol applet;
drawfuzzy(fuzzycontrol applet){
this.applet=applet;
}
public void reset(){
fm=0;
fn=0;
fheight1=0;
fheight2=0;
fi=0;
fj1=260;
fj2=260;
i=0;
m=0;
n=0;
height1=0;
height2=0;
```

```
j1=40;
j2=40;
timevalue=0;
timeindex=0;
timeleft=0;
pointnumber1=0;
pointnumber2=0;
pointnumber3=0;
}
public void run() {
while(true){
applet.output.println("waiting");
try {
applet.instream.readFully(currLine);
} catch (Exception e){}
if (!applet.resetalready) {
for(i=0;i<3;i++) {
currchar1[i]=(char)currLine[i];
currchar2[i]=(char)currLine[i+3];
currchar3[i]=(char)currLine[i+6];
currchar4[i]=(char)currLine[i+9];
currchar5[i]=(char)currLine[i+12];
currchar6[i]=(char)currLine[i+15];}
//build a string by the chars
for(i=0;i<5;i++) {
currchar7[i]=(char)currLine[18+i];}
fvalue1=new String(currchar1);
fvalue2=new String(currchar2);
value1=new String(currchar3);
value2=new String(currchar4);
index1=new String(currchar5);
index2=new String(currchar6);
applet.ruletank1=Integer.parseInt(index1.trim());
applet.ruletank2=Integer.parseInt(index2.trim());
//convert string to int, i.e., the Y value.
fheight1=180-Integer.parseInt(fvalue1.trim());
fheight2=180-Integer.parseInt(fvalue2.trim());
height1=180-Integer.parseInt(value1.trim());
height2=180-Integer.parseInt(value2.trim());
//height1=180-Integer.parseInt(value1.trim());
//height2=180-Integer.parseInt(value2.trim());
timevaluestring=new String(currchar7);
//System.out.println(timevaluestring);
//convert string to int, i.e., the Y value.
timevalue=Integer.parseInt(timevaluestring.trim());
if(applet.settime20){
timevalue=0;
applet.settime20=false;}
System.out.println("timevalue is "+timevalue);
timeindex=timevalue/200;
timeleft=timevalue%200;
if (timeleft>100)timeindex++;
fj1=fj1+timeindex;
fj2=fj1;
```

```
j1=j1+timeindex;
j2=j1;
//System.out.println(fj1);
//System.out.println(j1);
applet.flx1[fm]=fj1;
applet.fly1[fm]=fheight1;
applet.flx2[fm]=fj2;
applet.fly2[fm]=fheight2;
applet.x1[fm]=j1;
applet.y1[fm]=height1;
applet.x2[fm]=j2;
applet.y2[fm]=height2;
if (applet.flx1[fm]<=310) {
pointnumber1++;}
else if (applet.flx1[fm]<=360) {
pointnumber2++;
}
else {
pointnumber3++;
}
if (applet.flx1[fm]>=410) {
applet.shift=fm-pointnumber1;
for (fn=0;fn<=fm-pointnumber1;fn++) {
applet.flx1[fn]=applet.flx1[fn+pointnumber1]-50;
applet.fly1[fn]=applet.fly1[fn+pointnumber1];
applet.flx2[fn]=applet.flx2[fn+pointnumber1]-50;
applet.fly2[fn]=applet.fly2[fn+pointnumber1];
applet.x1[fn]=applet.x1[fn+pointnumber1]-50;
applet.y1[fn]=applet.y1[fn+pointnumber1];
applet.x2[fn]=applet.x2[fn+pointnumber1]-50;
applet.y2[fn]=applet.y2[fn+pointnumber1];
}
fj1=applet.flx1[fm-pointnumber1];
fj2=fj1;
j1=applet.x1[fm-pointnumber1];
j2=j1;
fm=fm-pointnumber1;
pointnumber1=pointnumber2;
pointnumber2=pointnumber3;
pointnumber3=0;
applet.k++;
applet.flk++;
applet.fltemp=true;
applet.temp=true;
}
fm++;
applet.flm=fm;
applet.m=fm;
//convert string to int, i.e., the Y value.
applet.repaint();
}
else {
applet.resetalready=false;
}
```

```
//try {sleep(applet.samplerate);}
//catch(InterruptedException e){  }
}
}
}
/**class fuzzyrule extends Thread
{
byte[] currLine =new byte[6];
char[] currchar1=new char[3];
char[] currchar2=new char[3];
String value1;
String value2;
int i=0;
fuzzycontrol applet;
fuzzyrule(fuzzycontrol applet){
this.applet=applet;
}
public void run() {
while(true) {
try {applet.output1.println(applet.value);
applet.instream1.readFully(currLine);
} catch (Exception e){}
for(i=0;i<3;i++) {
currchar1[i]=(char)currLine[i];
currchar2[i]=(char)currLine[i+3];
}
//build a string by the chars
value1=new String(currchar1);
value2=new String(currchar2);
applet.ruletank1=Integer.parseInt(value1.trim());
applet.ruletank2=Integer.parseInt(value2.trim());
applet.repaint();
}
}
}
*/
public class fuzzycontrol extends java.applet.Applet implements
    MouseListener,MouseMotionListener {
String running="no";
boolean changetime=false;
int timeperiod=20;
int ruletank1=10;
int ruletank2=10;
int m=0;
int flm=0;
int n=0;
int fln=0;
int[] x1=new int[200];
int[] y1=new int[200];
int[] x2=new int[200];
int[] y2=new int[200];
int k=0;//use to change time
boolean temp=false;
boolean retemp=false;
```

```
int[] flx1=new int[200];
int[] fly1=new int[200];
int[] flx2=new int[200];
int[] fly2=new int[200];
int flk=0;//use to change time
boolean fltemp=false;
boolean refltemp=false;
Font f=new Font("TimesRoman", Font.BOLD,14);
int samplerate;
String controlvalue1;
String controlvalue2;
String value;
XCTextField set1=new XCTextField(4);
XCTextField set2=new XCTextField(4);
String setvalue1;
String setvalue2;
PrintStream output;
DataInputStream instream;
PrintStream output1;
DataInputStream instream1;
Button run=new Button("Run");
Button reset=new Button("Reset");
Button defau=new Button("Default");
Socket con;
Socket con1;
/** String url="http://vlab.ee.nus.edu.sg";
URL host;*/
drawfuzzy run1=new drawfuzzy(this);
//fuzzyrule run2=new fuzzyrule(this);
boolean suspendalready=false;
Color greencolor=new Color(204,255,204);
Color pinkcolor=new Color(248,199,248);
boolean first=true;
String tank1err="-10.0 -5.0 0.0 -5.0 0.0 5.0 0.0 5.0 10.0";
String tank2err="-10.0 -5.0 0.0 -5.0 0.0 5.0 0.0 5.0 10.0";
String tank1derr="-50.0 -25.0 0.0 -25.0 0.0 25.0 0.0 25.0 50.0";
String tank2derr="-50.0 -25.0 0.0 -25.0 0.0 25.0 0.0 25.0 50.0";
String tank1out="-10.0 -5.0 0.0 -5.0 0.0 5.0 0.0 5.0 10.0";
String tank2out="-10.0 -5.0 0.0 -5.0 0.0 5.0 0.0 5.0 10.0";
String tank1rule1="NL";
String tank1rule2="NL";
String tank1rule3="ZR";
String tank1rule4="NL";
String tank1rule5="ZR";
String tank1rule6="PL";
String tank1rule7="ZR";
String tank1rule8="PL";
String tank1rule9="PL";
String tank2rule1="NL";
String tank2rule2="NL";
String tank2rule3="ZR";
String tank2rule4="NL";
String tank2rule5="ZR";
String tank2rule6="PL";
```

```
String tank2rule7="ZR";
String tank2rule8="PL";
String tank2rule9="PL";
int tank1rulevalue1=-1;
int tank1rulevalue2=-1;
int tank1rulevalue3=0;
int tank1rulevalue4=-1;
int tank1rulevalue5=0;
int tank1rulevalue6=1;
int tank1rulevalue7=0;
int tank1rulevalue8=1;
int tank1rulevalue9=1;
int tank2rulevalue1=-1;
int tank2rulevalue2=-1;
int tank2rulevalue3=0;
int tank2rulevalue4=-1;
int tank2rulevalue5=0;
int tank2rulevalue6=1;
int tank2rulevalue7=0;
int tank2rulevalue8=1;
int tank2rulevalue9=1;
String tank1ruleindex1="-1";
String tank1ruleindex2="-1";
String tank1ruleindex3="0";
String tank1ruleindex4="-1";
String tank1ruleindex5="0";
String tank1ruleindex6="1";
String tank1ruleindex7="0";
String tank1ruleindex8="1";
String tank1ruleindex9="1";
String tank2ruleindex1="-1";
String tank2ruleindex2="-1";
String tank2ruleindex3="0";
String tank2ruleindex4="-1";
String tank2ruleindex5="0";
String tank2ruleindex6="1";
String tank2ruleindex7="0";
String tank2ruleindex8="1";
String tank2ruleindex9="1";
boolean clicktank1=false;
boolean clicktank2=false;
boolean resetrule=false;
boolean runornot=false;
int shift=0;
boolean resetalready=false;
boolean settime20=false;
public void init(){
this.addMouseListener(this);
this.addMouseMotionListener(this);
this.setBackground(greencolor);
set1.setForeground(Color.red);
set2.setForeground(Color.blue);
set1.setText("20");
set2.setText("20");
```

```
set1.button1=run;
set2.button1=run;
setLayout(new FlowLayout(FlowLayout.LEFT));
add(new Label("Set Point (20-230)mm"));
add(set1);
add(set2);
add(run);
add(reset);
//add(new Label("              "));
//add(new Label("              "));
//add(new Label("               "));
//add(defau);
}
public void start(){
try { /**host=new URL(url);*/
InetAddress add=InetAddress.getByName("137.132.165.77");
con= new Socket(add,5555);
instream=new DataInputStream(con.getInputStream());
output=new PrintStream(con.getOutputStream());
System.out.println(con);  }catch(Exception ex) {
System.out.println(ex);
}
try {
InetAddress add1=InetAddress.getByName("137.132.165.77");
con1= new Socket(add1,6666);
instream1=new DataInputStream(con1.getInputStream());
output1=new PrintStream(con1.getOutputStream());
System.out.println(con1);  }catch(Exception ex) {
System.out.println(ex);}
}
public String returnrunning(){
return running;
}
public void gettank1err(String t1err) {
tank1err=t1err;
controlvalue1=setvalue1+" "+"["+tank1ruleindex1+"
    "+tank1ruleindex2+" "+tank1ruleindex3+" "+tank1ruleindex4+"
    "+tank1ruleindex5+" "+tank1ruleindex6+" "+tank1ruleindex7+"
    "+tank1ruleindex8+" "+tank1ruleindex9+" "+tank1err+"
    "+tank1derr+" "+tank1out+"]";
controlvalue2=setvalue2+" "+"["+tank2ruleindex1+"
    "+tank2ruleindex2+" "+tank2ruleindex3+" "+tank2ruleindex4+"
    "+tank2ruleindex5+" "+tank2ruleindex6+" "+tank2ruleindex7+"
    "+tank2ruleindex8+" "+tank2ruleindex9+" "+tank2err+"
    "+tank2derr+" "+tank2out+"]";
value="fuzzy@"+controlvalue1+"&"+controlvalue2;
System.out.println(value);
}
public void gettank2err(String t2err){
    tank2err=t2err;
controlvalue1=setvalue1+" "+"["+tank1ruleindex1+"
    "+tank1ruleindex2+" "+tank1ruleindex3+" "+tank1ruleindex4+"
    "+tank1ruleindex5+" "+tank1ruleindex6+" "+tank1ruleindex7+"
```

```
    "+tank1ruleindex8+" "+tank1ruleindex9+" "+tank1err+"
    "+tank1derr+" "+tank1out+"]";
controlvalue2=setvalue2+" "+"["+tank2ruleindex1+"
    "+tank2ruleindex2+" "+tank2ruleindex3+" "+tank2ruleindex4+"
    "+tank2ruleindex5+" "+tank2ruleindex6+" "+tank2ruleindex7+"
    "+tank2ruleindex8+" "+tank2ruleindex9+" "+tank2err+"
    "+tank2derr+" "+tank2out+"]";
value="fuzzy@"+controlvalue1+"&"+controlvalue2;
}
public void gettank1derr(String t1derr) {
tank1derr=t1derr;
controlvalue1=setvalue1+" "+"["+tank1ruleindex1+"
    "+tank1ruleindex2+" "+tank1ruleindex3+" "+tank1ruleindex4+"
    "+tank1ruleindex5+" "+tank1ruleindex6+" "+tank1ruleindex7+"
    "+tank1ruleindex8+" "+tank1ruleindex9+" "+tank1err+"
    "+tank1derr+" "+tank1out+"]";
controlvalue2=setvalue2+" "+"["+tank2ruleindex1+"
    "+tank2ruleindex2+" "+tank2ruleindex3+" "+tank2ruleindex4+"
    "+tank2ruleindex5+" "+tank2ruleindex6+" "+tank2ruleindex7+"
    "+tank2ruleindex8+" "+tank2ruleindex9+" "+tank2err+"
    "+tank2derr+" "+tank2out+"]";
value="fuzzy@"+controlvalue1+"&"+controlvalue2;
}
public void gettank2derr(String t2derr) {
    tank2derr=t2derr;
controlvalue1=setvalue1+" "+"["+tank1ruleindex1+"
    "+tank1ruleindex2+" "+tank1ruleindex3+" "+tank1ruleindex4+"
    "+tank1ruleindex5+" "+tank1ruleindex6+" "+tank1ruleindex7+"
    "+tank1ruleindex8+" "+tank1ruleindex9+" "+tank1err+"
    "+tank1derr+" "+tank1out+"]";
controlvalue2=setvalue2+" "+"["+tank2ruleindex1+"
    "+tank2ruleindex2+" "+tank2ruleindex3+" "+tank2ruleindex4+"
    "+tank2ruleindex5+" "+tank2ruleindex6+" "+tank2ruleindex7+"
    "+tank2ruleindex8+" "+tank2ruleindex9+" "+tank2err+"
    "+tank2derr+" "+tank2out+"]";
value="fuzzy@"+controlvalue1+"&"+controlvalue2;
}
public void gettank1out(String t1out) {
    tank1out=t1out;
controlvalue1=setvalue1+" "+"["+tank1ruleindex1+"
    "+tank1ruleindex2+" "+tank1ruleindex3+" "+tank1ruleindex4+"
    "+tank1ruleindex5+" "+tank1ruleindex6+" "+tank1ruleindex7+"
    "+tank1ruleindex8+" "+tank1ruleindex9+" "+tank1err+"
    "+tank1derr+" "+tank1out+"]";
controlvalue2=setvalue2+" "+"["+tank2ruleindex1+"
    "+tank2ruleindex2+" "+tank2ruleindex3+" "+tank2ruleindex4+"
    "+tank2ruleindex5+" "+tank2ruleindex6+" "+tank2ruleindex7+"
    "+tank2ruleindex8+" "+tank2ruleindex9+" "+tank2err+"
    "+tank2derr+" "+tank2out+"]";
value="fuzzy@"+controlvalue1+"&"+controlvalue2;
}
public void gettank2out(String t2out) {
    tank2out=t2out;
```

```
controlvalue1=setvalue1+" "+"["+tank1ruleindex1+"
    "+tank1ruleindex2+" "+tank1ruleindex3+" "+tank1ruleindex4+"
    "+tank1ruleindex5+" "+tank1ruleindex6+" "+tank1ruleindex7+"
    "+tank1ruleindex8+" "+tank1ruleindex9+" "+tank1err+"
    "+tank1derr+" "+tank1out+"]";
controlvalue2=setvalue2+" "+"["+tank2ruleindex1+"
    "+tank2ruleindex2+" "+tank2ruleindex3+" "+tank2ruleindex4+"
    "+tank2ruleindex5+" "+tank2ruleindex6+" "+tank2ruleindex7+"
    "+tank2ruleindex8+" "+tank2ruleindex9+" "+tank2err+"
    "+tank2derr+" "+tank2out+"]";
value="fuzzy@"+controlvalue1+"&"+controlvalue2;
}
public boolean action(Event evt,Object arg) {
String label=(String)arg;
if (evt.target instanceof Button) {
if(label.equals("Run")) { //judge=true;
run.setLabel("Stop");
runornot=true;
setvalue1=set1.getText();
setvalue2=set2.getText();
int sp1=Integer.parseInt(setvalue1);
int sp2=Integer.parseInt(setvalue2);
if(sp1>230) {
sp1=230;
setvalue1="230";
set1.setText("230");
okdialog.createokdialog("        Set Point is 20-230mm!");}
else if (sp1<0) {
sp1=0;
setvalue1="20";
set1.setText("20");
okdialog.createokdialog("        Set Point is 20-230mm!");
}
else if (sp2>230) {
sp2=230;
setvalue2="230";
set2.setText("230");
okdialog.createokdialog("        Set Point is 20-230mm!");
}
else if (sp2<0) {
sp2=0;
setvalue2="20";
set2.setText("20");
okdialog.createokdialog("        Set Point is 20-230mm!");
}
controlvalue1=setvalue1+" "+"["+tank1ruleindex1+"
    "+tank1ruleindex2+" "+tank1ruleindex3+" "+tank1ruleindex4+"
    "+tank1ruleindex5+" "+tank1ruleindex6+" "+tank1ruleindex7+"
    "+tank1ruleindex8+" "+tank1ruleindex9+" "+tank1err+"
    "+tank1derr+" "+tank1out+"]";
controlvalue2=setvalue2+" "+"["+tank2ruleindex1+"
    "+tank2ruleindex2+" "+tank2ruleindex3+" "+tank2ruleindex4+"
    "+tank2ruleindex5+" "+tank2ruleindex6+" "+tank2ruleindex7+"
```

```
   "+tank2ruleindex8+" "+tank2ruleindex9+" "+tank2err+"
   "+tank2derr+" "+tank2out+"]";
value="fuzzy@"+controlvalue1+"&"+controlvalue2;
output1.println(value);
System.out.println(value);
if(run1.isAlive()) run1.resume();
else run1.start();
// if(run2.isAlive()) run2.resume();
// output.println("run1 resume now!");
// else run2.start();
suspendalready=false;
running="yes";
}
if(label.equals("Stop")) {
//output.println(label);
//judge=false;
run.setLabel("Run");
run1.suspend();
//run2.suspend();
suspendalready=true;
//runornot=false;
output1.println("stop@");
running="no";
}
if(label.equals("Reset")) {
ruletank1=10;
ruletank2=10;
first=true;
runornot=false;
if(!suspendalready){run1.suspend();//run2.suspend();
}
resetalready=true;
settime20=true;
run1.reset();
run.setLabel("Run");
set1.setText("20");
set2.setText("20");
output1.println("reset@");
temp=false;
retemp=true;
fltemp=false;
refltemp=true;
m=0;
flm=0;
k=0;
flk=0;
tank1err="-10.0 -5.0 0.0 -5.0 0.0 5.0 0.0 5.0 10.0";
tank2err="-10.0 -5.0 0.0 -5.0 0.0 5.0 0.0 5.0 10.0";
tank1derr="-50.0 -25.0 0.0 -25.0 0.0 25.0 0.0 25.0 50.0";
tank2derr="-50.0 -25.0 0.0 -25.0 0.0 25.0 0.0 25.0 50.0";
tank1out="-10.0 -5.0 0.0 -5.0 0.0 5.0 0.0 5.0 10.0";
tank2out="-10.0 -5.0 0.0 -5.0 0.0 5.0 0.0 5.0 10.0";
tank1ruleindex1="-1";
tank1ruleindex2="-1";
```

```
tank1ruleindex3="0";
tank1ruleindex4="-1";
tank1ruleindex5="0";
tank1ruleindex6="1";
tank1ruleindex7="0";
tank1ruleindex8="1";
tank1ruleindex9="1";
tank2ruleindex1="-1";
tank2ruleindex2="-1";
tank2ruleindex3="0";
tank2ruleindex4="-1";
tank2ruleindex5="0";
tank2ruleindex6="1";
tank2ruleindex7="0";
tank2ruleindex8="1";
tank2ruleindex9="1";
tank1rule1="NL";
tank1rule2="NL";
tank1rule3="ZR";
tank1rule4="NL";
tank1rule5="ZR";
tank1rule6="PL";
tank1rule7="ZR";
tank1rule8="PL";
tank1rule9="PL";
tank2rule1="NL";
tank2rule2="NL";
tank2rule3="ZR";
tank2rule4="NL";
tank2rule5="ZR";
tank2rule6="PL";
tank2rule7="ZR";
tank2rule8="PL";
tank2rule9="PL";
repaint();}
}
return true;
}
public void mouseMoved(MouseEvent e) {
if(!runornot) {
int x=e.getX();
int y=e.getY();
if ( (x>500 && x<575 && y>90 && y<165)||(x>620 && x<695 && y>90 &&
    y<165)) {
setCursor(Cursor.getPredefinedCursor(Cursor.HAND_CURSOR));
}
else {
setCursor(Cursor.getPredefinedCursor(Cursor.DEFAULT_CURSOR));
}
}
}
public void mouseDragged(MouseEvent e) {}
public void mouseEntered(MouseEvent e) {}
public void mousePressed(MouseEvent e) {}
```

```
public void mouseReleased(MouseEvent e) {}
public void mouseClicked(MouseEvent e) {
if(!runornot){ if(e.getClickCount()==1) {
if(e.getModifiers()==MouseEvent.BUTTON1_MASK) {
int mousex=e.getX();
int mousey=e.getY();
if (mousex<525 && mousex>500 && mousey<115 && mousey>90) {
if (tank1rule1=="NL")  {
tank1rule1="ZR";
tank1rulevalue1=0;
tank1ruleindex1=String.valueOf(tank1rulevalue1);
}
else if(tank1rule1=="ZR") {
tank1rule1="PL";
tank1rulevalue1=1;
tank1ruleindex1=String.valueOf(tank1rulevalue1);
}
else if(tank1rule1=="PL") {
tank1rule1="NL";
tank1rulevalue1=-1;
tank1ruleindex1=String.valueOf(tank1rulevalue1);
}
clicktank1=true;
repaint();
}
else if(mousex<550 && mousex>525 && mousey<115 && mousey>90) {
if (tank1rule2=="NL")  {
tank1rule2="ZR";
tank1rulevalue2=0;
tank1ruleindex2=String.valueOf(tank1rulevalue2);
}
else if(tank1rule2=="ZR") {
tank1rule2="PL";
tank1rulevalue2=1;
tank1ruleindex2=String.valueOf(tank1rulevalue2);
}
else if(tank1rule2=="PL") {
tank1rule2="NL";
tank1rulevalue2=-1;
tank1ruleindex2=String.valueOf(tank1rulevalue2);
}
clicktank1=true;
repaint();
}
else if( mousex<575 && mousex>550 && mousey<115 && mousey>90) {
if (tank1rule3=="NL") {
tank1rule3="ZR";
tank1rulevalue3=0;
tank1ruleindex3=String.valueOf(tank1rulevalue3);
}
else if(tank1rule3=="ZR") {
tank1rule3="PL";
tank1rulevalue3=1;
tank1ruleindex3=String.valueOf(tank1rulevalue3);
```

```
}
else if(tank1rule3=="PL") {
tank1rule3="NL";
tank1rulevalue3=-1;
tank1ruleindex3=String.valueOf(tank1rulevalue3);
}
clicktank1=true;
repaint();}
else if(mousex<525 && mousex>500 && mousey<140 && mousey>115) {
if (tank1rule4=="NL") {
tank1rule4="ZR";
tank1rulevalue4=0;
tank1ruleindex4=String.valueOf(tank1rulevalue4);
}
else if(tank1rule4=="ZR") {
tank1rule4="PL";
tank1rulevalue4=1;
tank1ruleindex4=String.valueOf(tank1rulevalue4);
}
else if(tank1rule4=="PL") {
tank1rule4="NL";
tank1rulevalue4=-1;
tank1ruleindex4=String.valueOf(tank1rulevalue4);
}
clicktank1=true;
repaint();
}
else if(mousex<550 && mousex>525 && mousey<140 && mousey>115) {
if (tank1rule5=="NL") {
tank1rule5="ZR";
tank1rulevalue5=0;
tank1ruleindex5=String.valueOf(tank1rulevalue5);
}
else if(tank1rule5=="ZR") {
tank1rule5="PL";
tank1rulevalue5=1;
tank1ruleindex5=String.valueOf(tank1rulevalue5);
}
else if(tank1rule5=="PL") {
tank1rule5="NL";
tank1rulevalue5=-1;
tank1ruleindex5=String.valueOf(tank1rulevalue5);
}
clicktank1=true;
repaint();
}
else if(mousex<575 && mousex>550 && mousey<140 && mousey>115) {
if (tank1rule6=="NL") {
tank1rule6="ZR";
tank1rulevalue6=0;
tank1ruleindex6=String.valueOf(tank1rulevalue6);
}
else if(tank1rule6=="ZR") {
tank1rule6="PL";
```

```
tank1rulevalue6=1;
tank1ruleindex6=String.valueOf(tank1rulevalue6);
}
else if(tank1rule6=="PL") {
tank1rule6="NL";
tank1rulevalue6=-1;
tank1ruleindex6=String.valueOf(tank1rulevalue6);}
clicktank1=true;
repaint();
}
else if(mousex<525 && mousex>500 && mousey<165 && mousey>140) {
if (tank1rule7=="NL") {
tank1rule7="ZR";
tank1rulevalue7=0;
tank1ruleindex7=String.valueOf(tank1rulevalue7);
}
else if(tank1rule7=="ZR") {
tank1rule7="PL";
tank1rulevalue7=1;
tank1ruleindex7=String.valueOf(tank1rulevalue7);
}
else if(tank1rule7=="PL") {
tank1rule7="NL";
tank1rulevalue7=-1;
tank1ruleindex7=String.valueOf(tank1rulevalue7);}
clicktank1=true;
repaint();
}
else if(mousex<550 && mousex>525 && mousey<165 && mousey>140) {
if (tank1rule8=="NL") {
tank1rule8="ZR";
tank1rulevalue8=0;
tank1ruleindex8=String.valueOf(tank1rulevalue8);}
else if(tank1rule8=="ZR") {
tank1rule8="PL";
tank1rulevalue8=1;
tank1ruleindex8=String.valueOf(tank1rulevalue8);
}
else if(tank1rule8=="PL") {
tank1rule8="NL";
tank1rulevalue8=-1;
tank1ruleindex8=String.valueOf(tank1rulevalue8);}
clicktank1=true;
repaint();
}
else if(mousex<575 && mousex>550 && mousey<165 && mousey>140) {
if (tank1rule9=="NL") {
tank1rule9="ZR";
tank1rulevalue9=0;
tank1ruleindex9=String.valueOf(tank1rulevalue9);
}
else if(tank1rule9=="ZR") {
tank1rule9="PL";
tank1rulevalue9=1;
```

```
tank1ruleindex9=String.valueOf(tank1rulevalue9);
}
else if(tank1rule9=="PL") {
tank1rule9="NL";
tank1rulevalue9=-1;
tank1ruleindex9=String.valueOf(tank1rulevalue9);}
clicktank1=true;
repaint();
}
else if(mousex<645 && mousex>620 && mousey<115 && mousey>90) {
if (tank2rule1=="NL") {
tank2rule1="ZR";
tank2rulevalue1=0;
tank2ruleindex1=String.valueOf(tank2rulevalue1);
}
else if(tank2rule1=="ZR") {
tank2rule1="PL";
tank2rulevalue1=1;
tank2ruleindex1=String.valueOf(tank2rulevalue1);
}
else if(tank2rule1=="PL") {
tank2rule1="NL";
tank2rulevalue1=-1;
tank2ruleindex1=String.valueOf(tank2rulevalue1);
}
clicktank2=true;
repaint();
}
else if(mousex<670 && mousex>645 && mousey<115 && mousey>90) {
if (tank2rule2=="NL") {
tank2rule2="ZR";
tank2rulevalue2=0;
tank2ruleindex2=String.valueOf(tank2rulevalue2);
}
else if(tank2rule2=="ZR") {
tank2rule2="PL";
tank2rulevalue2=1;
tank2ruleindex2=String.valueOf(tank2rulevalue2);
}
else if(tank2rule2=="PL") {
tank2rule2="NL";
tank2rulevalue2=-1;
tank2ruleindex2=String.valueOf(tank2rulevalue2);}
clicktank2=true;
repaint();
}
else if(mousex<695 && mousex>670 && mousey<115 && mousey>90) {
if (tank2rule3=="NL") {
tank2rule3="ZR";
tank2rulevalue3=0;
tank2ruleindex3=String.valueOf(tank2rulevalue1);
}
else if(tank2rule3=="ZR") {
tank2rule3="PL";
```

```
tank2rulevalue3=1;
tank2ruleindex3=String.valueOf(tank2rulevalue3);
}
else if(tank2rule3=="PL") {
tank2rule3="NL";
tank2rulevalue3=-1;
tank2ruleindex3=String.valueOf(tank2rulevalue3);
}
clicktank2=true;
repaint();
}
else if(mousex<645 && mousex>620 && mousey<140 && mousey>115) {
if (tank2rule4=="NL")  {
tank2rule4="ZR";
tank2rulevalue4=0;
tank2ruleindex4=String.valueOf(tank2rulevalue4);
}
else if(tank2rule4=="ZR")  {
tank2rule4="PL";
tank2rulevalue4=1;
tank2ruleindex4=String.valueOf(tank2rulevalue4);
}
else if(tank2rule4=="PL") {
tank2rule4="NL";
tank2rulevalue4=-1;
tank2ruleindex4=String.valueOf(tank2rulevalue4);
}
clicktank2=true;
repaint();
}
else if(mousex<670 && mousex>645 && mousey<140 && mousey>115) {
if (tank2rule5=="NL") {
tank2rule5="ZR";
tank2rulevalue5=0;
tank2ruleindex5=String.valueOf(tank2rulevalue5);
}
else if(tank2rule5=="ZR")  {
tank2rule5="PL";
tank2rulevalue5=1;
tank2ruleindex5=String.valueOf(tank2rulevalue5);
}
else if(tank2rule5=="PL")  {
tank2rule5="NL";
tank2rulevalue5=-1;
tank2ruleindex5=String.valueOf(tank2rulevalue5);
}
clicktank2=true;
repaint();
}
else if (mousex<695 && mousex>670 && mousey<140 && mousey>115) {
if (tank2rule6=="NL")  {
tank2rule6="ZR";
tank2rulevalue6=0;
tank2ruleindex6=String.valueOf(tank2rulevalue6);
```

```
}
else if(tank2rule6=="ZR") {
tank2rule6="PL";
tank2rulevalue6=1;
tank2ruleindex6=String.valueOf(tank2rulevalue6);
}
else if(tank2rule6=="PL") {
tank2rule6="NL";
tank2rulevalue6=-1;
tank2ruleindex6=String.valueOf(tank2rulevalue6);
}
clicktank2=true;
repaint();
}
else if(mousex<645 && mousex>620 && mousey<165 && mousey>140) {
if (tank2rule7=="NL")  {
tank2rule7="ZR";
tank2rulevalue7=0;
tank2ruleindex7=String.valueOf(tank2rulevalue7);
}
else if(tank2rule7=="ZR") {
tank2rule7="PL";
tank2rulevalue7=1;
tank2ruleindex7=String.valueOf(tank2rulevalue7);
}
else if(tank2rule7=="PL") {
tank2rule7="NL";
tank2rulevalue7=-1;
tank2ruleindex7=String.valueOf(tank2rulevalue7);
}
clicktank2=true;
repaint();
}
else if(mousex<670 && mousex>645 && mousey<165 && mousey>140) {
if (tank2rule8=="NL")  {
tank2rule8="ZR";
tank2rulevalue8=0;
tank2ruleindex8=String.valueOf(tank2rulevalue8);
}
else if(tank2rule8=="ZR") {
tank2rule8="PL";
tank2rulevalue8=1;
tank2ruleindex8=String.valueOf(tank2rulevalue8);
}
else if(tank2rule8=="PL") {
tank2rule8="NL";
tank2rulevalue8=-1;
tank2ruleindex8=String.valueOf(tank2rulevalue8);
}
clicktank2=true;
repaint();
}
else if(mousex<695 && mousex>670 && mousey<165 && mousey>140) {
if (tank2rule9=="NL") {
```

```
tank2rule9="ZR";
tank2rulevalue9=0;
tank2ruleindex9=String.valueOf(tank2rulevalue9);
}
else if(tank2rule9=="ZR") {
tank2rule9="PL";
tank2rulevalue9=1;
tank2ruleindex9=String.valueOf(tank2rulevalue9);
}
else if(tank2rule9=="PL") {
tank2rule9="NL";
tank2rulevalue9=-1;
tank2ruleindex9=String.valueOf(tank2rulevalue9);
}
clicktank2=true;
repaint();
}
}
}
controlvalue1=setvalue1+" "+"3"+" "+tank1ruleindex1+"
    "+tank1ruleindex2+" "+tank1ruleindex3+" "+tank1ruleindex4+"
    "+tank1ruleindex5+" "+tank1ruleindex6+" "+tank1ruleindex7+"
    "+tank1ruleindex8+" "+tank1ruleindex9+" "+tank1err+"
    "+tank1derr+" "+tank1out;
controlvalue2=setvalue2+" "+"3"+" "+tank2ruleindex1+"
    "+tank2ruleindex2+" "+tank2ruleindex3+" "+tank2ruleindex4+"
    "+tank2ruleindex5+" "+tank2ruleindex6+" "+tank2ruleindex7+"
    "+tank2ruleindex8+" "+tank2ruleindex9+" "+tank2err+"
    "+tank2derr+" "+tank2out;
System.out.println(controlvalue1);
System.out.println(controlvalue2);
}
}
public void mouseExited(MouseEvent e){}
public void stop() {
run1.stop();
output.println("0 0");
try {con.close();
con1.close();}catch(Exception e){}
}
synchronized public void update (Graphics g) {
if(clicktank1) {
g.clipRect(500,90,75,75);
}
if(clicktank2) {
g.clipRect(620,90,75,75);
}
paint(g);
}
synchronized public void paint(Graphics g) {
if(changetime) {
g.setColor(greencolor);
g.fillRect(35,185,500,30);
changetime=false;
```

```
}
g.setColor(pinkcolor);
g.fillRect(500,90,75,75);
g.fillRect(620,90,75,75);
if(temp) {
g.setColor(greencolor);
g.fillRect(30,50,200,180);
for (n=0;n<shift;n++) {
g.setColor(Color.red);
g.drawLine (x1[n+1],y1[n+1],x1[n],y1[n]);
g.setColor(Color.blue);
g.drawLine (x2[n+1],y2[n+1],x2[n],y2[n]);
}
temp=false;
}
if(retemp) {
g.setColor(greencolor);
g.fillRect(30,50,200,180);
retemp=false;}
/**   if(j==180){k=k+30;
g.setColor(Color.lightGray);
g.fillRect(30,30,190,125);
} */
//g.setColor(Color.black);
g.setColor(Color.black);
g.drawString(String.valueOf(k*10),35,195);
//g.drawString(String.valueOf(k+5),50,145);
g.drawString(String.valueOf((k+1)*10),85,195);
//g.drawString(String.valueOf(k+15),100,145);
g.drawString(String.valueOf((k+2)*10),135,195);
//g.drawString(String.valueOf(k+25),150,145);
g.drawString(String.valueOf((k+3)*10),185,195);
//height, time axis
g.drawLine(40,180,210,180);
g.drawLine(40,60,40,180);
// on time axis
//g.drawLine(55,128,55,132);
g.drawLine(90,178,90,182);
//g.drawLine(105,128,105,132);
g.drawLine(140,178,140,182);
//g.drawLine(155,128,155,132);
g.drawLine(190,178,190,182);
g.drawString("(s)",210,195);
g.drawString("t",215,185);
g.drawString("u",20,65);
g.drawString("(v)",44,65);
//on height axis
g.drawLine(38,80,42,80);
g.drawString("10",15,85);
g.drawLine(38,130,42,130);
g.drawString("5",20,134);
//g.drawLine(108,96,112,96);
//g.drawString("100",85,101);
g.drawString("0",20,180);
```

```
int xcoords1[]={40,35,45,40};
int ycoords1[]={60,68,68,60};
int xcoords2[]={210,202,202,210};
int ycoords2[]={180,175,185,180};
g.fillPolygon(xcoords1,ycoords1,4);
g.fillPolygon(xcoords2,ycoords2,4);
if(m==0)m=0;
else if (m==1) {
g.setColor(Color.red);
g.drawLine(x1[m-1],y1[m-1],x1[m-1],y1[m-1]);
g.setColor(Color.blue);
g.drawLine(x2[m-1],y2[m-1],x2[m-1],y2[m-1]);
}
else {
g.setColor(Color.red);
g.drawLine(x1[m-2],y1[m-2],x1[m-1],y1[m-1]);
g.setColor(Color.blue);
g.drawLine(x2[m-2],y2[m-2],x2[m-1],y2[m-1]);
}
if(fltemp) {
g.setColor(greencolor);
g.fillRect(240,50,200,180);
for (fln=0;fln<shift;fln++) {
g.setColor(Color.red);
g.drawLine (flx1[fln+1],fly1[fln+1],flx1[fln],fly1[fln]);
g.setColor(Color.blue);
g.drawLine (flx2[fln+1],fly2[fln+1],flx2[fln],fly2[fln]);
}
fltemp=false;
}
if(refltemp) {
g.setColor(greencolor);
g.fillRect(240,50,200,180);
refltemp=false;
}
g.setColor(Color.black);
g.drawString(String.valueOf(flk*10),255,195);
//g.drawString(String.valueOf(k+5),50,145);
g.drawString(String.valueOf((flk+1)*10),300,195);
//g.drawString(String.valueOf(k+15),100,145);
g.drawString(String.valueOf((flk+2)*10),355,195);
//g.drawString(String.valueOf(k+25),150,145);
g.drawString(String.valueOf((flk+3)*10),405,195);
//height, time axis
g.drawLine(260,180,430,180);
g.drawLine(260,60,260,180);
// on time axis
//g.drawLine(55,128,55,132);
g.drawLine(310,178,310,182);
//g.drawLine(105,128,105,132);
g.drawLine(360,178,360,182);
//g.drawLine(155,128,155,132);
g.drawLine(410,178,410,182);
g.drawString("(s)",430,195);
```

```
g.drawString("t",435,185);
g.drawString("(mm)",264,65);
g.drawString("y",245,65);
//on height axis
g.drawLine(258,80,262,80);
g.drawString("300",235,85);
g.drawLine(258,113,262,113);
g.drawString("200",235,118);
g.drawLine(258,146,262,146);
g.drawString("100",235,151);
g.drawString("0",230,180);
int flxcoords1[]={260,255,265,260};
int flycoords1[]={60,68,68,60};
int flxcoords2[]={430,422,422,430};
int flycoords2[]={180,175,185,180};
g.fillPolygon(flxcoords1,flycoords1,4);
g.fillPolygon(flxcoords2,flycoords2,4);
if (flm==0) flm=0;
else if (flm==1) {
g.setColor(Color.red);
g.drawLine(flx1[flm-1],fly1[flm-1],flx1[flm-1],fly1[flm-1]);
g.setColor(Color.blue);
g.drawLine(flx2[flm-1],fly2[flm-1],flx2[flm-1],fly2[flm-1]);
}
else {
g.setColor(Color.red);
g.drawLine(flx1[flm-2],fly1[flm-2],flx1[flm-1],fly1[flm-1]);
g.setColor(Color.blue);
g.drawLine(flx2[flm-2],fly2[flm-2],flx2[flm-1],fly2[flm-1]);
}
if (ruletank1<10) {
if (ruletank1==1) {
g.setColor(Color.red);
g.fillRect(500,90,25,25);
g.setColor(Color.black);
g.drawString(tank1rule1,505,110);
}
else{g.setColor(pinkcolor);
g.fillRect(500,90,25,25);
g.setColor(Color.black);
g.drawString(tank1rule1,505,110);}
if(ruletank1==2) {
g.setColor(Color.red);g.fillRect(525,90,25,25);
g.setColor(Color.black);
g.drawString(tank1rule2,530,110);
}
else {
g.setColor(pinkcolor);
g.fillRect(525,90,25,25);
g.setColor(Color.black);
g.drawString(tank1rule2,530,110);
}
if (ruletank1==3) {
g.setColor(Color.red);g.fillRect(550,90,25,25);
```

```
g.setColor(Color.black);
g.drawString(tank1rule3,555,110);
}
else {
g.setColor(pinkcolor);
g.fillRect(550,90,25,25);
g.setColor(Color.black);
g.drawString(tank1rule3,555,110);}
if (ruletank1==4) {
g.setColor(Color.red);g.fillRect(500,115,25,25);
g.setColor(Color.black);
g.drawString(tank1rule4,505,135);}
else{g.setColor(pinkcolor);
g.fillRect(500,115,25,25);
g.setColor(Color.black);
g.drawString(tank1rule4,505,135);}
if(ruletank1==5) {
g.setColor(Color.red);g.fillRect(525,115,25,25);
g.setColor(Color.black);
g.drawString(tank1rule5,530,135);
}
else {
g.setColor(pinkcolor);
g.fillRect(525,115,25,25);
g.setColor(Color.black);
g.drawString(tank1rule5,530,135);
}
if(ruletank1==6) {
g.setColor(Color.red);g.fillRect(550,115,25,25);
g.setColor(Color.black);
g.drawString(tank1rule6,555,135);}
else{g.setColor(pinkcolor);
g.fillRect(550,115,25,25);
g.setColor(Color.black);
g.drawString(tank1rule6,555,135);
}
if(ruletank1==7) {
g.setColor(Color.red);g.fillRect(500,140,25,25);
g.setColor(Color.black);
g.drawString(tank1rule7,505,160);}
else{g.setColor(pinkcolor);
g.fillRect(500,140,25,25 );
g.setColor(Color.black);
g.drawString(tank1rule7,505,160);}
if(ruletank1==8) {
g.setColor(Color.red);g.fillRect(525,140,25,25);
g.setColor(Color.black);
g.drawString(tank1rule8,530,160);
}
else {
g.setColor(pinkcolor);
g.fillRect(525,140,25,25 );
g.setColor(Color.black);
g.drawString(tank1rule8,530,160);
```

```
}
if(ruletank1==9) {
g.setColor(Color.red);g.fillRect(550,140,25,25);
g.setColor(Color.black);
g.drawString(tank1rule9,555,160);}
else{g.setColor(pinkcolor);
g.fillRect(550,140,25,25 );
g.setColor(Color.black);
g.drawString(tank1rule9,555,160);
}
}
if(ruletank2<10) {
if (ruletank2==1) {
g.setColor(Color.blue);g.fillRect(620,90,25,25);
g.setColor(Color.black);
g.drawString(tank2rule1,625,110);}
else{g.setColor(pinkcolor);
g.fillRect(620,90,25,25 );
g.setColor(Color.black);
g.drawString(tank2rule1,625,110);}
if(ruletank2==2) {
g.setColor(Color.blue);g.fillRect(645,90,25,25);
g.setColor(Color.black);
g.drawString(tank2rule2,650,110);}
else{g.setColor(pinkcolor);
g.fillRect(645,90,25,25 );
g.setColor(Color.black);
g.drawString(tank2rule2,650,110);
}
if(ruletank2==3) {
g.setColor(Color.blue);g.fillRect(670,90,25,25);
g.setColor(Color.black);
g.drawString(tank2rule3,675,110);}
else{g.setColor(pinkcolor);
g.fillRect(670,90,25,25 );
g.setColor(Color.black);
g.drawString(tank2rule3,675,110);}
if (ruletank2==4) {
g.setColor(Color.blue);g.fillRect(620,115,25,25);
g.setColor(Color.black);
g.drawString(tank2rule4,625,135);}
else{g.setColor(pinkcolor);
g.fillRect(620,115,25,25 );
g.setColor(Color.black);
g.drawString(tank2rule4,625,135);}
if(ruletank2==5) {
g.setColor(Color.blue);g.fillRect(645,115,25,25);
g.setColor(Color.black);
g.drawString(tank2rule5,650,135);}
else{g.setColor(pinkcolor);
g.fillRect(645,115,25,25 );
g.setColor(Color.black);
g.drawString(tank2rule5,650,135);}
if(ruletank2==6) {
```

```
g.setColor(Color.blue);g.fillRect(670,115,25,25);
g.setColor(Color.black);
g.drawString(tank2rule6,675,135);}
else{g.setColor(pinkcolor);
g.fillRect(670,115,25,25 );
g.setColor(Color.black);
g.drawString(tank2rule6,675,135);
}
if(ruletank2==7) {
g.setColor(Color.blue);g.fillRect(620,140,25,25);
g.setColor(Color.black);
g.drawString(tank2rule7,625,160);}
else{g.setColor(pinkcolor);
g.fillRect(620,140,25,25 );
g.setColor(Color.black);
g.drawString(tank2rule7,625,160);
}
if(ruletank2==8) {
g.setColor(Color.blue);g.fillRect(645,140,25,25);
g.setColor(Color.black);
g.drawString(tank2rule8,650,160);}
else{g.setColor(pinkcolor);
g.fillRect(645,140,25,25 );
g.setColor(Color.black);
g.drawString(tank2rule8,650,160);
}
if(ruletank2==9) {
g.setColor(Color.blue);g.fillRect(670,140,25,25);
g.setColor(Color.black);
g.drawString(tank2rule9,675,160);}
else{g.setColor(pinkcolor);
g.fillRect(670,140,25,25 );
g.setColor(Color.black);
g.drawString(tank2rule9,675,160);
}
}
g.setColor(Color.black);
g.drawString("Err",485,80);
g.drawString("NL",505,85);
g.drawString("ZR",530,85);
g.drawString("PL",555,85);
g.drawString("DErr",465,95);
g.drawString("NL",480,110);
g.drawString("ZR",480,135);
g.drawString("PL",480,160);
g.drawString(tank1rule1,505,110);
g.drawString(tank1rule2,530,110);
g.drawString(tank1rule3,555,110);
g.drawString(tank1rule4,505,135);
g.drawString(tank1rule5,530,135);
g.drawString(tank1rule6,555,135);
g.drawString(tank1rule7,505,160);
g.drawString(tank1rule8,530,160);
g.drawString(tank1rule9,555,160);
```

```
g.drawString("Err",605,80);
g.drawString("NL",625,85);
g.drawString("ZR",650,85);
g.drawString("PL",675,85);
g.drawString("DErr",585,95);
g.drawString("NL",600,110);
g.drawString("ZR",600,135);
g.drawString("PL",600,160);
g.drawString(tank2rule1,625,110);
g.drawString(tank2rule2,650,110);
g.drawString(tank2rule3,675,110);
g.drawString(tank2rule4,625,135);
g.drawString(tank2rule5,650,135);
g.drawString(tank2rule6,675,135);
g.drawString(tank2rule7,625,160);
g.drawString(tank2rule8,650,160);
g.drawString(tank2rule9,675,160);
if(clicktank1) {
g.setColor(pinkcolor);
g.fillRect(500,90,75,75);
g.setColor(Color.black);
g.drawString(tank1rule1,505,110);
g.drawString(tank1rule2,530,110);
g.drawString(tank1rule3,555,110);
g.drawString(tank1rule4,505,135);
g.drawString(tank1rule5,530,135);
g.drawString(tank1rule6,555,135);
g.drawString(tank1rule7,505,160);
g.drawString(tank1rule8,530,160);
g.drawString(tank1rule9,555,160);
clicktank1=false;
}
if (clicktank2) {
g.setColor(pinkcolor);
g.fillRect(620,90,75,75);
g.setColor(Color.black);
g.drawString(tank2rule1,625,110);
g.drawString(tank2rule2,650,110);
g.drawString(tank2rule3,675,110);
g.drawString(tank2rule4,625,135);
g.drawString(tank2rule5,650,135);
g.drawString(tank2rule6,675,135);
g.drawString(tank2rule7,625,160);
g.drawString(tank2rule8,650,160);
g.drawString(tank2rule9,675,160);
clicktank2=false;
}
g.setColor(Color.gray);
g.drawLine(500,90,575,90);
g.drawLine(500,115,575,115);
g.drawLine(500,140,575,140);
g.drawLine(500,90,500,165);
g.drawLine(525,90,525,165);
g.drawLine(550,90,550,165);
```

```
g.drawLine(500,165,575,165);
g.drawLine(575,165,575,90);
g.drawLine(620,90,695,90);
g.drawLine(620,115,695,115);
g.drawLine(620,140,695,140);
g.drawLine(620,90,620,165);
g.drawLine(645,90,645,165);
g.drawLine(670,90,670,165);
g.drawLine(620,165,695,165);
g.drawLine(695,165,695,90);
g.setFont(f);
g.setColor(Color.red);
g.drawString("Tank1",80,65);
g.drawString("Tank1",300,65);
g.drawString("Tank1",520,65);
g.setColor(Color.blue);
g.drawString("Tank2",130,65);
g.drawString("Tank2",350,65);
g.drawString("Tank2",640,65);
}
}
```

Appendix C. Source Codes for Coupled-Tank Control

C.1 `fuzzycontrol.m`

```
if first==1
  tank1lasterr=0;
  tank1derr=0;
  tank1err=0;
  Tank1Index=0;
  %Tank1Out=0;
  tank1rulearray=tank1input(1:9);
  tank1errarray=tank1input(10:18);
  tank1derrarray=tank1input(19:27);
  tank1outarray=tank1input(28:36);
  tank2lasterr=0;
  tank2derr=0;
  tank2err=0;
  Tank2Index=0;
  %Tank2Out=0;
  tank2rulearray=tank2input(1:9);
  tank2errarray=tank2input(10:18);
  tank2derrarray=tank2input(19:27);
  tank2outarray=tank2input(28:36);
  n=3;
  for i=1:n
    tank1rulematrix(i,:)=tank1rulearray((i-1)*n+1:i*n);
    tank1errmatrix(i,:)=tank1errarray((i-1)*n+1:i*n);
    tank1derrmatrix(i,:)=tank1derrarray((i-1)*n+1:i*n);
    tank1outmatrix(i,:)=tank1outarray((i-1)*n+1:i*n);
    tank2rulematrix(i,:)=tank2rulearray((i-1)*n+1:i*n);
    tank2errmatrix(i,:)=tank2errarray((i-1)*n+1:i*n);
    tank2derrmatrix(i,:)=tank2derrarray((i-1)*n+1:i*n);
    tank2outmatrix(i,:)=tank2outarray((i-1)*n+1:i*n);
  end
  ErrScale=1;
```

```
          DerrScale=50;
          OutScale=10;
          DiscreteNumber=100;
          tank1errmatrix=tank1errmatrix/ErrScale;
          tank1derrmatrix=tank1derrmatrix/DerrScale;
          tank1outmatrix=tank1outmatrix/OutScale;
          tank2errmatrix=tank2errmatrix/ErrScale;
          tank2derrmatrix=tank2derrmatrix/DerrScale;
          tank2outmatrix=tank2outmatrix/OutScale;
          first=0;
      end
      tank1derr=tank1err-tank1lasterr;
      tank1lasterr=tank1err;
      tank2derr=tank2err-tank2lasterr;
      tank2lasterr=tank2err;
      Tank1Index =
          getindex(tank1errmatrix,tank1derrmatrix,tank1err,tank1derr);
      Tank2Index =
          getindex(tank2errmatrix,tank2derrmatrix,tank2err,tank2derr);
      for i=1:n
        if i==1
          tank1Err(1,i) =
          getleft(tank1errmatrix(i,2),tank1errmatrix(i,3),tank1err);
          tank1DErr(1,i) =
          getleft(tank1derrmatrix(i,2),tank1derrmatrix(i,3),tank1derr);
          tank2Err(1,i) =
          getleft(tank2errmatrix(i,2),tank2errmatrix(i,3),tank2err);
          tank2DErr(1,i) =
          getleft(tank2derrmatrix(i,2),tank2derrmatrix(i,3),tank2derr);
        elseif i==n
          tank1Err(1,i) =
          getright(tank1errmatrix(i,1),tank1errmatrix(i,2),tank1err);
          tank1DErr(1,i) =
          getright(tank1derrmatrix(i,1),tank1derrmatrix(i,2),tank1derr);
          tank2Err(1,i) =
          getright(tank2errmatrix(i,1),tank2errmatrix(i,2),tank2err);
          tank2DErr(1,i) =
          getright(tank2derrmatrix(i,1),tank2derrmatrix(i,2),tank2derr);
        else
          tank1Err(1,i) =
          getcenter(tank1errmatrix(i,1),tank1errmatrix(i,2),
          tank1errmatrix(i,3),tank1err);
          tank1DErr(1,i) =
          getcenter(tank1derrmatrix(i,1),tank1derrmatrix(i,2),
          tank1derrmatrix(i,3),tank1derr);
          tank2Err(1,i) =
          getcenter(tank2errmatrix(i,1),tank2errmatrix(i,2),
          tank2errmatrix(i,3),tank2err);
          tank2DErr(1,i) =
          getcenter(tank2derrmatrix(i,1),tank2derrmatrix(i,2),
          tank2derrmatrix(i,3),tank2derr);
        end
      end
      for i=1:n
```

```
  for j=1:n
    Row=(i-1)*n+j;
    tank1Column=tank1rulematrix(i,j)+(n+1)/2;
    tank2Column=tank2rulematrix(i,j)+(n+1)/2;
    tank1Temp1(Row,tank1Column)=min(tank1Err(1,j),tank1DErr(1,i));
    tank2Temp1(Row,tank2Column)=min(tank2Err(1,j),tank2DErr(1,i));
  end
end
for i=1:n
  tank1Temp2(1,i)=max(tank1Temp1(:,i));
  tank2Temp2(1,i)=max(tank2Temp1(:,i));
end
for i=1:n
  if i==1
    for j=1:DiscreteNumber
        tank1Temp3(i,j) =
        min(tank1Temp2(1,i),getleft(tank1outmatrix(i,2),
        tank1outmatrix(i,3),j*2/DiscreteNumber-1));
        tank2Temp3(i,j) =
        min(tank2Temp2(1,i),getleft(tank2outmatrix(i,2),
        tank2outmatrix(i,3),j*2/DiscreteNumber-1));
    end
  elseif i==n
    for j=1:DiscreteNumber
        tank1Temp3(i,j) =
        min(tank1Temp2(1,i),getright(tank1outmatrix(i,1),
        tank1outmatrix(i,2),j*2/DiscreteNumber-1));
        tank2Temp3(i,j) =
        min(tank2Temp2(1,i),getright(tank2outmatrix(i,1),
        tank2outmatrix(i,2),j*2/DiscreteNumber-1));
    end
  else
    for j=1:DiscreteNumber
        tank1Temp3(i,j) =
        min(tank1Temp2(1,i),getcenter(tank1outmatrix(i,1),
        tank1outmatrix(i,2),tank1outmatrix(i,3),
        j*2/DiscreteNumber-1));
        tank2Temp3(i,j) =
        min(tank2Temp2(1,i),getcenter(tank2outmatrix(i,1),
        tank2outmatrix(i,2),tank2outmatrix(i,3),
        j*2/DiscreteNumber-1));
    end
  end
end
tank1NumSum=0;
tank1DenSum=0;
tank2NumSum=0;
tank2DenSum=0;
for i=1:DiscreteNumber
  tank1Temp4=max(tank1Temp3(:,i));
  tank1NumSum=tank1NumSum+i*tank1Temp4;
  tank1DenSum=tank1DenSum+tank1Temp4;
  tank2Temp4=max(tank2Temp3(:,i));
  tank2NumSum=tank2NumSum+i*tank2Temp4;
```

```
      tank2DenSum=tank2DenSum+tank2Temp4;
   end
   tank1Temp5=(tank1NumSum/tank1DenSum)*2/DiscreteNumber-1;
   tank2Temp5=(tank2NumSum/tank2DenSum)*2/DiscreteNumber-1;
   Tank1Out=Tank1Out+tank1Temp5*1;
   Tank2Out=Tank2Out+tank2Temp5*1;
   if Tank1Out<0
      Tank1Out=0;
   end
   if Tank1Out>10
      Tank1Out=10;
   end
   if Tank2Out<0
      Tank2Out=0;
   end
   if Tank2Out>10
      Tank2Out=10;
   end
```

C.2 generalpre.m

```
   if first==1
      for i=1:n
         A(i,:)=a((i-1)*n+1:i*n);
         B(i,:)=b((i-1)*2+1:i*2);
         G(i,:)=g((i-1)*2+1:i*2);
      end
      for i=1:2
         C(i,:)=c((i-1)*n+1:i*n);
         D(i,:)=d((i-1)*2+1:i*2);
         H(i,:)=h((i-1)*2+1:i*2);
      end
      BG=[B G];
      DH=[D H];
      [AD, BGD] = C2D(A,BG,T);
      X=x';
      H1=0;
      H2=0;
      Qi1=0;
      Qi2=0;
   end
   RY=ry';
   H1=RY(1,1);
   H2=RY(2,1);
   H1=(H1-0.3568)/0.0406;
   H2=(H2-0.0378)/0.0412;
   X=AD*X+BGD*RY;
   U=C*X+DH*RY;
   u1=U(1,1);
   u2=U(2,1);
   %u1=6760.8*u1+53;
   %u2=6810.7*u2-1307.7;
```

```
Qi1=2020.7*(H1^0.5)+1144.3*sign(H1-H2)*(abs(H1-H2)^0.5)-53;
Qi2=2199.36*(H2^0.5)+1144.3*sign(H2-H1)*(abs(H1-H2)^0.5)+1307.7;
u1=Qi1/6760.8+u1;
u2=Qi2/6810.7+u2;
if u1<0
    u1=0;
end
if u2<0
    u2=0;
end
if u1>10
    u1=10;
end
if u2>10
    u2=10;
end
```

C.3 generalnopre.m

```
if first==1
  for i=1:n
    A(i,:) = a((i-1)*n+1:i*n);
    B(i,:) = b((i-1)*2+1:i*2);
    G(i,:) = g((i-1)*2+1:i*2);
  end
  for i=1:2
    C(i,:) = c((i-1)*n+1:i*n);
    D(i,:) = d((i-1)*2+1:i*2);
    H(i,:) = h((i-1)*2+1:i*2);
  end
  BG = [B G];
  DH = [D H];
  X=x';
end
RY = ry';
[AD, BGD] = C2D(A,BG,T);
X = AD*X+BGD*RY;
U = C*X+DH*RY;
u1 = U(1,1);
u2 = U(2,1);

if u1<0
   u1 = 0;
end
if u2<0
   u2 = 0;
end
if u1>10
   u1 = 10;
end
if u2>10
   u2 = 10;
end
```

References

1. Simione AH, Tuttle JM. Designing and implementing college-wide web-based course materials: a case study. *Proceedings of the 1997 North American Web Conference* (accessible at http://naweb.unb.ca/proceedings/1997/tuttle/tuttle.html), The University of New Brunswick, Frederiction, New Brunswick, Canada, 1997.

2. Pascoe R. Introducing WWW technology into tertiary teaching: a personal perspective. *Proceedings of the 1997 North American Web Conference* (accessible at http://naweb.unb.ca/proceedings/1997/pascoe/pascoe.html), The University of New Brunswick, Frederiction, New Brunswick, Canada, 1997.

3. Rosenblum J, Healy E. Developing an educational intranet. *Proceedings of the 1996 North American Web Conference* (accessible at http://naweb.unb.ca/proceedings/1996/zrosenblum.html) , The University of New Brunswick, Frederiction, New Brunswick, Canada, 1996.

4. Antsaklis P, Basar T, DeCarlo R, McClamroch NH, Spong M, Yurkovich S. Report on the NSF/CSS workshop on new directions in control engineering education. *IEEE Control Systems Magazine*, 19:53–8 (1999).

5. Poindexter SE, Heck BS. Using the web in your courses: what can you do? what should you do? *IEEE Control Systems Magazine*, 19:83–92 (1999).

6. Tilbury D, Luntz J, Messner W. Controls education on the WWW: tutorials for MATLAB and SIMULINK – web technology for controls education. *Proceedings of the 1998 American Control Conference*, Philadelphia, 1998, pp. 1304–9.

7. Crutchfield SG, Rugh WJ. Interactive exercises and demonstrations on the web for basic signals, systems, and control. *Proceedings of the 36th IEEE Conference on Decision and Control*, San Diego, 1997, pp. 3811–5.

8. Foss B, Eikass T, Hovd M. Merging physical experiments back into the learning arena. *Proceedings of the 2000 American Control Conference*, Chicago, 2000, pp. 2944–8.

9. Gillet D, Salzmann C, Latchman H, Crisalle O. Recent advances in remote experimentation. *Proceedings of the 2000 American Control Conference*; Chicago, 2000, pp. 2955–6.

10. Travis J. *Internet Applications in LabVIEW*. Englewood Cliffs, NJ: Prentice-Hall, 2000.

11. Junge TF, Schmid C. Web-based remote experimentation using a laboratory-scale optical tracker. *Proceedings of the 2000 American Control Conference*, Chicago, 2000, pp. 2951–4.

12. National Instruments Corporation. *Academic Solutions: Remote Experiment Control with LabVIEW*. Austin, TX: National Instruments Corporation, 2000.

13. Johnson GW. LabVIEW *Graphical Programming: Practical Applications in Instrumentation and Control*. New York: McGraw-Hill, 1994.

14. Stonick VL. Teaching signals and systems using the virtual laboratory environment in ECE at CMU. *Proceedings of the 1993 IEEE International Conference on Acoustics, Speech and Signal Processing*, New York: IEEE, 1993, pp. 36–39.

15. Hoffman CM, Houstis EN, Rice JR, Catlin AC, Gaitatzes M, Weerawarana S. SoftLab – a virtual laboratory for computational science. *Mathematics & Computers in Simulation*, 36:479–91 (1994).

16. Aktan B, Bohus CA, Crowl LA, Shor MH. Distance learning applied to control engineering laboratories. *IEEE Transactions on Education*, 39:320–6 (1996).

17. Werges S, Naylor DL. A networked instructional instrumentation facility. *Proceedings of the Annual Conference of the American Society for Engineering Education*, Milwaukee, 1997.

18. National Instruments Corporation. *Comprehensive solutions: LabVIEW software development*. Austin, TX: National Instruments Corporation, 2000.

19. Krause C. *From a Distance: Remote Operation of Research Equipment*. Research Report. Oak Ridge, TN: Oak Ridge National Laboratory, 2001.

20. Ko CC, Chen BM, Chen J, Zhuang Y, Tan KC. Development of a web-based laboratory for control experiments on a coupled tank apparatus. *IEEE Transactions on Education*, 44:76–86 (2001).

21. Ko CC, Chen BM, Hu SY, Ramakrishnan V, Cheng CD, Zhuang Y, Chen J. A web-based virtual laboratory on a frequency modulation experiment. *IEEE Transactions on Systems, Man, and Cybernetics – Part C*, 31:295–303 (2001).

22. Ramakrishnan V, Zhuang Y, Hu SY, Chen J, Ko CC, Chen BM, Tan KC. Development of a web-based control experiment for a coupled tank apparatus. *Proceedings of the 2000 American Control Conference*, Chicago, 2000, pp. 4409-13.

23. Zhang J, Chen J, Ko CC, Chen BM, Ge SS. A web-based laboratory on control of a two-degree-of-freedom helicopter. *Proceedings of the 40th IEEE Conference on Decision and Control*, Orlando, 2001, pp. 2821-6.

24. Ko CC, Chen BM, Ramakrishnan V, Zhuang Y, Hu SY, Chen J. An innovative advance in conducting experiments – virtual laboratories in the National University of Singapore. *Proceedings of the IFAC/IEEE Symposium on Advances in Control Engineering Education 2000*, Gold Coast, Australia, 2000.

25. Ladd E, O'Donnell J. *Using HTML 3.2, Java 1.1, and CGI*. Indianapolis, IN: Que Corporation, 1996.

26. Stevens WR. *UNIX Network Programming*. New York: Addison-Wesley, 2004.

27. Reynolds JK, Postel JB. Assigned numbers. *Request for Comments* 1700 (1994).

28. Hewlett-Packard Corporation. *User's Guide: HP8590 E-series & L-series Spectrum Analyzers*. Polo Alto, CA: Hewlett-Packard Corporation, 1995.

29. Hewlett-Packard Corporation. *Operating Guide: HP 53131A/132A Universal Counter*. Polo Alto, CA: Hewlett-Packard Corporation, 1995.

30. OR-X Limited. *Operating Manual: Model 620 Arbitrary Waveform Generator*. Rehovt, Israel: OR-X Limited, 1995.

31. Walnum C. *Java by Example*. Indianapolis, IN: Que Corporation, 1996.

32. National Instruments Corporation. *LabVIEW User Manual*. Austin, TX: National Instruments Corporation, 1998.

33. National Instruments Corporation. *GPIB Hardware Guide*. Austin, TX: National Instruments Corporation, 1999.

34. National Instruments Corporation. *Lab-PC-1200/AI User Manual*. Austin, TX: National Instruments Corporation, 1998.

35. National Instruments Corporation. *User Manual: DAQ-PCI E Series*. Austin, TX: National Instruments Corporation, 1997.

36. National Instruments Corporation. *Real-time Interface (RTI and RTI-MP) Implementation Guide*. Austin, TX: National Instruments Corporation, 1997.

37. Durkin JF. *Voice Enabling the Data Network: H.323, MGCP, SIP, QoS, SLAs, and Security*. Indianapolis, IN: Cisco Press; 2003.

38. Kumar V, Korpi M, Sengodan S. *IP Telephony with H.323: Architectures for Unified Networks and Integrated Services*. New York: Wiley, 2001.

39. Microsoft Corporation. *User Guide for Windows NetMeeting*. Redmond, WA: Microsoft Corporation, 2001.

40. American Dynamics Corporation. *Model 1641 Series Economical Receivers with Modular Code Board, Installation and Operating Instructions Manual*. Gaithersburg, MD: American Dynamics Corporation, 1998.

41. Palm WJ. *Modeling, Analysis, and Control of Dynamic Systems*. New York: John Wiley & Sons, Inc., 1998.

42. Kent Ridge Instruments. *User Manual for Coupled-tank Control Apparatus*. Singapore: Kent Ridge Instruments, 1997.

43. Stardust Technologies Incorporated. Multicast backgrounder – an IP multicast initiative, White Paper. Campbell, CA: Stardust Technologies Incorporated, 1997.

44. Waitzman D, Partridge C, Deering S. Distance vector multicast routing protocol. *Request for Comments* 1075 (1988).

45. Moy J. OSPF version 2. *Request for Comments* 2178 (1997).

46. Malkin G, Minnear R. RIPng for IPv6. *Request for Comments* 2080 (1997).

47. Ballardie A. Core based trees (CBT) multicast routing architecture. *Request for Comments* 2201 (1997).

48. Deering S. Host extensions for IP multicasting. *Request for Comments* 1112 (1989).

49. Postel J. Internet control message protocol. *Request for Comments* 792 (1981).

50. Hughes M. Multicast the chatwaves. http://www.javaworld.com/, 2001.

Index